MEDIA, FEMINISM, CULTURAL STUDIES

The Sacred Cinema of Andrei Tarkovsky
by Jeremy Mark Robinson

Liv Tyler
by Thomas A. Christie

The Cinema of Hayao Miyazaki
Jeremy Mark Robinson

Stepping Forward: Essays, Lectures and Interviews
by Wolfgang Iser

The Christmas Movie Book
by Thomas A. Christie

Wild Zones: Pornography, Art and Feminism
by Kelly Ives

'Cosmo Woman': The World of Women's Magazines
by Oliver Whitehorne

The Cinema of Richard Linklater
by Thomas A. Christie

Andrea Dworkin
by Jeremy Mark Robinson

Cixous, Irigaray, Kristeva: The Jouissance of French Feminism
by Kelly Ives

The Erotic Object: Sexuality in Sculpture From Prehistory to the Present Day
by Susan Quinnell

Women in Pop Music
by Helen Challis

Sex in Art: Pornography and Pleasure in Painting and Sculpture
by Cassidy Hughes

Erotic Art
by Cassidy Hughes

John Hughes
by Thomas A. Christie

Jean-Luc Godard: The Passion of Cinema / Le Passion de Cinéma
by Jeremy Mark Robinson

Genius and Loving It! Mel Brooks
by Thomas Christie

The Comic Art of Mel Brooks
by Maurice Yacowar

Marvelous Names
by P. Adams Sitney

The Art of Katsuhiro Otomo
by Jeremy Mark Robinson

Akira: The Movie and the Manga
by Jeremy Mark Robinson

The Art of Masamune Shirow (3 vols)
by Jeremy Mark Robinson

Detonation Britain: Nuclear War in the UK
by Jeremy Mark Robinson

Julia Kristeva: Art, Love, Melancholy, Philosophy, Semiotics
by Kelly Ives

Luce Irigaray: Lips, Kissing, and the Politics of Sexual Difference
by Kelly Ives

Helene Cixous I Love You: The Jouissance *of Writing*
by Kelly Ives

FORTHCOMING BOOKS

Naruto
Bleach
Hellsing
One Piece
Nausicaä of the Valley of the Wind
Tsui Hark
The Ecstatic Cinema of Tony Ching Siu-tung
The Twilight Saga
Jackie Collins and the Blockbuster Novel
Harry Potter

SALO, OR THE 120 DAYS OF SODOM

SALO, OR THE 120 DAYS OF SODOM

PIER PAOLO PASOLINI

POCKET MOVIE GUIDE

Jeremy Mark Robinson

CRESCENT MOON

Crescent Moon Publishing
P.O. Box 1312, Maidstone
Kent, ME14 5XU, Great Britain
www.crmoon.com

First published 2022.
© Jeremy Mark Robinson 2022.

Set in Times New Roman 9 on 12pt.
Designed by Radiance Graphics.

The right of Jeremy Mark Robinson to be identified as the author of this book has been asserted generally in accordance with sections 77 and 78 of the Copyright, Designs and Patents Act 1988.

All rights reserved. No part of this book may be reprinted or reproduced, stored in a retrieval system, or transmitted, in any form or by any means, electronic, mechanical, photocopying, recording or otherwise, without permission from the publisher.

British Library Cataloguing in Publication data available for this title.

ISBN-13 9781861718525

CONTENTS

Acknowledgements ✤ 9
Abbreviations ✤ 9

PART ONE ✤ PIER PAOLO PASOLINI

1 Introduction ✤ 14
2 Pier Paolo Pasolini: Biography ✤ 16
3 The Works of Pier Paolo Pasolini ✤ 59
4 Aspects of Pasolini's Cinema ✤ 83

PART TWO ✤ SALO, OR THE 120 DAYS OF SODOM

1 *Salò, or The 120 Days of Sodom* ✤ 139

APPENDICES

Quotes By Pier Paolo Pasolini ✤ 218
Notes On Renaissance Artists ✤ 220
Filmography: *Salò* ✤ 227
Filmography and Bibliography: Pier Paolo Pasolini ✤ 231
Bibliography ✤ 235

ACKNOWLEDGEMENTS

To the authors and publishers quoted.
To the copyright holders of the illustrations.

ABBREVIATIONS

ES Enzo Siciliano, *Pier Paolo Pasolini*
PP *Pasolini On Pasolini*

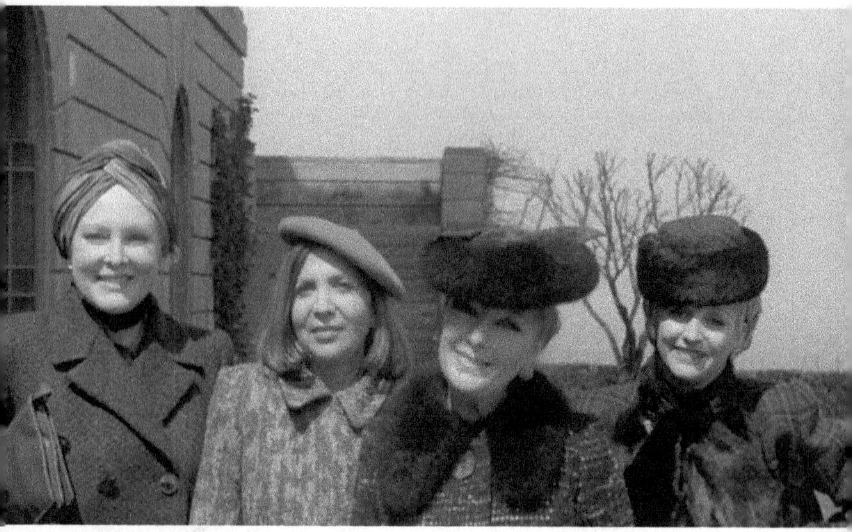

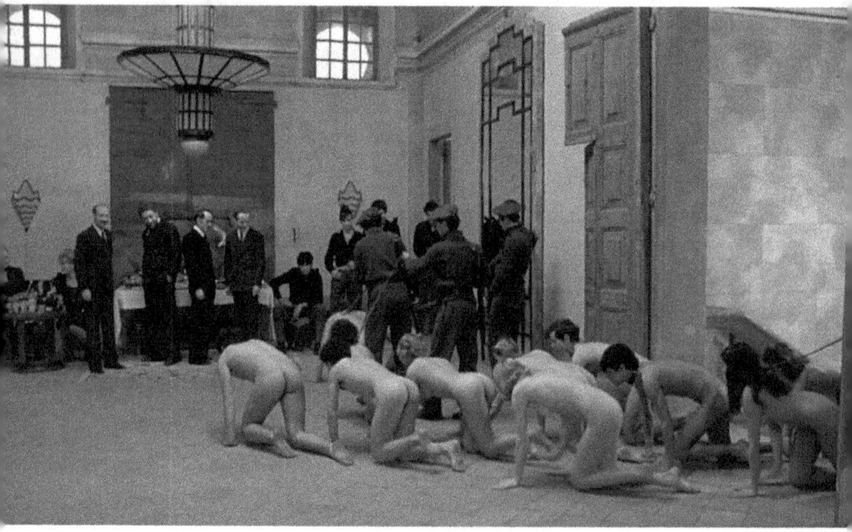

PART ONE
✥
PIER PAOLO PASOLINI

Oso alzare gli occhi
sulle cime secche degli alberi:
non vedo il Signore, ma il suo lume
che brilla sempre immenso.

(Daring to lift my eyes
towards the dry treetops,
I don't see God, but his light
is immensely shining.)

Pier Pasolo Pasolini, 'Mystery' (1945)[1]

---

[1] Trans. A.P. Nicolai, C.U.N.Y., Brooklyn.

1

INTRODUCTION

This study focusses on *Salò, or The 120 Days of Sodom* directed by Pier Paolo Pasolini. However, it should be remembered that he was also a poet, novelist, essayist and playwright. Indeed, there is still a huge interest in Pasolini as a poet and writer, and there are as many articles and books about Pasolini's writing as there are about his cinema. (For many, it is Pasolini the poet who is more valuable culturally than Pasolini the filmmaker – which's a *very* unusual situation for a film director who's regarded as a major player in Italian and European cinema). But Pasolini is one of those filmmakers, like Orson Welles or Jean-Luc Godard, who is so enormously talented and full of life, they produced major works in a number of areas, not only in cinema.

There are plenty of approaches to the work of Pier Paolo Pasolini – I have focussed on the cinema, and Pasolini as a filmmaker. Another obvious approach is to consider the gay, queer and homosexual elements in Pasolini's work (as I have done so much of this elsewhere, I have left that approach aside).

I began my study of Pasolini's cinema (*Pasolini: Il Cinema di Poesia/ The Cinema of Poetry*) in the early 2000s, and added to it over the years, including in 2011, 2015 and 2017 (when it was nearly complete). It has been difficult to finish – partly because Pasolini is a fascinating filmmaker and artist, and there always seems to be more to say about his work. This book is an offshoot of my main study of Pasolini, which has been rewritten and expanded numerous times, and has demanded an enormous amount of work to complete.

2

PIER PAOLO PASOLINI: BIOGRAPHY

LIFE.

Pier Paolo Pasolini was born on March 5, 1922, in Bologna, Italy. He died on November 2, 1975, in Ostia, Rome (he was buried in Casarsa, in his beloved Friuli). Italy, by the way, has a population of 57 million (in 1997), and a land mass of 116,341 square miles. The country was re-unified in 1870.

Pier Paolo Pasolini looks like one of the characters in his movies: the suave, chiselled, sometimes gaunt features (beautiful cheekbones!), the short, dark hair, and those beady eyes that don't miss a thing. Pasolini comes across in interviews (and in his films) as an aristocrat – an artist, surely, but debonair, sophisticated and clever. He appears highly educated, intellectual, outspoken, but also mischievous and very individual (people compared him to a priest – and of course he played priests in his movies).

He was a slim, rangy guy, 5' 6" (with those prominent cheekbones and piercing dark eyes, he was often compared to actor Jack Palance: the street kids of Roma called him *Giacche Palànce*).[2] He prided himself on keeping active into middle-age, and being able to

---
[2] Jack Palance in his red Alfa Romeo in *Contempt* (1963) is strikingly reminiscent of Pier Paolo Pasolini.

play soccer.[3]

Later, when he was a film director (starting late, at age 39), Pier Paolo Pasolini was certainly an intimidating presence, with a formidable reputation – like Cecil B. DeMille, Erich von Stroheim or Akira Kurosawa. Very confident, very smart, a great talker and interviewee, a leader on set, with no doubts from anyone about who was the primary creator and author.

It's clear, if you know anything about Pier Paolo Pasolini, that he was a very bright guy from an early age. He doesn't seem to have been afflicted by a lack of self-confidence – certainly with regard to his own work (which affects writers almost as a matter of course). Pasolini happily, in his twenties, takes on any big subject he likes.

Pasolini's background was bourgeois – ironic, considering how passionately he detested the bourgeoisie. His mother, Susanna Colussi, was born in 1891 and died in 1981. His father Carlo Alberto Pasolini (1892-1958) was a lieutenant in the Italian Army[4] (consequently, like many military families, they moved around a good deal). They married in 1921. For Pasolini, his father was 'overbearing, egoistic, egocentric, tyrannical and authoritarian' (PP, 13).

Pier Paolo Pasolini's relationship with his mother Susanna Colussi, and hers with him, has been described as unhealthily eroticized: according to Enzo Siciliano, Susanna invested far too much in her son emotionally: she gave Pasolini what she withheld from her husband Carlo Alberto (ES, 33). The theme of (hints of) incestuous relations between mothers and sons crop up in Pasolini's work (in *Mamma Roma*, obviously; some Pasolini movies, such as *Theorem*, play the incestuous fantasy literally and explicitly).

Pier Paolo Pasolini's brother Guidalberto (b. 1925) died in WWII (in 1945), when he was part of the Resistance. In the war, Pasolini was taken prisoner by

---
[3] Tho', like everybody, he also disliked ageing (the bad teeth, the thinning hair), and dressed younger than his years.
[4] His father had once prevented an assassination attempt on Benito Mussolini.

the Germans, but escaped back to Friuli. WWII looms very large over all of Pasolini's work.

Pier Paolo Pasolini described himself as a child as stubborn, capricious, naïve, credulous, easily enthusiastic, and also shy and awkward (ES, 45). As a boy, Pasolini lived in Bologna, Belluno, Conegliano, Casarsa della Delizia (in Friuli), Cremona, Scandiano and Reggio Emilia.[5] From 1950, Pasolini made Rome[6] his home (PP, 19).

Apart from literature[7] (he formed a literature club at high school), Pier Paolo Pasolini enjoyed football. As a child Pasolini studied music (piano and violin) briefly.

Pier Paolo Pasolini worked as a teacher in the late 1940s and early 1950s. Pasolini had a number of teaching posts, and the teacher in him never left – it was always a part of his movies, for instance (indeed, a character such as the talking bird in *The Hawks and the Sparrows* was entirely a teacher figure). And in interviews, Pasolini can't help coming across at times like an instructor.

That Pier Paolo Pasolini was a highly, passionately politicized artist is obvious: his passion for political issues runs throughout his movies and his poetry, his interviews, his essays, and pretty much everything he did or said publicly. Pasolini is always talking about Italian society, Italian culture, about Communism in Italy, about how Italy is becoming modernized, about Italy losing something when it embraces new technologies, etc. If there's an opportunity for rumin-ating on contemporary, Italian culture and society, Pasolini will take it.

Among the important friends in Pier Paolo Pasolini's life were:

Laura Betti (1927-2004).

---

[5] As a youth, Pier Paolo Pasolini said he grew up in Bologna, Parma, Conigilano, Belluno, Sacile, Idria, Cremona and other towns in Northern Italy (PP, 11).

[6] Pasolini bought a country retreat at Chai, near Viterbo, which Dante Ferretti had re-modelled for him.

[7] Pasolini's early literary idols included Rimbaud, Dostoievsky, Tolstoy, Shakespeare, Novalis and Coleridge.

Alberto Moravia (1907-1990).[8]
Elsa Morante (1912-1985).
Franco Citti (1938-2016).
Sergio Citti (1933-2005).
Susanna Colussi, mother (1891-1981).
Ninetto Davoli (b. 1948).

One of Pier Paolo Pasolini's first lovers was the fourteen year-old Tonuti Spagnol, whom Pasolini had met in Versuta (where he and his mom Susanna Colussi had retreated during the bombings of WW2). Pasolini tended to go for much younger lovers (like Ninetto Davoli later, 26 years younger than him).

Way before Pier Paolo Pasolini began to write for movies and then to direct them, he was deeply into poetry, into writing, and into literature. Way back in the 1940s, when Pasolini was in his twenties (and during WWII), he was already publishing poetry, writing essays,[9] reviews, and memorials (such as for his brother Guido who died in the war at the hands of Communists).

Another of Pier Paolo Pasolini's passions, long before he became enamoured of cinema, was Friuli: Friuli the place, the landscape, and the local people (and, later, the Friulian dialect). Pasolini moved away from Bologna (which he associated with his father) to Friuli.

Pier Paolo Pasolini had grown up around Casarsa, near Pordenone, in the Friuli-Venezia Giulia region, right up in the Northern corner of Italy. Yugoslavia is not far off to the East, with the Alps to the North; Venice isn't too far away (the Venice Film Festival looms large in Pasolinu's career). Friuli is a region that prides itself on being somewhat distanced from Italy. Friuli is known for its peasant culture, which Pasolini revered (tho' it has been disappearing for many decades).

Pier Paolo Pasolini was thus a kid from the sticks, not a city kid at all, not the sophisticated urbanite of Italy's great cities (Milan, Bologna,[10] Venice, Rome, nor

---

[8] The *dolce vita* set included Federico Fellini, Pier Paolo Pasolini, Luchino Visconti, Alberto Moravia *et al*.
[9] In his essays and articles for magazines over the years Pier Paolo Pasolini discussed Giuseppe Ungaretti, Umberto Saba, and Gianna Manzaini.
[10] Tho' he was born in Bologna.

the Southern country that he later loved – Napoli, Sicily). Rather, it was a world of small towns and villages and the countryside, bicycle rides, flirting with girls, reading books, writing poetry in dialect ('peace and quiet, girls, mental concentration, fields, idleness, drink', Pasolini noted in a letter of 1940, when he was 18).

But it was also the Friulian dialect (*friulano*) that Pier Paolo Pasolini fell in love with, and Friulian culture. Pasolini was a keen connoisseur of dialects; he composed works in dialect (such as his early poetry), and also employed dialects in his cinema.

Pier Paolo Pasolini was a devotee of language like many modern poets and writers. One thinks of Rainer Maria Rilke, André Gide, Lawrence Durrell, Henry Miller, Alain Robbe-Grillet, Samuel Beckett, etc – writers for whom language and communication itself was a mysterious and utterly compelling force in their lives. Language, as French feminist Hélène Cixous remarked, is the key. For Cixous (who is loved and loathed by feminists nearly as energetically as Andrea Dworkin or Princess Diana), writing is absolutely crucial, and central. Writing is oxygen to Cixous, she must write to live. Cixous asserted in "Difficult Joys" that

> writing, writing poetically, treating language as one of the most important things in the world, today sounds mad. Yet for human beings it is the first most important thing.[11]

Pier Paolo Pasolini was one of those filmmakers who, had he been unable to continue to make movies, would've been quite happy writing (Woody Allen and Ingmar Bergman come to mind).[12] Jean-Luc Godard also took that view: for him, filmmaking and writing were part of the same thing anyway. Writing was 'already a

---
[11] "Difficult Joys", in H. Wilcox, 1990, 23.
[12] There are, of course, some famous film directors who found writing very difficult to do – Steven Spielberg, David Lean, Stanley Kubrick – filmmakers who couldn't write their own scripts, who had to have collaborators and writers. But of course most directors *do not* write their own scripts at all.

way of making films,' Godard said in 1962 of his time as a film critic, 'for the difference between writing and directing is quantative not qualitative'.[13] Godard often said he wouldn't stop creating if cinema died: he would move into TV, and if that disappeared, he would move into writing again (ibid., 171).

Other areas which Pasolini might've explored had he lived longer would include opera – several of his contemporaries took up directing live opera performances (Luchino Visconti, Ken Russell, Andrei Tarkovsky, Robert Altman – and even Federico Fellini, who disliked opera, came around to it. Fellini claimed that he only liked Nino Rota's music, and didn't like anything else. In the 1980s, however, Fellini decided he liked opera after all).[14]

Another area was pop promos – maybe too capitalist for Pier Paolo Pasolini, but the right pop act and the right deal might've attracted Pasolini to direct some pop videos. (One of the appeals was that they could be done in a single day, often had a decent budget, and were guaranteed exhibition and an audience).

DVD, Blu-ray and home releases of movies seem an ideal platform for Pier Paolo Pasolini to talk about his works. Some of the most valuable contributions that film directors make are to audio commentaries about their movies (such as Ken Russell, Oliver Stone, Werner Herzog, Mamoru Oshii and Stephen Sommers). Pasolini relating the stories of making *The Gospel According To Matthew* and *The Arabian Nights* would be a treat. (However, some film directors pointedly refuse to talk in audio commentaries about their films, such as Steven Spielberg and Woody Allen. For them, the works speak for themselves).

---

13 *Godard On Godard*, 171.
14 *And the Ship Sails On* (1983) featured an opera star along with other singers, and many other references to opera, and Fellini planned a documentary about opera in 1987 (there were invitations to direct operas, such as at Covent Garden and in Milan).

PASOLINI AND HIS FATHER

The revolt against the Father, against his own father Carlo Alberto Pasolini, was a violent one for Pier Paolo Pasolini, and it coloured much of his work. 'The public aspect of Pasolini's poetry will take the form of a struggle against all repressive and authoritarian conventions', remarked Enzo Siciliano (ES, 43), and it was his father that inaugurated that rebellion. (It was the loss/ rejection of the father, Siciliano reckoned, that was fatal for Pasolini, a loss and a pain that never left him).

Pier Paolo Pasolini associated his father and the father image with 'all the symbols of authority and order, of fascism, of the bourgeoisie'.[15] Pasolini defined his father as 'a nationalist and a fascist', and conventional (PP, 14).

According to his biographer, Pier Paolo Pasolini's father Carlo Alberto was stricken by his son's gay lifestyle:

> he was overwhelmed by the drama of Pier Paolo, by the "scandal," and accepted it with grief. It brought him to a kind of insanity. He drank more and more, and at night cried out that his wife did not love him. (ES, 40)

As Pier Paolo Pasolini put it, he had placed himself 'in a relationship of rivalry and hatred towards my father', which made it easier for him to examine that relationship, compared to that with his mother, which was more latent (PP, 119). For Pasolini, 'everything ideological, voluntary, active and practical in my actions as a writer depends on my struggle with my father' (ibid., 120). Pasolini was thus conscious of using his deep-seated feelings as engines for his creative work (in the way that André Gide said that everything could be material or fuel for a writer. Famously, Gide remarked that as he was living his life he was also considering how it could be exploited in his writing).

According to Sam Rohdie, Pier Paolo Pasolini

---
15 Quoted in J. Duflot, 22.

associated Northern Italia and Bologna with his father, with the bourgeoisie, with fascism, with technology, with capitalism, and with the Law of the Father. That was not the Italy that Pasolini enshrined, but the one he wanted to move away from. Pasolini's Italy was of the South, of Rome and Napoli and Calabria: the South was alive, it was peasants, it was a link to the past, it was non-technological, it was not capitalist (13). However, Bologna has long been a stronghold for the Italian Communist Party (it has held the city since 1945).

That Pier Paolo Pasolini's cinema exhibits a major father complex is clear to all. The ambiguous, anxious attitude towards fathers, father figures, the Sins of the Fathers, and the older generation, is everywhere. In *Pigsty,* the only words spoken in the 15th century tale are when the chief protagonist (Pierre Clementi) announces just as he's about to die: 'I killed my father, I ate the flesh of humans, I shivered with joy' (or something similar). Killing the father – the atmosphere of *Oedipus Rex* and *Theorem* was still in the air, perhaps (these movies – *Pigsty, Theorem, Medea* and *Oedipus Rex* are perhaps Pasolini's most concentrated attacks on the figure of the father).

POETRY AND LITERATURE

Pier Paolo Pasolini was writing poetry and articles from an early age: it's as if, as with poets such as Emily Dickinson or William Shakespeare, he had always written poetry. It was one of the fundamental creative activities in his life. He became disillusioned with politics, with the cultural life in contemporary Italy, with intellectuals, with the passing of the old world (as he saw it – but it had been decaying for 100s of years), yet his poetry remained central to his existence.

Pier Paolo Pasolini's poetry is in free verse – long,

rambling lines and stanzas in the modernist tradition (recalling poets such as Walt Whitman and D.H. Lawrence, who preferred to write in lengthy, loose lines).

Pier Paolo Pasolini's first artistic efforts in the public arena included publishing a literary magazine (in 1941), and his own poems (*Versi a Casarsa*, 1941). He was editor of *Il Setaccio* (*The Sieve*).

By the late 1940s, Pasolini was writing and publishing regularly: *The Diaries*; *Quaderni Rossi*; the play *Il Cappellano*; and *The Cries*, a poetry book. Pasolini's novels (still in print) include *Ragazzi de Vita* (1955)[16] and *Una Vita Violenta* (1959) (both of which have been filmed).

Pier Paolo Pasolini's novel *Ragazzi di Vita* was 'a succès de scandale, drawing positive reviews, heated sales, hostile editorials, and even legal action for obscenity', remarked Shawn Levy in *Dolce Vita Confidential* (190). *Boys of Life* had a run-in in 1956 with the public prosecution office for being 'obscene'. Among the defenders of *Ragazzi di Vita* were Giuseppe Ungaretti, Carlo Bo, Pietro Bianchi and Livio Garzanti.

Reviewing *Una Vita Violenta*, Mario Montanana (a Communist senator), wondered that

> Pasolini does not like poor people, that he despises in general the inhabitants of the Roman shanty-towns, and despises our party even more. The hero, Tommasino, is in reality a juvenile delinquent of the worst kind: thief, robber, pederast.

Enzo Siciliano called Pier Paolo Pasolini a

> frantically manneristic writer – and of a baroque mannerism, a lover of asymmetry, of tormented versifications of topical matter, who made of his style a shining example of the forbidden, who delighted in a "poetics of regression" in order to break the gilded trappings of twentieth-century academicism. (ES, 398)

---

[16] Andrea Di Marco sued Pier Paolo Pasolini for libel in relation to *Ragazzi di Vita* in April, 1962.

An unfinished novel (of 1948), *Amado Mio*, contained autobiographical resonances, coalescing around its central character, Desiderio. In *Amado Mio*, Pasolini secreted 'the meaning of his own obsession,' according to Enzo Sciliano: 'to become father to his boy, so that the latter would mirror, by returning his embrace, all his unsatisfied longings for a son' (114).

The early work, *Amado Mio*, contains a pæan to Rita Hayworth in *Gilda*, as it plays to a cinema of rowdy, young Italians, by moonlight, in the open-air, with the boisterous crowd getting turned on. As the narrator of *Amado Mio* tells it,

> before the image of Gilda something wondrously shared enveloped all the spectators... Rita Hayworth with her huge body, her smile, her breasts of a sister and a prostitute – equivocal and angelic – stupid and mysterious with that nearsighted gaze of hers, cold and tender to the point of languor...

Pasolini was a passionate advocate of Friuli – he was a member of the Friulian Language Academy, the Association for the Autonomy of Friuli, and contributed to the magazine *Stroligùt di cà da l'aga*. Pasolini learnt how to speak Friulian as an adult – it wasn't part of his upbringing: it became part of his poetry – 'I learnt it as a sort of mystic act of love' (PP, 15).

Among Pier Paolo Pasolini's early influences were William Shakespeare (*Macbeth*), whom he discovered at 14,[17] and of course Italy's two giant poets, Francesco Petrarch and Dante Alighieri. Other favourites were André Gide (such as his novel *The Immoralist*[18]), Barbey d'Aurevilly, Niccolò Tommaseo, Johann Wolfgang von

---

[17] With *Macbeth* Pasolini entered the world of books, visiting the stalls in the Portici della Morte in Bologna to buy used books.

[18] A novel tailor-made for Pasolini, evoking a spiritual journey from Northern Europe to the South, the breakdown of a marriage, the discovery of homosexual encounters in North Africa, and the development of an Existential, outsider persona. Classically, André Gide begins his tale with the anti-hero's father's death, a very Pasolinian device (instantly adding a welter of œdipal associations and an evocation of the Law of the Father). Pasolini didn't need to adapt *The Immoralist* – he lived it (tho' it would have been fascinating to see Pasolini take on Gide).

Goethe, Lautréamont and *Les Chants de Maldoror* (inevitably), Arthur Schopenhauer (his pithy, proto-Existential philosophy is a favourite with many European intellectuals), Villiers de l'Isle-Adam, and Daniell Bartoli (*Uomo al punto*).

As a youth, Pier Paolo Pasolini said he had consumed adventure stories, like many other children, but in his mid-teens discovered Fyodor Dostoievsky, William Shakespeare, Arthur Rimbaud, and authors who were somewhat regarded as rebellious, standing outside of the fascist society of Italy (PP, 17).

There are so many references to the work of Dante Alighieri in Pier Paolo Pasolini's output it's a wonder that he didn't produce a feature film of the *Divina Commedia* (or at least a TV documentary). However, there *are* elements of *The Divine Comedy* in *The Decameron*, in the finale of *The Canterbury Tales,* with its devils, the traveller and his guide (in *The Hawks and the Sparrows* and the 'trilogy of life' films), and of course the *tableaux* from Renaissance art in *La Ricotta* and *The Gospel According To Matthew*.

The significance of Pier Paolo Pasolini's works are often interpreted as a group, and in relation to one another, rather than taken as single pieces to be seen in isolation. Thus, *Accattone* is always related to Pasolini's novels of the rough Roman youth, and the Marxism in *The Gospel According To Matthew* and *Oedipus Rex* is related to Pasolini's political statements. (This interconnectedness was of course encouraged by the maestro himself).

'THE BOURGEOISIE ARE ALWAYS WRONG': MARXISM AND ANTI-BOURGEOIS POLITICS

> I don't think you can make an unpolitical movie. Your politics are going to show by permission or omission, so that the best you can do is to try and focus on them in some way in your movie, organise it so that it doesn't happen totally by accident.

Warren Beatty

Only Jean-Luc Godard among comparable filmmakers has a deeper and more visceral loathing of the bourgeoisie than Pier Paolo Pasolini. Oh, how Pasolini *hated* everything bourgeois! – 'I nourish a visceral, deep, irreducible hatred for the bourgeoisie, its self-importance, its vulgarity; it is an ancient hatred, or if you like, a religious one', Pasolini asserted.[19]

As with Jean-Luc Godard, an ingredient of Pier Paolo Pasolini's politics is not so much Marxism as anti-bourgeoisism, anti-capitalism, and anti-consumerism. It is – again like Godard – partly *against things* for the sake of it: *against* the bourgeoisie, *against* consumerism.[20] And it's a politics that is *for* revolution, *for* change, for the sake of it, to turn things upside-down, and to oppose whatever's on offer. (But *how* would Pasolini stem the tide of consumerism and the social decline of his beloved Italy? He doesn't say – because he can't say – because no one can say. Pasolini offers nothing to replace contemporary, capitalist society. His utoptian project is about rewriting or enshrining the past, or the 'Third World').

Pasolini acknowledged that Marxism was a system imposed from the top down by an *élite*, like other political/ philosophical systems. But it gave the illusion that an individual mattered, or had an effect on the system. Andrew Sarris reckoned that 'Italian cinema as a whole – is primarily a Marxist cinema with a deep sense of doubt' (D. Georgakas, 236).

---

19 Quoted in J. Duflot, 22.
20 However, Pasolini was happy to drive flashy sports cars, one of the loudest symbols of consumer-capitalism.

The aim of shocking the bourgeoisie (that childish goal of too many leftist/ Marxist artists), may derive in part from the attempt at reaching a realm where the bourgeoisie and their ideals do not go. That is, to go beyond the limits of what is accepted by bourgeois society, into the crude, the ultra-violent, the bestial.

It's typical that Pier Paolo Pasolini would side with the policemen in the political unrest of 1968, rather than with the student protesters. Why? Because Pasolini thought the students were bourgeois, and the cops were true working class people.

However, that part of the Pasolini Legend isn't the whole story: Pasolini's famous views about the police (expressed in a poem) were modified by his sceptical views of the police as enforcers of the law in Italy, and his sympathies with the political aspects of the counter-culture (Pasolini, the subject of many run-ins with the Italian authorities, held a sceptical view of the *carabinieri*).[21] Subsequently, Pasolini's verses were employed by right-leaning groups and commentators., and twisted around, missing the irony and paradox that Pasolini was exploring.

On his Marxism, Pier Paolo Pasolini reminded Oswald Stack that in Italy everybody is a Marxist, and everybody is a Catholic (PP, 22). 'Pasolini's Marxist critique is sadly too narrow in its view of bourgeois neurosis as a symptom of class decadence under advanced capitalism', according to John Orr in *Contemporary Cinema* (1998, 8).

It's ironic for a left-wing and Marxist radical author like Pier Paolo Pasolini that often for his material he took on very traditional, conservative and right-wing texts and authors: the *Bible*, Ancient Greek mythology, Islamic stories, Geoffrey Chaucer and Giovanni Boccaccio. In fact, historical cinema tends to be conservative at the least, and often right-wing, too (this conservatism doesn't only reflect the markets of commercial cinema).

---

[21] See an interesting article by Luca Peretti on Pasolini and Communism: "Remembering Pier Paolo Pasolini" (jacobinmag.com).

The decline of the ideological investment in Communism, socialism and Marxism in the 1970s, following the height of the idealism and activism of the late 1960s, was something that many intellectuals and artists had to face. Hayao Miyazaki, Jean-Luc Godard, Milos Forman, and many Eastern European filmmakers, as well as Pier Paolo Pasolini, confronted the fact that in some societies Communism and Marxism were not only not working, they were becoming as damaging as the mythologies and ideologies they opposed to, or were created in opposition to (such as Western capitalism).

The dream was over. Between the heady days of 1968 (manning the barricades, the student/ youth riots, the anti-Vietnam War protests, the civil rights marches), and the mid-1970s, it was a rapid decline.

'Pasolini's interventions were extreme and unflagging, pleasing to practically nobody across the political spectrum, and, uniquely, were intricately inscribed with the fact of his sexual difference', noted Gary Indiana (14).[22] True – left-wingers and Communists found just as much to get irritated by in Pasolini's pronouncements in the political arena as right-wingers and conservatives. (And Pasolini likely secretly enjoyed the fact that his views wound up leftists as well as rightists).

SOUTHERN ITALY

Pier Paolo Pasolini had a very idealized view of Southern Italy, or rural Italy, or pre-industrial Italy, of peasant Italy, of an Italy before television, cars and two World Wars. It was an Italy that never really existed, but which he wanted to exist. It was an Italy that he loved – the Italy of regions, and regional dialects and languages.

---

[22] For Indiana, Pier Paolo Pasolini was the wrong sort of gay artist – a Marxist who criticized the political system who wasn't like Franco Zeffirelli, a raging queen (and thus harmless).

It was if Pasolini saw himself as born out of his time – he might've been happier in the mediæval era, say, or the Renaissance (I think Pasolini would've got along just fine in the Ancient Roman period – and so would Federico Fellini and Walerian Borowczyk!).

A Northern Italian (he was born in Bologna), Pier Paolo Pasolini revered the South, of Naples, of Calabria. Of course he spent most of his adult life in the Eternal City; yet he always maintained the links to the countryside (keeping a Summer house, for instance).

It was no surprise that Pasolini opted to stage his most well-known movie, *The Gospel According To Matthew*, in Southern Italy, using many non-actors who were chosen by the maestro and his casting team for their interesting faces (as with Federico Fellini).

Accattone had inaugurated numerous approaches to cinema which Pier Paolo Pasolini would pursue throughout his career: a cast of unknowns and non-actors, low budgets, filming on location (and adapting existing settings), and employing recorded music, often classical (rather than specially composed scores).

Choosing unknown performers was about achieving some kind of reality, or a non-fictionalized, non-embellished reality: Pier Paolo Pasolini said in 1973:

> I pick actors whose sheer physical presence suffices to convey this sense of reality. I do not pick them at random but in order to offer examples of reality.[23]

Pasolini wanted the real thing, without making it pretty or cute. I can't think of another filmmaker who so loved extras, or who gave more screen time in terms of close-ups to extras – except perhaps Federico Fellini. And Pier Paolo Pasolini was especially fond of anybody who looked odd – terrible teeth, warts on lips, wall eyes, scars, and faces wrinkled by the Southern Italian sunshine.

The casting directors on Pier Paolo Pasolini's movies deserve all the credit coming their way for

---

[23] P. Pasolini, *The Guardian*, Aug 13, 1973.

gathering such an extraordinary collection of actors and amateurs (such as Alberto di Stefanis, who cast *The Decameron*). Using non-actors is part of the Neo-realist film tradition – such as the Roberto Rossellini film *Francesco* (1950), co-written by Fellini. Movies like *Francesco* showed Pasolini how you could adapt a religious subject for the cinema without stars or professional actors.

Pasolini was happy to direct non-professional actors thru scenes, beat-by-beat, in the Italian cinema manner (by coaxing them from beside the *macchina fotografica*). It worked wonders – Enrique Irazoqui as Jesus in *The Gospel According To Matthew*, for instance. But sometimes it failed: Giuseppe Gentile might possess the sportsman's physique to look like the mythical hero Jason in *Medea*, but he sure can't act.

For Sam Rohdie, the extras in the 'trilogy of life' movies didn't need to act, they just needed to 'be', to appear on camera – their appearance was their characterization and their performance. (It's a version of Pasolini's notion of 'realism' – you simply show reality, and show people as people, and the process of cinema does the rest).

'A SEARCH FOR MAGIC': TRAVELS WITH PASOLINI

Pier Paolo Pasolini's is a cinema of journeys and voyages, eternally restless – films as a continuous search for locations (and as what we could term location scouting movies, Pasolini's are some of the finest). But also a search for the sacred, 'a search for magic', a search for mythology. And it's a quest for a place where those things still hold sway. A search for a time, too, an era of magic and the poetic.

Certainly the exotic is a big draw in Pier Paolo Pasolini's cinema, and for the director too. He did not shoot in North America (tho' he enjoyed visiting it), but took his productions to North Africa, the Middle East, India and Nepal (as well as the wildly alien, end-of-the-line wildernesses of dear, old England!).

Always Pier Paolo Pasolini goes South and East – to Africa, the Middle East, India (and Southern Italy), rather than North, to Germany, Scandinavia, Russia... Some have associated the North in Pasolini's æsthetics to his father, and the Law of the Father (i.e., Northern Italy, Bologna, etc).[24] The journey East and South, when taken from Europe, is towards the sun, to heat, to the desert, to the exotic, to the ancient world, to Islam, to old religions, to old mythologies.

As well as India, Pier Paolo Pasolini also visited Africa several times: Kenya in Jan, 1961 and Jan, 1962 (as well as Sudan); Ghana, Guinea and Nigeria in 1963; Africa again in 1970 (for the *Oresteia* film); and Israel and Jordan in 1963 (when he was planning to film *The Gospel According To Matthew* in the Holy Land).

When Pier Paolo Pasolini and his writer chums Alberto Moravia and Elsa Morante visited India in December, 1960, it wasn't for a particular film or book project (tho' a book, *The Scent of India,* duly appeared, as well as a short documentary later, *Notes For a Film In India*, 1969).

PASOLINI THE POET

Was Pier Paolo Pasolini a believer or a non-believer? In what? – in God? Love? Death? Art? Life? Terms like belief, or atheism, or agnosticism, or non-belief, just don't do justice to Pasolini's multi-faceted personality and works. The man and his art were much more complicated than that (also, there are many levels of

---

[24] Pasolini's beloved Friuli was in the North, of course, but not grouped with the North for Pasolini – it was beyond-the-North.

'belief', and ways of 'believing').

Pier Paolo Pasolini was a mass of contradictions only to the extent that many (most?) humans are contradictory. Can a Marxist believe in God? What is the relation between Marxism and materialism to religion and the spirit? These and many other questions have been discussed in relation to Pasolini. As he put it in 1966:

> If you know that I am an unbeliever, then you know me better than I do myself. I may be an unbeliever, but I am an unbeliever who has a nostalgia for a belief.

You only have to look at a couple of movies directed by Pier Paolo Pasolini to see there is a wealth of romance, nostalgia, spirituality, desire and yearning. What was Pasolini's 'religion'? What did he 'believe in'?

Poetry.

If there *are* contradictions, that's because Pier Paolo Pasolini was certainly a contradictory personality. Like Orson Welles, Rainer Fassbinder, Jean-Luc Godard and Andrei Tarkovsky (among filmmakers), Pasolini was a complex person – no single view, no one opinion, no philosophy on its own can sum him up, or condense his views into a coherent whole. (Indeed, every single biographical sketch online, in documentaries, books and newspapers always stresses the seemingly contradictory elements of the Pasolini Legend: religion plus Marxism plus homosexuality plus radical cinema, etc etc etc etc etc).

If there's one single word I would use for Pier Paolo Pasolini, it is poetry. He poeticizes life, poeticizes the world and everything in it. 'To make films is to be a poet', he asserted (PP, 154). 'Pasolini's defence of poetry was a political act of complete committment' (S. Rohdie, 89). Poetry and the poet's life sums up many aspects of Pasolini's personality, and also his approach to art, and to cinema, but it doesn't crystallize everything. With Pasolini, you are always aware of depths and levels below the surface. He may talk a lot in interviews, he may appear forthcoming and affable on camera in interviews (or as the interviewer in his own movies, when he won't shut up or let the interviewee get a word in edgeways), but there are whole oceans of things you don't know about, whole continents where acts, thoughts, ideas and gestures are hidden, or will never be found out, and as everybody who knew Pasolini personally eventually dies as the years pass, we won't know.

With Pier Paolo Pasolini, the legend has become enormous, and of course Pasolini fed it no end in his lifetime, as with filmmakers such as Orson Welles, Alfred Hitchcock, Ken Russell, Jean-Luc Godard and Werner Herzog. Those filmmakers liked nothing better than talking about themselves and their work. There should be a sub-category of film directors who luxuriate in their own eccentricities, in rattling out the same stories and anecdotes. The brief moments of self-deprecation (Ingmar Bergman, Woody Allen, Andrei Tarkovsky, Steven Spielberg) don't fool us for a moment.

In Enzo Siciliano's 1978 biography, Pier Paolo Pasolini comes across as a *very* complex individual: he was a mass of contradictions. Nothing could be simple with Pasolini. There were always a number of levels to consider at the same time.

Pier Paolo Pasolini's relationship with his father Carlo Alberto Pasolini was ambiguous, anxious and filled with conflicting emotions. Pasolini spoke of loving his father until his was three years-old; then came a crisis, and he fell out of love, forever. It was during the time that Susanna was pregnant with Pasolini's brother Guido. What exactly happened isn't clear; certainly it is a classic case of oedipal rebellion, with the father as the erotic rival with the boy for the mother's love (it may have been the Freudian primal scene, Enzo Siciliano wondered, of stumbling upon his parents making love in the kitchen). And it is also a (jealous) rivalry with the younger brother.

There's no need to explore the love-hate relation with the father and the Law of the Father in P.P. Pasolini's art here, because it's plastered all over his films and his poetry. Pasolini's movies are in part a psychoanalytical investigation into the relationship with the father figure. The movies are their own therapy, their own psychoanalytical cases. The depictions of fathers and the Sins of the Fathers is so obvious it doesn't require any gloss here.

Ditto with his mother – there's no need to explore Pier Paolo Pasolini's relation with his beloved mother, Susanna Colussi Pasolini. That Pasolini adored his mom comes over strongly in his poetry and cinema.

> The mark which has dominated all my work is this longing for life, this sense of exclusion, which doesn't lessen but augments this love of life.
> (Interview in a documentary, late 1960s)

PASOLINI AND RELIGION

> I suffer from the nostalgia of a peasant-type religion, and that is why I am on the side of the servant. But I do not believe in a metaphysical god. I am religious because I have a natural identification between reality and God. Reality is divine. That is why my films are never naturalistic. The motivation that unites all of my films is to give back to reality its original sacred significance.
>
> Pier Paolo Pasolini (1968)

Whatever he may have said in interviews or written in essays and poetry, Pier Paolo Pasolini was certainly fascinated by many aspects of religion and Catholicism. The imagery and themes of Catholicism, for instance, run throughout his movies – and not because he was Italian, or because he was brought up amongst

Catholicism.

You can think of Pier Paolo Pasolini's 'religion' as being poetry; but even here, the crossovers between religion and poetry are numerous, and have been explored by 1,000s of commentators. Enzo Siciliano called Pasolini 'a profoundly religious man, but in his religion the vocative "God" was absent' (ES, 396).

As commentators have noted, Pier Paolo Pasolini's religious faith wasn't in Catholicism, it was in Communism. For him, Communism was natural, inevitable, essential, a way of looking at the world that explained (and fed) his nostalgia for the peasant world, his dissatisfaction with modern life, his hatred of advanced capitalism, his sympathy with the under-class, and his distrust of authority. And there was a social aspect to Communist politics for Pasolini: it brought him together with intellectuals, of course, but he also 'frequented the dance halls on the "red" outskirts of the city' (as Enzo Siciliano explained [162]). Pasolini continued to vote for the Partito Comunista Italiano (Italian Communist Party) and contribute to its publications (though his relationship with the Partito Comunista Italiano was troubled at times).

Of course, being an intellectual and highly educated observer, Pier Paolo Pasolini was inevitably highly critical of the Church, but he was also intrigued by many issues that the Church was linked to. Social control, and State authority, for instance, or issues such as morality and sexual ethics, or the role that Catholicism had in the political and social formation of young people. (And of course, Pasolini was steeped in Catholic art, to the point where it would have probably been absolutely impossible for him to eradicate all traces of that cultural absorption).

In 1971, he said:

> The Church will probably be able to continue for centuries to come if it creates an ecclesiastic assembly that continually negates and re-creates itself. My criticism is against the Church as power

as it is today. I said that when I was a boy I
believed, I prayed... but it wasn't anything very
serious. I think there're some facets in my character
that have something of a mystifying quality. I'd
say this is a part of the trauma that dominates my
existence. Nature doesn't seem natural to me, it is a
sort of an act between me and the naturalness of
nature. (1971)

Whether Pier Paolo Pasolini personally 'believed' or not is not the issue, is not important, and is not even interesting. It's what Pasolini *did* with those beliefs or non-beliefs that's valuable, it's how Pasolini engaged with institutions such as religion, Catholicism, the State, education, Communism, Marxism, and capitalism that's interesting. But even those big issues are not especially compelling on their own, unless, at least for commercial cinema, they are combined with or put into drama, fiction, stories and characters.

'Christianity was part of his moral reasoning, the part that obliged him to interrogate himself (albeit in the guise of a country priest) on the unrelenting demands of the body', Enzo Siciliano noted, *pace Amado Mio* (121).

Pier Paolo Pasolini said he tended to see the world in too reverential, too childlike terms – if he had any religion, he remarked, it would be a vague mystical response to the world (including objects and nature as well as people [PP, 14]).

PASOLINI THE OUTSIDER

The feeling of not fitting in anywhere in the modern world can be found throughout Pier Paolo Pasolini's writings and films (and it makes his work appealing to modern audiences). You can see how Pasolini would be right at home in the Middle Ages (as an assistant to

Dante Alighieri or Giotto, say, or in the Ancient Roman world, as a poet rival to, say, Petronius or Ovid) – yet, even here, Pasolini would probably still feel that he didn't fit in, would still have that consuming, near-tragic experience of otherness. Pasolini is an exile in his own life, where his poems and films offer a commentary, a layer, a musing on the discontinuities between his life and his art, his life and his heart, his life and his relationships.

We are all exiles, says French philosopher Julia Kristeva. Her experience of displacement (from her homeland of Bulgaria) was an ingredient in her notion of the 'cosmopolitan' individual, the 'intellectual dissident'. As Kristeva knew, strangeness or otherness (being a foreigner) is fundamental to being human: as Kristeva put it, *étrangers à nous-mêmes* (we are strangers to ourselves).[25]

Some of the forerunners of Pier Paolo Pasolini's lifestyle, which combined outsider status, an eccentric and highly individual cultural trajectory, and a homosexual lifestyle, included Oscar Wilde and André Gide. A touchstone for Pasolini, Gide (1869-1951) was cited by Pasolini as an important influence. Easy to see why: early Gide works such as *The Immoralist* and *Fruits of the Earth* are like early Pasolini movies,[26] with their Existentialist, outsider protagonists, their fashionable (French) avant gardism, their depictions of older, white, European guys falling for young, Arab boys (plus the inevitable guilt and post-coital self-loathing), their Catholic/ post-Catholic *milieu*, their high culture and literary allusions, and their enshrinement of the poetry of being alive.

If you enjoy Pier Paolo Pasolini's movies, you will love André Gide's novels (and vice versa). As Pasolini was a 'filmmaker's filmmaker' (like Orson Welles, F.W.

---

[25] In *Strangers to Ourselves,* Julia Kristeva describes the foreigner as the 'cold orphan', motherless, a 'devotee of solitude', a 'fanatic of absence', alone even in a crowd, arrogant, rejected, yet oddly happy (4-5). The stranger is always in motion, doesn't belong anywhere, to 'any time, any love' (7).

[26] *The Immoralist* is ideal for the Pasolinian treatment. Indeed, *Theorem* has the feel of *The Immoralist*.

Murnau or Sergei Paradjanov), so Gide was very much a 'writer's writer' (as with Rainer Maria Rilke, Francesco Petrarch or Samuel Beckett). C.P. Cavafy, the 20th century Greek poet of lyrical, homoerotic nostalgia, is another reference point for Pier Paolo Pasolini (there are numerous affinities between the two).

PASOLINI THE ICONOCLAST

A controversial figure even today, Pier Paolo Pasolini had run-ins with the Italian authorities many times (he was brought to trial on several occasions). His works were condemned for their blasphemy and obscenity. An early encounter with the authorities occurred when he was accused of pædophilia and homosexuality – with the Ramuscello boys in Casarsa. It was this incident that partly encouraged Pasolini to leave Bologna and to live in Rome (see below).

Altho' critics and admirers found some of Pier Paolo Pasolini's writing and movie-making extreme, it wasn't, compared to some authors: William Burroughs, Marco Vassi, Henry Miller, or even Paul Bowles.

There's no doubt that part of Pier Paolo Pasolini enjoyed shocking people, or simply winding them up – he did it in his newspaper articles, in his poetry, in his movies, and in his documentaries. And he succeeded many times: the number of controversies that Pasolini was involved with is very high – compared to most of his contemporaries (either in literature or cinema).

Things seemed to happen to Pasolini.

> Wholly a man of his time [wrote Enzo Siciliano], he chose to live in the enemy camp, launching polemics and accusations, pushing his intolerable personal situation to the point of paradox, and not troubling himself about anything else. (ES, 399-400)

Pier Paolo Pasolini saw himself as something of an outsider in Italian culture, a 'disturber of the peace', someone whose contributions were unwanted. Yes – but that didn't stop Pasolini pouring out pronouncements and movies and poems and books! Pasolini wasn't going to hurry home, slam the door and vow never to talk to the press or anyone else again for the rest of his life! He was not someone who could keep quiet. (Instead, Pasolini glorified in attention of all kinds: he was one of those filmmakers who revel in the attention – look at his interviews – you see the same enjoyment of adulation in Orson Welles, in Jean-Luc Godard, in Steve Spielberg, in Francis Coppola, etc).

Pier Paolo Pasolini was involved in a brawl in Rome, at nighttime in a rough part of the city (Via di Panico). The case came to trial on Nov 15, 1961 (around the time that *Accattone* opened in cinemas). Pasolini was charged with 'aiding and abetting', but was fully acquitted.[27] Enzo Siciliano speaks of this period as having 'a climate of persecution', when 'hysteria grew around the public figure of Pasolini' (248).

Yet another brush with the law occurred when Pier Paolo Pasolini was accused of holding up a gas station with a gun (!). The accusations came from Bernardino De Santis, a boy working at the garage, who said that Pasolini had used a black pistol to hold up the garage. The trial took place in Latina on July 3, 1962. (Once again, Pasolini's defence used the concept of research – Pasolini often defended himself by saying that he was researching places and people for future projects). Further scandals are noted below.

Few Italian artists in the same era were attacked and criticized more than Pasolini. 'Pasolini remained uninterruptedly in the hand of judges from 1960 to 1975', as Stefano Rodotà put it in *Pasolini: Judicial Report, Persecution, Death* (1977). Magazines and newspapers such as *Il Borghese, Oggi, Gente* and *Lo Specchio* regularly slandered him. Among Pasolini's loudest

---

[27] According to Laura Betti in the *Who Says the Truth Shall Die* documentary, Pasolini was accused some 33 times of different crimes but he was always acquitted. Yet the Italian press kept going after him.

critics were Maria Predassi (writing as Gianna Preda) and Giose Rimanelli (writing as A.G. Solari).

But why? asked Wu Ming in a 2016 article:

> Why such a persecution? Because he was homosexual? He was certainly not the only one amongst artists and writers. Because he was homosexual and communist? Yes, but this isn't enough either. Because he was homosexual, communist and expressed himself openly against the bourgeoisie, government, Christian Democracy, fascists, judges and police? Yes, this is enough. It would have been enough anywhere, let alone in Italy, and in that Italy.

PASOLINI AND HOMOSEXUALITY: THE PERCEPTION OF PASOLINI'S IDENTITY

It's striking how many commentators on the work of Pier Paolo Pasolini mention his sexual identity (i.e., his homosexuality). As if they are now professional, psychoanalytical experts on sexuality and gender (almost all film critics are not). There is something patronizing about this, as well as something of the tabloid journalist's pig's nose for snuffling out sensationalism (yes, and the bastard was gay, too!). As if to be gay is automatically to be weird, 'other', or perverted.

Every frigging biographical sketch I've read about Pier Paolo Pasolini mentions his sexuality. Yes, even those critics who are supposed to be (1) intellectual, (2) well-read, and (3) critical/ perceptive. And they often depict Pasolini's sexual preferences as 'dark', or exotic, or odd. Were they? And how can anybody know?! Why is his sexual identity seen as such a big deal? Hell, maybe Pasolini just liked sex! As Spike Milligan said: 'people like to fuck'.

The issue of homosexuality in relation to

Pasolini's media persona is very minor compared to his public critiques and attacks on institutions such as the Christian Democrat party in Italy, on the bourgeoisie, on consumer capitalism, etc.

There are so many assumptions and damaging views in the way that the personality of Pier Paolo Pasolini has been discussed. However, it's true that in some respects the media image of Pier Paolo Pasolini conforms to the stereotype of the ageing homosexual who preys upon boys. Many observers have attested to that, how, according to the Pasolini Legend, he would go out night after night in search of rough trade (often in one of his sports cars). Boys that hung around the Termini railroad station in the centre of Roma, or in the *borgate*, or the bathhouses along the River Tiber (such as the Ciriola below Castel Sant' Angelo).[28] Boys that wouldn't be brought back home, because home meant his beloved Mamma. (His preference was for *ragazzi* with a roguish smile, curly hair on their foreheads, plenty of vitality, and often a reputation as bad boys, as petty criminals).[29]

Famous filmmakers who were homosexual include F.W. Murnau, Jean Cocteau, Andy Warhol, Rainer Werner Fassbinder, Kenneth Anger, George Cukor, James Whale, and more recently, James Ivory, Joel Schumacher, and Pasolini's fellow Italians Luchino Visconti and Franco Zeffirelli (also, Visconti and Zeffirelli didn't, as with Pasolini, hide their sexual identity[30]).

Discussing the idea of the romantic couple in 1970, Pasolini pointed out that societies reject what challenges the norms and the rules – and that includes homosexuality:

---

28 Pier Paolo Pasolini was sometimes accompanied by his friend Sandro Penna: they had a joky contest over who could tup the most boys.
29 In Great Britain, in legal history, male homosexuality has been the subject of several laws, including the law on sodomy of 1533 (in Henry VIII's reign), the 1861 and 1885 laws on sodomy and gross indecency; the 1898 Vagrancy Act, the Sexual Offences Act of 1967, and the Criminal Justice Bill of 1991 (however, lesbianism has been largely invisible and unacknowledged).
30 However, Visconti and Zeffirelli didn't loudly criticize the State, the Church and other Italian institutions like Pasolini.

> Homosexuality is a threat to society. It is inconceivable in any organisms or community, no matter how free. (1970)

Enzo Siciliano in his biography portrays Pier Paolo Pasolini as someone tormented by his passions, his predilections for young, raw boys. 'Pasolini lived in the torment of not being able to give it [his eros] what it demanded of him. And the demand was obscure, indeed dark and nocturnal' (ES, 391).

In 1948, Pier Paolo Pasolini described his homosexuality as something other:

> I was born to be calm, balanced, natural: my homosexuality was something added, it lay outside, it had nothing to do with me. I've always seen it as something beside me like an enemy, I've never felt it to be within me.

Pier Paolo Pasolini revered the rugged, working class *ragazzi* of Rome, Calabria and Friuli, but however much he liked to hang around with them (and have sex with them), he was never one of them. Pasolini was always the intellectual, always the poet, always the guy who wrote newspapers columns and directed movies. He was never a street kid, was never one of the tough, poor *ragazzi* that he liked to cruise at night.

For some observers, Pier Paolo Pasolini was the classic predatory homosexual, the older, gay man who takes to exploring the streets of cities and towns at night looking for willing youths to share the momentary pleasures of sex. It was a habit that Pasolini found hard to break: he enjoyed the danger of it, as well as the ecstasy (he would return from his secretive nighttime jaunts battered and bruised sometimes). According to Enzo Siciliano, most times the erotic encounters consisted of fellatio and masturbation.

Sometimes Pier Paolo Pasolini had to be rescued from his nightly adventures, sore and bleeding (producer Alfredo Bini and production manager Eliseo Boschi would respond to telephone calls to go get

Pasolini from some nocturnal spree that'd turned sour – in Africa and the Middle East as well as in Rome). 'I'm leading not a violent but an extremely violent life', Pasolini wrote in a letter of Oct 5, 1959 (ES, 141).

Pier Paolo Pasolini did have heterosexual experiences. One was with a young mother from Viterbo. Another was with a girl at the beach. Another was with Mariella Bauzano in the early 1950s. And as a kid Pasolini had flirted with girls (and referred to them in his letters). However, Enzo Siciliano wondered if some of these 'girls' were in fact boys (ES, 52).

There were also a number of social and criminal scandals, some of which involved under-age youths and sexuality – which were linked to Pasolini's homosexual practices.

When he was 19, Pier Paolo Pasolini was accused by a neighbourhood child's father of pederasty, when he offered the child some ice cream (this occurred in Bologna in 1941). Pasolini insisted that his intentions were innocent.

One of the biggest scandals in Pier Paolo Pasolini's life, and one which changed the course of his life, occurred in 1949 in Casarsa (his home), when Pasolini (then 27) was overheard talking to some 16 year-old lads in Ramuscello (outside of San Vito al Tagliamento). What happened with the boys at Ramuscello ('probably mutual masturbation', Enzo Siciliano reckoned [135]), which Pasolini had enjoyed (he called it an unforgettable evening), became public when complaints were made to the *carabineri.* In December, 1950, the court acquitted Pasolini of the charges of corrupting minors, but he was convicted of committing lewd acts. In April, 1952, the appeals court absolved Pasolini due to insufficient evidence (ES, 135).

Pier Paolo Pasolini trotted out a defence he used again in later scandals a few times: he was conducting research for a novel, he claimed: 'I was trying an erotic and literary experiment, under the influence of a book I had been reading'. Even if he cited a big cultural name like André Gide, it seems a pretty flimsy excuse.

Pier Paolo Pasolini's erotic encounter with the Ramuscello boys had other repercussions – such as Pasolini's ousting from the Communist Party, which he found very upsetting (he revered Communism). Pasolini lost his teaching job (as well as the financial security it brought).

The scandal tore into Pier Paolo Pasolini's family – his father went ballistic, raging all night about his son, and his mother locked herself in her room ('Yesterday morning my mother almost went out of her mind, my father is in an unbearable state – I heard him weeping and moaning all night', Pasolini wrote to Ferdinando Mautino). To a friend called over for solace, Giuseppe Zigaina, Pasolini confessed he wanted to kill himself (ES, 137). It was the repercussions of this event that precipitated the move to Roma with his mother, where he remained for the rest of his life.

The pattern of this early scandal of 1949 – Pier Paolo Pasolini preying upon young boys, the social intolerance of homosexuality it evoked, and Pasolini's intellectual defence of his actions – would be repeated a few times in his life.

Another incident involving young boys occurred on July 10, 1960, in Anzio, when Pier Paolo Pasolini was thought to have propositioned some boys in the harbour (the parents of the boys filed a complaint). One of the striking aspects about the career of Pier Paolo Pasolini is that he didn't give up in the face of several scandals.

HOMOSEXUALITY IN PASOLINI'S CINEMA

Critics have noted that although he was a gay filmmaker, homosexuality is not often portrayed in Pier Paolo Pasolini's cinema. Well, there are obvious instances, such as the condemned, male homosexuals in the witchhunting sequence in *The Canterbury Tales*, where one of the victims is publicly burnt to death (while an older one buys himself out), and in *Theorem,* homosexual relationships are explored in more depth (but in *Theorem* the homosexuality is with a visitor who is part-god, part-devil – not an 'average' relationship at all!).

But when you look closer, there are further levels of homosexual elements in Pier Paolo Pasolini's cinema. The preponderance of male brotherhoods, for instance, of men being men together, which you can see in *The Canterbury Tales*, *The Decameron*, *Accattone* and, yes, in *The Gospel According To Matthew*. The homosocial relationships are right in the foreground from Pasolini's debut (*Accattone*) onwards. Indeed, *Accattone* is a very gay movie from that perspective (even down to the way that women are treated – their maltreatment further bolsters the homosocial bonds of the guys).

And look at the way that Pier Paolo Pasolini includes so many rough and ready youths in his movies (the *ragazzi* of his 1950s novels), and how the camera lingers over them at length. Pasolini is very fond of close-ups of young *ragazzi* smiling into the camera, as part of the conventional shot-reverse-shot editing pattern of cinema, yes, but the amount of screen time given over to close-ups of attractive, macho young men is very striking.

Brotherhoods and male bonding are fundamental to many other filmmakers' work – it's central to Westerns, to the crime and gangster genres, to the war genre, to action cinema, and is a key element in the cinema of Sam Peckinpah, Howard Hawks, John Woo, Ringo Lam, Martin Scorsese, Francis Coppola, etc etc.

I'm reminded of Michelangelo Merisi da Caravaggio,[31] probably *the* painter (at least in Italy), of beautiful, tough, young men. The homosexuality of Caravaggio is another aspect, of course, but in terms of

---

[31] Other writers have noted the affinities between Pier Paolo Pasolini and Caravaggio: Cesare Garboli drew attention to the similarities, with the art historian Roberto Longhi as the intermediary (Longhi had organized an important exhibition of Caravaggio in Milan in 1951).

the art itself, Caravaggio's work is certainly a forerunner of this element in Pier Paolo Pasolini's cinema. And the other artist is of course Michelangelo Buonarroti, the towering genius of the Renaissance, who made the male nude the most sublime, erotic thing you've ever seen (visit the Musée de Louvre to see the *Dying Slave* sculptures, truly orgasmic works of art).

And Pier Paolo Pasolini and his crews did film many men nude. Within the context of heterosexual encounters, that male nudity has a justification. And Pasolini was unusual among many film directors is putting an equal amount of male nudity on screen as female nudity in love scenes (male actors can be more reluctant to disrobe completely – and of course, there are double standards in most cinema, where an actor will stay partially clad, while an actress is fully naked).

As well as nudity,[32] Pier Paolo Pasolini and the camera teams also focussed on the male genitals. In *The Arabian Nights* there are quite a few close-ups of genitals (as well as the usual thrusting butts in sex scenes of heterosexual cinema). *The Arabian Nights* probably contains the most male nudity in Pasolini's cinema, along with *Salò*.

Despite the beauty of Pasolini's imagery, his exaltation of bodies (and men in particular), there isn't much erotic pleasure in some of his works, and sexuality is tied, via his personality, 'to a realm of suffering' which 'inflects his work with melancholy and morbidity', according to Gary Indiana (16).

Pasolini identified with the victim, not the perpetrator, some observed; his masochism was to sympathize with the down-trodden – in Italia, that meant the sub-proletariat (Pasolini invested his social hopes in the sub-proletariat).

Feminists have discussed the male gaze (voyeurism, the look, etc), and wondered if there can be a female gaze in cinema. That there is a homosexual, lesbian, queer and bisexual gaze – or, I would prefer to

---

[32] Nobody can miss the fact that Pier Paolo Pasolini's last four films are jammed with nudity and sex. (And also in *Theorem* and *Pigsty*).

call it a multi-sexual gaze (why stop at two or three genders?) – is clear from the films of Pier Paolo Pasolini, Walerian Borowczyk and Ken Russell.

I'm not talking about the sexual preferences of the filmmakers, but of the gaze, the looks, the desire and the structure of their works. For example, although Ken Russell, Francis Coppola, Martin Scorsese, Bernardo Bertolucci and Michael Powell were heterosexual (at least according to their autobiographies and colleagues and wives and girlfriends), some of their works are supremely gay, queer, lesbian and homosexual.

Pier Paolo Pasolini, though, was not particularly interested in foregrounding that aspect of his personality in his cinema. What does come across, though, and very strongly, is the aspect of *desire*. Sexual desire, desire for life. Which's often intensely romantic and poetic, sometimes nostalgic, sometimes ironic, sometimes masochistic, and sometimes vitriolic.

The most unbridled expression of desire in Pier Paolo Pasolini's work is in the three 'life' movies, 1971, 1972 and 1974. But the desire on display is nearly all heterosexual (*Salò* explores desire within an eccentric, S/M environment).

PASOLINI CRITICISM

A huge amount of articles, essays and books have appeared about the works of Pier Paolo Pasolini, focussing on his poetry, his novels, his essays/statements and his movies. In short, Pasolini has been taken *very* seriously, with critics and journos assuming that he is an important figure with significant things to say. I would imagine that Pasolini himself would be stunned, delighted, and perhaps embarrassed by the number of pieces written about his work, and how he has been placed in the same company as many of his cultural heroes.

I would recommend, as the first point of call, the amazing biography by Enzo Siciliano (sadly out of print). Among the studies of Pier Paolo Pasolini's films, Sam Rohdie, B. Babington, Pamela Grace, Philip Kolker, John Orr, A. Pavelin, and Gary Indiana are useful.

There are far fewer biographies of Pier Paolo Pasolini in print than one might think. In fact, for years no biographies have been in print in English. The biography by Enzo Siciliano, *Pasolini,* published in 1978 by Rizzoli (in Italian), is among the finest (it was translated in 1982, and published in 1987). Retrospectives of Pasolini's work were mounted at the Museum of Modern Art in 2012 and the British Film Institute in 2013.

Enzo Siciliano concentrates very much on Pier Paolo Pasolini the public figure in Italian cultural life, and on Pasolini's poetry: there is far less in his biography on Pasolini's cinema, for instance, than on Pasolini's poems (Siciliano quotes from the poetry at length). Siciliano also employs the poems in a problematic manner: to illustrate Pasolini's thoughts and even some of his experiences. Assessing and explaining someone's life through their poetry is full of difficulties, filled with assumptions about what poetry is, how it works, how poets write poems, and how poetry relates to the poet's life.

In short, poetry is not autobiography, or documentary, or history. Very often it has no relation to the poet's life whatsoever. Robert Graves called poetry a 'spiritual autobiography', but even that is not always the case.

With Pier Paolo Pasolini, however, some of his poems definitely do reflect upon his experiences, and many poems do express his own views. But it's still a very stylized, literary kind of mirror, reflecting back only what the poet chooses.

Pier Paolo Pasolini has been discussed widely in cinema circles, but when you look into it, there are far fewer really good books about Pasolini's cinema than one might expect (certainly compared to contemporaries such as Jean-Luc Godard or Orson Welles). And many of the best studies are now out of print (including Enzo Siciliano's essential biography).

In studies of the cinema of Pier Paolo Pasolini's cinema, the context and the references tend to be Neo-realism, and to that select band of Italian filmmakers who have been exported and critically revered: Fellini, Rossellini, Visconti, Antonioni, de Sica, Bertolucci, etc.

Sure – those are the great artists of Italian cinema of the 1950s to 1970s. But they are not really representative of Italian cinema of that era. Rather, cinema in Italy of the 50s through 70s was a thriving industry of remakes, sequels, rip-offs, exploitation movies, *mondo* movies, populist comedies (hugely popular), *James Bond* cash-ins, and endless genre movies (Spaghetti Westerns, *gialli* (horror/ thriller), crime, erotica, and of course the *peplum/* sword & sandal movies), plus the many visiting productions from North America (resulting in the 'Hollywood On the Tiber' cycle). If a movie – from anywhere – was successful, Italian cinema dived in and had a cash-in movie filmed and released within weeks (same with the Hong Kong film business).

We don't think of Pasolini as a director of sequels and franchises, but he *did* sequelize his own movies: *Mamma Roma* follows up *Accattone*, *The Hawks and the Sparrows* led to further collaborations with Totò (in the short films for anthologies, and a feature-length sequel to *The Hawks and the Sparrows* was planned), *Medea* is a follow-up to *Oedipus Rex,* and the 'trilogy of life' pictures can be regarded as a film series.

Pier Paolo Pasolini distanced himself from Neo-realist cinema; while Neo-realism was dead in Italy, it had migrated to England and France, Pasolini noted (PP, 137). He didn't like the British version of the New Wave at all (very few Europeans did!), tho' of course he greatly admired Jean-Luc Godard.

Inevitably, Pasolini would be critical of Neo-realist cinema and distance himself from it (as Federico Fellini and Bernardo Bertolucci did), partly because we know that Pasolini (and Fellini and Bertolucci) didn't like being part of a group, or being pigeon-holed and labelled.

However, Pasolini, like Fellini, certainly employed some of the formal approaches of Neo-realism (even if he denied using them): in her 2005 essay on *Rome: Open City*, Marcia Landy listed some of the styles and subjects of Neo-realist cinema:

> a predominant use of location shooting, deep-focus and long-take photography, non-professional actors, a loose form of narration, and a documentary look, plus in the intermingling of fiction and nonfiction, the privileging of marginal and subaltern groups, and a focus on contemporary situations. (J. Geiger, 404)

The decline of the Neo-realist form of cinema coincided with the changes in Italian society after WWII. As David Cook explained in *A History of Narrative Film*:

> In practice, it was a cinema of poverty and pessimism firmly rooted in the immediate postwar period. When times changed and economic conditions began to improve, neorealism lost first its ideological basis, then its subject matter. (453)

Another factor was the Andreotti Law, instituted in response to the glut of North American movies in Italy in 1949. The Andreotti Law taxed imported films and promoted home-grown products. (Several European nations have attempted to control American cultural imports and promote their national arts).

CRITICS ON PASOLINI

For David A. Cook (in *A History of Narrative Film*), at his best Pier Paolo Pasolini 'succeeded in creating an intellectual cinema in which metaphor, myth, and narrative form all subserved materialist ideology' (1990, 633).

Gary Indiana described Pasolini as:

Indefatigably productive, ingenious, exasperating, narcisstically didactic, slyly self-promoting, abject, generous, exploitative, devoted to the wretched of the earth with honest fervor and deluded romanticism...

Pierre Leprohon, in one of the standard books on Italian cinema (1972), was suspicious of the merits of Pier Paolo Pasolini's work: 'originality, violence, controversiality and a taste for (often confused) symbols', Leprohon asserted, with anachronistic music, and it's deliberately, irritatingly mystifying (207).

For David Thomson (an idiosyncratic and not always reliable film critic), Pier Paolo Pasolini's films weren't up to the level of his theories and poetry: there was too much portentousness in Pasolini's imagery, Thomson reckoned, adding:

His strident compositions were clumsy and monotonous, and his appetite for faces often overrode the ability to edit shots together fluently. The style was top-heavy, just as the meanings of his films were too literary, too immediate, and too inconsistent. (1995, 575-6)

Of course I don't agree with any of that. 'Monotonous'?! Hardly. And why is being 'too immediate' a problem? But you could agree that some of the imagery and the *mise-en-scène* didn't match up with the grand themes and issues, that sometimes the imagery is too grandiose for the stories and the characters (or vice versa).

THE DEATH OF PIER PAOLO PASOLINI

> How would I define myself? It's like asking the definition of infinity. There's an interior infinity and an exterior infinity. When I think of myself, I think of something infinite. It's impossible to define myself. For you I'm definable but for me I'm infinite. I'm the mirror of exterior infinity, it's impossible for me to define myself. I could create... some slogans, a few funny things in conversations, in salons, perhaps... I could quote something Elsa Morante said about me: "I'm a narcissistic individual who has a happy love of myself." I must add that I have an unhappy love for the world. Or maybe, I could say I'm a true devil, not a false devil like Sanguineti or the *avant garde* writers.
>
> Pier Paolo Pasolini (1966)

The death of Pier Paolo Pasolini at age 53 has loomed large in his legend (as with the deaths of figures such as Marilyn Monroe, Jim Morrison, Jimi Hendrix and Bruce Lee). The details are still shrouded in mystery and controversy. No one knows precisely what happened, or will confess the truth. (It does seem as if some people *do* know who was responsible, but refuse to say). Anyway, nobody can agree exactly what went on that fateful night of November 1-2, 1975.

Some of the events of the night of Nov 1 and Nov 2, 1975 are agreed upon: that Pier Paolo Pasolini picked up the 17 year-old hustler Giuseppe Pelosi in Rome; that they ate in a restaurant; and that they drove in Pasolini's sports car to Ostia (a typical evening for Pasolini, thus far).

After that, there are many versions of what happened. That Pasolini was beaten and run over by his own car seems certain.

Other details of the murder have come to light:

• the green sweater that didn't belong to Pasolini in the car;

• the bloody handprint on the roof of the car;

• that witnesses claimed they saw at least one

motorbike and possibly a car following Pasolini's vehicle;

• that a skinny kid could not have killed the bigger, athletic Pasolini;

• that Pelosi didn't have any blood on him;

• that the damage sustained by Pasolini was far beyond what Pelosi could have inflicted;

• that, if other people were involved, the murder seems inept;

• that the motives are obscure – for Giuseppe Pelosi, but also for other groups (such as a local gang).

Giuseppe Pelosi confessed to Pier Paolo Pasolini's murder (and was duly imprisoned). Pelosi claimed that Pasolini had proposed things that he didn't want to do (including, preposterously, sodomy with a wooden stake). Pelosi's motives for the murder have never been explained satisfactorily.

In 2005, Giuseppe Pelosi retracted his confession, which he claimed had been made due to threats to his family. Pelosi gave more names in 2008.

Several high profile members of Italian society have asked that the case be re-opened, including former mayors and lawyers, as well as journalists.

When the case was re-opened in 2005, Sergio Citti, Pier Paolo Pasolini's long-time lover and colleague, said that Pasolini had been going to meet someone who had stolen reels of the film *Salò* (with a view to extorting money). Others have also reckoned that film canisters stolen on Aug 27, 1975 from the Technicolor lab in Rome might've been involved (as well as *Salò*, some of the negatives of *Casanova* were taken – 74 cans of film. Some have suggested that the thieves mistook the negatives of *Salò* for those from *Casanova*. Producer Alberto Grimaldi (he was producing both films) refused to pay the thieves the half a billion Lire they demanded).

The extortion scenario doesn't make total sense – not least because it's the producers, the production companies and the studios who control the money in the film industry, not directors. Also, killing someone means you won't get the money you're extorting. That

Pasolini would go to meet some small-time crooks intent on extracting some Lire out of him at night in a lonely spot like Ostia seems unconvincing.

Several theories have been proposed for the death of Pier Paolo Pasolini. That he irritated some groups (and institutions) is well-known – that his views were not welcome in some quarters of Italian society; that he was known as a Marxist and Communist who criticized the social and political status quo; that he wrote articles published in Aug, 1975 which criticized Christian Democrats and other right-wing organizations for the decline of Italian society, etc. But then, many writers and artists have stirred up controversy (and some were louder and more outspoken than even Pasolini). And being a Communist in Italy is common (Pasolini remarked that everyone in Italy was a Catholic, and a Communist).

Anyway, one or more neo-fascist groups have been put forward as possible culprits, plus a local criminal gang (partly because witnesses said several people (perhaps five) murdered Pier Paolo Pasolini, not Giuseppe Pelosi on his own. Laura Betti and others have claimed that a car containing four people followed Pasolini's vehicle). Links have also been suggested between neo-fascist groups and the Italian secret services. (The neo-fascist connection makes sense – it was neo-fascist groups that caused trouble at screenings of Pasolini's films in the early 1960s).

For Bernardo Bertolucci and others, it was a kind of public execution, an over-the-top act of punishment, probably backed by conservative groups in Italy who wanted Pasolini silenced, or to make an example of him. Bertolucci wondered if the perpetrators even knew what they were doing, or if they knew of the real motives behind the murder they were hired to carry out. Certainly, whoever killed Pasolini knew that they could get away with it, that they wouldn't be caught, that they had a scapegoat lined up, and that Pasolini's supporters would not have the means to bring them to justice.

The death of Pier Paolo Pasolini has provided

plenty of speculation and gossip-mongering. Inevitably commentators refer to his homosexuality, to his habit of cruising or seeking out rough trade, to his apparent sadomasochism (even with suggestions of a kind of suicide), to the brutality of his last film, *Salò,* and so on. But the sex/ masochism angle, though sensational, isn't the whole story by any means.

With its combination of spectacle, sex and mystery, Pasolini's murder is a 500-word newspaper piece that writes itself. When you add in aspects such as conspiracy, or extortionists, or neo-fascist groups, or political organizations such as Christian Democrats, you have an explosive cocktail that damns segments of Italian society. Pretty much every piece on Pasolini mentions his sensational demise.

Even philosophers such as Julia Kristeva have had their say (in *Tales of Love*):

> Masochism, which, we are told, is essentially and originally feminine, is a submissiveness to the Phallus that the soulosexual knows well and can assume until death in order to become the "true" woman – passive, castrated, nonphallic – that his/ her mother was not. Mishima, mistaking himself for Saint Sebastian, and even Pasolini, allowing himself to be executed by a hoodlum on an Italian beach, carry to the limit the slavish moment of male eroticism appended to a deathful veneration of the Phallus. (78)

Pasolini on set:
with opera superstar Maria Callas during Medea (above).
And with Enrique Irazoqui during The Gospel (below).

Pasolini and Welles during Curd Cheese (1963).

3

THE WORKS OF PIER PAOLO PASOLINI

> I love life fiercely, desperately... Love of life for me has become a more tenacious vice than cocaine. I devour my existence with an insatiable appetite.
>
> Pier Paolo Pasolini[1]

Pier Paolo Pasolini directed thirteen feature films (one is a documentary), and also many shorter pieces, including contributions to anthology movies. His feature movies are:

Beggar (*Accattone*, 1961)
Mother Rome (*Mamma Rome*, 1962)
Love Meetings (a.k.a. *Lessons In Love = Comizi d'Amore*, 1964)
The Gospel According To Matthew (*Il Vangelo Secondo Matteo*, 1964)
The Hawks and the Sparrows (*Uccellacci e Uccellini*, 1966)
Oedipus Rex (*Edipo Re*, 1967)
Theorem (*Teorma*, 1968)
Pigsty (*Porcile*, 1969)

---

[1] In L. Valentin, "Tête-à-Tête avec Pier Paolo Pasolini", *Lui*, April, 1970. Andrea Dworkin used that Pasolini quote – 'I love life so fiercely, so desperately' – in her novels.

Medea (*Medea*, 1969)

The Decameron (*Il Decamerone*, 1971)

The Canterbury Tales (*I Racconti di Canterbury*, 1972)

The Arabian Nights (*Il Fiore Delle Mille e Una Notte*, 1974)

Salò, or The 120 Days of Sodom (*Salò, o le Centoventi Giornate di Sodoma*, 1975)

Pier Paolo Pasolini's contributions to episode or anthology[2] movies are:

The Anger (*La Rabbia*, 1963)

Curd Cheese (*La Ricotta*, episode in *RoGoPaG*, 1963)

The Earth Seen From the Moon (*La Terra Vista Dalla Luna*, episode in *The Witches = Le Streghe*, 1967)

What Are the Clouds? (*Che Cosa Sono le Nuvole?*, episode in *Caprice Italian Style = Capriccio all'Italiana*, 1968)

The Sequence of the Flower Field (*La Sequenza del Fiore di Carta*, episode in *Love and Anger = Vangelo '70/ Amore e Rabbia*, 1969)

Pier Paolo Pasolini's shorter works include:

Location Hunting In Palestine (*Sopralluoghi in Palestina Per Il Vangelo Secondo Matteo*, 1965)

Notes For a Film In India (*Appunti Per un Film Sull'India*, 1969)

Notes For a Garbage Novel (*Appunti Per un romanzo dell'immondizia*, 1970)

Notes Towards an African Oresteia (*Appunti Per un'Orestiade Africana*, 1970)

The Walls of Sana'a (*Le Mura di Sana'a*, 1971)

12 December 1972 (*12 Dicembre 1972*, 1972)

---

2 Advantages for filmmakers with anthology movies included: they didn't have to originate them or raise the cash – the producer did all of that; they could be filmed in one or two weeks; they could dig out unmade ideas; they could write their own scripts or come up with their own ideas; and they often had more freedom than with a feature film.

Pasolini and the Shape of the City (*Pasolini e la forma della città,* 1975)

✳

Pier Paolo Pasolini's 1955 novel *Ragazzi di vita* was adapted into a movie by Jacques-Laurent Bost and Pasolini: *La Notte Brava* (a.k.a. *Bad Girls Don't Cry,* a.k.a. *The Big Night*, Mauro Bolognini, 1959). It was produced by Antonio Cervi and Oreste Jacovini for Ajace Film and Franco-London Film. In the cast were: Rosanna Schiaffino, Laurent Terzieff, Jean-Claude Brialy, Franco Interlenghi, Antonella Lauldi, Mylène Demengeot and Elsa Martinelli.

A chapter from *Ragazzi di vita* was adapted in *La Canta dell Marane* (1960, dir. Cecilia Mangini). It was produced by Giorgio Patara.

Una Vita Violenta (*A Violent Life,* dirs. Paolo Heusch and Brunello Rondi) was adapted by Ennio De Concini, Franco Brusati, Paolo Heusch, Brunello Rondi and Franco Solinas in 1962. *A Violent Life* was produced by Aera Films/ Zebra Film.

✳

Pier Paolo Pasolini worked on about 15 scripts b4 directing his first feature, *Accattone*, in 1961. As a screenwriter, Pasolini contributed to movies (working with many other writers) such as:

• *La Donna del Fiume* (1954, with 5 other writers: Bassani, Franchina, Vancini, Altovitti and Soldati),

• *Il Prigioniero della Montagna* (1955, with Trenker and Bassani),

• *Nights of Cabiria* (1956, alongside 3 other writers: Fellini, Flaiano and Pinnelli),

• *Marisa la Civetta* (1957, with 2 writers: Demby and Bolognini),

• *A Farewell To Arms* (1957, with Ben Hecht and John Huston),

• *Giovani Mariti* (1958, with 5 other writers: Currelli, Martino, Bolognini, Franciosa and Camanile),

• *La Notte Brava* (1959, with Jacques-Laurent Bost),

• *Marte di un Amico* (1960, with 5 other writers: Berto, Biancoli, Rossi, Guerra and Riganti),

- *I Bell'Antonio* (1960, with Brancati, Bolognini and Visentini),
- *La Lunga Notte del '43* (1960, with Bassani, Vancini and Concini),
- *La Giornata Balorda* (1960, with Moravia and Visconti),
- *Il Carro Armato dell'8 Settembre* (1960, with Baratti, Bertolini and Questi),
- *La Ragazza In Vetrina* (1961, with Cassuto, Emmer, Sonego, Martino and Marinucci),
- *The Grim Reaper* (1962, a.k.a. *La Commare Secca*,[3] with Citti and Bertolucci),

He also co-wrote with Sergio Citti the films *Ostia* (1970) and *Storie Scellerate* (1973), both of which Citti directed.

✼

Pier Paolo Pasolini's books of poetry include:
Poesie e Casarsa (1942)
Diarii (1945)
Tal cour di un frut (1953/ 1974)
La Meglio gioventù (1954)
Le Ceneri di Gramsci (1957)
L'Usignolo della chiesa cattolica (1958)
La Religione del mio tempo (1961)
Poesia in forma di rosa (1964)
Trasumanar e organizzar (1971)
La Nuova gioventù (1975)
and *Roman Poems* (1986)
Pier Paolo Pasolini's fiction and narratives include:
Amado Mio - Atti Impuri (1948/ 1982)
Ragazzi di vita (*The Ragazzi*, 1955)
Una Vita Violenta (*A Violent Life*, 1959)
A Dream of Something (1962)
Roman Nights and Other Stories (1965)
Reality (*The Poets' Encyclopedia*, 1979)

---

[3] Pier Paolo Pasolini had conceived *The Grim Reaper* (writing a five-page treatment), but decided to make *Mamma Roma* instead. Producer Antonio Cervi had bought the project from Pasolini, and decided to let Bernardo Bertolucci have a go at directing it, after seeing the script he had commissioned from Bertolucci and Sergio Citti. Bertolucci admitted that his first film as director (he was only 21), *The Grim Reaper*, was made very much in the Pasolinian mold.

Petrolio (1992)

Pier Paolo Pasolini's volumes of essays and writings include: *Passione e ideologia* (1960), *Canzoniere italiano, poesia popolare italiana* (1960), *Empirismo eretico* (1972), *Scritti corsari* (1975), *Lettere luterane* (1976), *Le belle bandiere* (1977), *Descrizioni di descrizioni* (1979), *Il caos* (1979), *La pornografia è noiosa* (1979) and *Lettere (1940–1954)* (*Letters, 1940-54*, 1986).

Pier Paolo Pasolini directed plays. In Turin he directed a version of *Orgia* in November, 1968. The cast included Laura Betti, Luigi Mezzanotte and Nelide Giammarco.

Pier Paolo Pasolini's theatre work includes: *Orgia* (1968), *Porcile* (1968), *Calderón* (1973), *Affabulazione* (1977), *Pilade* (1977), and *Bestia da stile* (1977).

Films/ TV shows/ documentaries have been made after Pier Paolo Pasolini's death from his works (some have quoted from his poems and plays), including:

Laboratorio teatrale di Luca Ronconi (1977)
Mulheres... Mulheres (1981)
Calderon (1981)
Die Leiche murde nie gefunden (1985)
L'altro enigma (1988)
Who Killed Pasolini? (1995)
Complicity (1995)
Il pratone del casilino (1996)
Le bassin de J.W. (1997)
Una disperata vitalità (1999)
Orgia (2002)
Salò: Yesterday and Today (2002)
Pasolini prossimo nostro (2006)
'Na specie de cadavere lunghissimo (2006)
La rabbia di Pasolini (2008)
Pilades (2016)

Of the thirteen features directed by Pier Paolo Pasolini, only one is an acknowledged masterpiece: *The Gospel According to St Matthew* (taking its place alongside meisterwerks such as *8 1/2*, *The Searchers*,

Sunrise, Ran, Rashomon, Ordet, Persona, Vertigo, The Magnificent Ambersons, Citizen Kane and *The Godfather*). Some Pasolini pictures are highly regarded (*Theorem, Salò, Accattone*), some are minor (*Mamma Roma*), some deserve to be much better known (*The Arabian Nights, Medea, Oedipus Rex*), some are almost wilfully obscure (*The Canterbury Tales, Theorem*), some are very patchy (*The Hawks and the Sparrows,* parts of the 'trilogy of life' films), only parts of *Pigsty* are any good,[4] and one is a disaster (*Love Meetings*). But only *The Gospel According To Matthew* has become an out-and-out classic, that can take its place in the top ten lists of the critical academy. *The Gospel According To Matthew* is no. 30 in *Sight & Sound*'s 2012 poll of top movies among directors, and is included in the Vatican's list of important films (which the Pontifical Council For Social Communications produced in 1995, for the 100th anniversary of cinema). Other Italian films on the Vatican's list are *Rome: Open City, Bicycle Thieves, The Road, 8 1/2, The Leopard* and a forerunner of *The Gospel, Francesco.*

And of Pier Paolo Pasolini's short fiction films (for anthology movies), most are disappointing (*The Witches, Capriccio all'Italiana, Love and Anger*), with only two attaining greatness (*Curd Cheese* and *The Anger*).

However, some critics and filmmakers have put *Salò* into their top ten lists, and Bernardo Bertolucci places *Accattone* in there (as have some other critics). Occasionally a film like *The Arabian Nights* or *Oedipus the King* makes it into a critic's top ten. (The Italian movies that regularly crop up in top ten movie lists include *The Leopard, The Road, Bicycle Thieves, La Dolce Vita, The Conformist, Voyage To Italy* and *Rome, Open City*. The single most beloved Italian movie around the world for film critics and film directors is definitely *8 1/2*, the astonishing and enormously

---

[4] Yes, we know that *Pig Fry* is a poetical-political-polemical fable, a savage satire about survival and being human and capitalist consumerism and why aren't there any cafés on Mount Etna where you get a cheeseburger and a decent cup of coffee?

entertaining exploration of a modern film director in crisis helmed by Federico Fellini – closely followed by *La Dolce Vita*).

One should note, too, that directing 13 pictures over 15 years (from 1961-1975) is very productive (plus the anthology pieces and the documentaries). I wish that Pier Paolo Pasolini had started directing earlier (he was 40 when *Accattone* was released), and also that we might have seen the incredible work that Pasolini would no doubt have created from 1975 onwards (his *St Paul*, his *Socrates* – even, maybe, his *Terms of Endearment 3,* his *X-Men 6,* his *Star Trek 9*).

PASOLINI AS EUROPEAN *AUTEUR*

Although Pier Paolo Pasolini is classed with other European *auteurs* as a maker of small-scale art films (as if only North American or internationally-financed pictures could be 'epic' or large scale), in fact many of Pasolini's films as director have an enormous scope (and they were also part-financed by American companies). Sure, some of Pasolini's pictures are intimate and small-scale, but many of them happily contend with hundreds of extras, props, animals, costumes and a huge number of different locations and sets. In many movies directed by Pasolini the frame is teeming with human life – in the mediæval trilogy and in *The Gospel According To Matthew*. Pasolini, in some ways, is the European equivalent of Cecil B. DeMille or D.W. Griffith as a creator of historical epics.

Of course, there have been plenty of European, costume epic films over the years, but Pier Paolo Pasolini's films are very different from those international movies which are usually co-productions between, say, French, Italian, German, Spanish, Swedish or British film companies. Pasolini's films do not have the style, flavour or feel of the typical 'Euro-pudding' with their starry casts, glamour, and self-conscious apeing of Hollywood cinema.[5] Instead, Pasolini goes completely his own way, doesn't pander to creating star parts or scene-stealing cameos, doesn't cast U.S. actors, doesn't have easy-to-follow plots, doesn't shoot in English (or mid-Atlantic), and his cinematic approach is instantly recognizable (and has proved inimitable – very few film directors have the vision, the guts, the energy, the sheer stubbornness or, crucially, the *patience* to pursue that kind of grand, vast filmmaking).

Some of Pier Paolo Pasolini's Italian contemporaries produced large-scale historical films: Federico Fellini, Bernardo Bertolucci and Luchino Visconti, for instance. But Bertolucci's historical epics, from *1900* to *The Last Emperor* and *The Sheltering Sky*, were always commercial, European-American productions (in style and casting, if not in financing). Incredible as many of Bertolucci's later movies were, they were always slickly and glossily turned out, more than half in love with the creation of finely-crafted visuals (what Jean-Luc Godard called the cinema of Max Factor, his comments *pace Schindler's List*. Pasolini thought that Bertolucci had sold out to commercialism with *Last Tango In Paris*). Luchino Visconti's later films also have that eager eye on the international market. (Notice too that Pasolini doesn't do the usual thing of recreating the past accurately of historical movies: no, he preferred to produce characters and settings by analogy. Thus, the *Bible* wouldn't be filmed in Israel or Palestine, but in Calabria and Sicily).

Comparing the cinema of Pier Paolo Pasolini with that of Bernardo Bertolucci,[6] Bruce Kawin and Gerald Mast (in *A Short History of the Movies*) assert that Pasolini's movies are

> more abstract, more elliptical, more complexly

---

[5] However, Pasolini's later films were part-financed by American companies.
[6] Pier Paolo Pasolini remarked that Bertolucci's 'real master is Godard' (*Pasolini On Pasolini*, 138).

structured, and more ferociously aggressive moral-
political investigations, enlivened and propelled
by dazzling bursts of unforgettable imagery...
(338)

In his history of Italian cinema, Gian Brunetta remarked that

Of the entire generation of 1960s filmmakers, none stood out like Pier Paolo Pasolini. He was a postwar one-man band, capable ot transforming everything he touched into gold, from painting, poetry, and narartive to cinematography. Even his life and death were works of art. (238)

Somehow, Pier Paolo Pasolini's films remained stubbornly his own, far more idiosyncratic and eccentric than most of his contemporaries, except filmmakers such as Federico Fellini (Fellini's films were always highly self-conscious and comical in their evocations of history – *Fellini Satyricon*, for example, or *Roma*). Sometimes reaching for camp eccentricity appears laboured and clunky in cinema; for Pasolini, as for Fellini, Walerian Borowczyk and Ken Russell, it seems almost effortless (indeed, it is their natural habitat; when people drew attention to the vulgarity, the eccentricity, the eroticism and the silliness of their movies, they would reply, eh? I don't know what you mean. Because for them, it was natural to make movies like that!).

No doubt Pier Paolo Pasolini was a powerful talent in cinema, but let's not forget that he was aided by some of the greatest artists in Italian cinema, some of whom have been called geniuses: Danilo Donati (costumes), Dante Ferretti (production designer), Nino Baragli (editor), Sergio Citti (writer/ director), Giuseppe Rotunno and Tonino Delli Colli (photographers) and Ennio Morricone (composer).

There must have been times when Pier Paolo Pasolini's producers pleaded with the *auteur* to at least include some big names in some cameos, or to cast one or two star actors. But no, Pasolini simply didn't. However, he and his casting directors did put some well-known faces into his movies, include Silvana Mangano, Anna Magnani, Terence Stamp, Orson Welles, Totò, Hugh Griffith, Jean-Pierre Léaud, and Maria Callas. (And of course Pasolini helped to make Franco Citti a star, at least in Italy).

But I'm sure some of Pier Paolo Pasolini's producers wished he'd used plenty more stars, or used them in the conventional way (that would be the instinct of Italian producers such as Dino de Laurentiis and Carlo Ponti). There would be all sorts of factors involved here, not least money – the budgets of some of Pasolini's movies were small, compared to big, international co-productions, and to Hollywood A-pictures. Also, I would guess that some film stars wouldn't want to appear in the kind of movies that Pasolini was making (and also, they wouldn't do some of the things that the movies required, such as nudity. Sure, Marlon Brando might bugger Maria Schneider in *Last Tango In Paris*, but he did it fully clothed!).

It's intriguing to note that Pier Paolo Pasolini made three ancient world movies: *The Gospel According To Matthew*, *Medea* and *Oedipus Rex*, and three Middle Ages movies: *The Arabian Nights*, *The Decameron* and *The Canterbury Tales*. He was very happy in distant history (most filmmakers, if they film historical periods, go back to the mid or early 20th century (often their early years, or that of their parents), or to the 19th century[7] at most). Indeed, the last significant work that Pasolini produced that was set in the contemporary period in feature movies was one half of *Porcile* (the other half was set in the 15th century). His next four films after 1969 were historical pieces.

You can easily discern the influence of the cinema of Pier Paolo Pasolini on filmmakers such as Sergei Paradjanov (a huge admirer of Pasolini), Federico

---

[7] Pier Paolo Pasolini's works are steeped in Victoriana – the hysterical melodrama, the Gothicism and Romanticism, the early Industrial Revolution, the emerging metropolises, the industrialization of desire in mass prostitution, early capitalism, etc.

Fellini, Francis Coppola, Oliver Stone, Terry Gilliam (and the Monty Python team),[8] Derek Jarman, Peter Greenaway, Bernardo Bertolucci, Martin Scorsese, Jeunet and Caro, Guillermo del Toro and Abel Ferrara. In 2003 Gian Brunetta noted Pasolini's continuing impact on Italian filmmakers such as Mario Martone, Luigi Faccini, Nico d'Alessandria, Aurelio Grimaldi, Pappi Corsicato, Daniele Ciprí and Franco Maresco (239).

> Pasolini's life's work and his cinema continue to speak to us thanks to his cultural nomadism, his ability to mix and hybridize all codes, his asystematic working method, and his ability to tap into the pulse and capture the soul of minorities and regional identity. (239)

FIRST WORKS IN CINEMA

In Bologna, Pier Paolo Pasolini saw some of the classics for the first time: Charlie Chaplin, Jean Renoir, René Clair, etc. 'That's where my great love for the cinema started' (PP, 30). Films like *Rome, Open City* and *Bicycle Thieves*[9] made a big impact on the young Pasolini (ibid.).

Pier Paolo Pasolini had written his first film script in 1945 (aged 23), called *I calzon* or *Lied*. When he arrived in Roma (in 1950), he began writing movie scripts professionally. Some of the early screenplays were co-written (such as *La Donna del Fiume*, with Giorgio Bassani).

In the mid-1950s, Pier Paolo Pasolini was working

---

[8] One can see the influence of Pier Pasolini Pasolini in the Ancient Greek sequence in *Time Bandits* (Terry Gilliam, 1981), or in Monty Python's *Life of Brian* (the desert sequences in both films also allowed the two Terrys (Jones and Gilliam) to recreate Pasolini, whom they loved, as well as a bit of the Biblical epics – *Ben-Hur* and *The Ten Commandments*).

[9] He went to Udine (from Casarsa) specially to see *Bicycle Thieves*. He wasn't so young, tho' – *Bicycle Thieves* was released in 1948, when Pasolini was 26.

in movies as a scriptwriter. He published his key works in this period – such as *Ragazzi di vita* and his poetry book *La Meglio gioventù.*

When Pier Paolo Pasolini was dating Sergio Citti in the mid-1950s, he became friendly with many of the *ragazzi* of the *borgate*, the real-life street kids who would become non-professional actors in his first movies, from *Accattone* onwards.

Pier Paolo Pasolini was most productive in the years prior to his entry into film production, according to his biographer Enzo Siciliano: from 1953 to 1961. This was the period when he published novels (*Ragazzi di Vita, Una Vita Violenta*), poetry (*La Ceneri di Gramsci, La Religione del mio tempo*), 13 film scripts, translations (*Oresteia*), and magazine articles (such as for *Officina*).

SCRIPTS

All of the movies that Pier Paolo Pasolini wrote before taking up directing with *Accattone* were *co*-written: Pasolini was *not* the sole screenwriter on *La Donna del Fiume, Il Prigioniero della Montagna, Le Notti di Cabiria, Marisa La Civetta*, etc. Instead, he was part of writing teams which included Basilio Franchina, Florestano Vancini, Antonio Altovitti and Mario Soldati (*La Donna del Fiume*), Luis Trenker, and Giorgio Bassani (*Il Prigioniero della Montagna*), Federico Fellini, Ennio Flaiano and Tullio Pinelli (*Nights of Cabiria*), etc. Other films Pasolini contributed to were: *The Big Night, La Giornata balorda, Giovani mariti, Morte di un amico, Il Carro armato dell '8 settembre, La Ragazza in vetrina* and *La Cantata delle marane.* Pasolini worked with Bassani (1916-2000) on several films, including *Una Notte del' 43.* Bassani dubbed Orson Welles in *Curd Cheese,* and he wrote the novel *Il*

Giardino dei Finzi-Contini (later filmed by Vittorio de Sica).

It's also worth noting that before he started to direct with *Accattone*, Pier Paolo Pasolini had already had some of his works made into movies – though he didn't direct them. A chapter of the important Pasolini novel *Ragazzi di Vita* was adapted in *La Canta dell Marane* (1960, dir. Cecilia Mangini), and *Ragazzi di Vita* was made into a movie in 1959, as *La Notte Brava* (= *The Big Night,* dir. Mauro Bolognini), and *Una Vita Violenta* (= *A Violent Life*) was filmed by Ennio De Concini, Franco Brusati, Paolo Heusch, Brunello Rondi and Franco Solinas in 1962 (*Una Vita Violenta*, dir. Paolo Heusch and Brunello Rondi).

✻

Only a very few filmmakers write and direct their movies. I don't mean co-write, I mean who are the sole writers of their films. And even fewer filmmakers write and direct *from their own ideas* (i.e., they come up with the fundamental concept). Because most movies are adapted from existing material, whether it's comic-books, plays, books, computer games, TV shows, musicals, newspaper articles, or even theme park rides (plus remakes, sequels, reboots, etc).

And Pier Paolo Pasolini is no different: although we think of him as an *auteur*, writing and directing his movies (each one with the possessive credit: '*un film scritto e diretto da*'), in fact maybe half of his movies are based on existing material. They do not come from ideas and stories that Pasolini has conceived himself. Instead, they are adaptations – usually of classic literature: mediæval literature in three movies (the 'trilogy of life' series), three ancient world sources (*The Gospel According To Matthew*, *Medea* and *Oedipus Rex*), and the Marquis de Sade (*Salò*). So Pasolini didn't invent the concepts, the characters, the stories, the situations, the themes, the settings, the interactions, the relationships or many other elements of those adaptations.

The movies that are based on Pier Paolo Pasolini's

own ideas and stories include: *The Hawks and the Sparrows, Accattone, Mamma Roma, Theorem, Curd Cheese, The Earth Seen From the Moon* and *Pigsty*. Also, Pasolini did *not* write everything himself: he co-authored his scripts with writers such as Dacia Maraini, Pupi Avati, Giorgio Bassani, and Sergio Citti.

Pier Paolo Pasolini didn't take up pot-boilers, sleazy novels, airport fiction, computer games, theme park rides, TV comedies, sit-coms, radio shows, comicbooks or the backs of cereal packets to adapt into movies: he took up the very greatest literature, heavyweight authors like Sophocles, Euripides, Aeschylus, the *Bible*, Giovanni Boccaccio, Geoffrey Chaucer, the Marquis de Sade and *The Thousand and One Nights*. Well, that's a *very* impressive list! Nobody can doubt the high ambition or the seriousness of the master's approach!

For Jean-Luc Godard, all of the work in making a film is *already done* before the cameras started rolling. The real work of making the film was the scriptwriting and the preparation. 'Most people think they work only when the camera is rolling, but that's not it. When the camera rolls, everything is done already'.[10] That certainly applies to Pasolini – it's all about the conception and the writing.

FLAWS IN PASOLINI'S CINEMA

I am writing about the movies directed by Pier Paolo Pasolini primarily as movies, as movie experiences, in a deliberately simple and direct manner. But of course there are *thematic* and *narrative* and *political* and *psychological* and *theoretical* perspectives to these films which are rich and inspiring.

However, there are times in watching a Pasolini

---

[10] *Interviews*, 1998, 174.

movie when you think:

This is twaddle.[11]

I don't care if he's a major poet and political rebel and cultural iconoclast! It's as if Dante Alighieri directed *Deep Throat*!

Observers of the Legend and Cult of Pasolini in the early 1970s might've looked at the 'trilogy of life' movies with exasperation and dismay: when is Pasolini, they might've thought, going to stop bothering with these silly saucy frolics and get back to something worthy of his immense talents, like *Medea* or *Oedipus Rex*? (Well, Pasolini *did* come back to something very serious after the three Middle Ages romps, but it was *Salò, or The 120 Days of Sodom*! – a film that was so far in the other direction, it wasn't what audiences were expecting, and probably not what the Pasolini admirers wanted).

Unfortunately, with the less-than-successful movies in the Pier Paolo Pasolini canon – such as *Love Meetings, The Hawks and the Sparrows, Pigsty* and *The Canterbury Tales* – it becomes more difficult to sustain the hi-falutin' theoretical approach. I mean, if you didn't know that Pasolini directed *The Canterbury Tales,* would we even be discussing it today? Wouldn't it have been relegated to the marginal critical discourses of cult movies or *mondo* cinema? An entertaining, weird, over-the-top slice of 1970s kitsch, but ultimately small potatoes?

Not *everything* by a great filmmaker has to be 'great' (or can be 'great'), does it?[12] Orson Welles completed twelve features (a comparable number with Pier Paolo Pasolini's thirteen features): seven are masterpieces, by my reckoning – *Kane, Ambersons, Othello, Touch, Macbeth, F For Fake* and *Shanghai* –

---

11 This thought – am I watching piffle? – occurs with many directors who are highly critically acclaimed – Steven Spielberg, Sergio Leone, Billy Wilder, Martin Scorsese, John Woo, Vincente Minnelli, even Alfred Hitchcock, John Ford and D.W. Griffith.

12 Like many filmmakers (such as Woody Allen, Tim Burton and Hayao Miyazaki), Pier Paolo Pasolini said he never went to see his own films (PP, 108). Sometimes he saw them at film festivals, but he'd never dared to go see one of his movies in a public theatre.

but his 1955 movie *Mr Arkadin* (a.k.a. *Confidential Report*) was, by his own admission, a failure (whichever you look at, in whichever botched, public domain version you get to see it, *Mr Arkadin* is incredibly disappointing). *Mr Arkadin* was an important personal project for Welles, but the post-production had been unhappy (a recurring motif in Welles' film career), and the film had been re-cut by the producer (Louis Dolivet).

Or take Francis Coppola: an all-round filmmaker with few peers and a truly colossal talent, Coppola has directed at least three masterpieces (*The Godfathers 1* and *2* and *Apocalypse Now*, though some would include *The Conversation*, and I would include more), but many critics found *Jack* (1996) perplexingly lightweight, and Coppola's two early movies – *Finian's Rainbow* (1968) and *You're a Big Boy Now* (1966) – are uneven (some would say mis-conceived and very dissatisfying – certainly *Finian's Rainbow*, as a Fred Astaire musical, is under-whelming).

To a degree, Pier Paolo Pasolini suffered like Orson Welles and Francis Coppola from a similar problem, seen in conventional critical terms: they were very successful early in their careers. Everything Welles did after *Citizen Kane* was compared with *Citizen Kane*, and his films never escaped that blinkered view from critics.[13] And Coppola is routinely satirized by critics as the man who directed *The Godfather* but went into artistic 'decline' in the 1980s with *The Cotton Club* and *One From the Heart*.

Rubbish, of course, but persistent rubbish.

Pier Paolo Pasolini, meanwhile, launched a filmmaking career with a minor masterwork, *Accattone*, and produced the staggering, 100% classic *The Gospel According To Matthew* three years later. As with Orson Welles and Francis Coppola and other filmmakers, early successes mean other movies can get made, but the stigma of early triumphs can colour the critical reception of later works. And in the case of Welles and

---

[13] Which is also applied all the time to Woody Allen, where audiences prefer his early, funny films.

Coppola, critics' emphasis on the early triumphs becomes obsessive (both Coppola and Welles became completely exasperated by everybody harking on about those early works, even while they appreciated that at least people were talking about them!).

I'm sure that the later films of Pier Paolo Pasolini tried the patience and devotion of even his most ardent admirers (as with the later work of Jean-Luc Godard, Walerian Borowczyk, Ken Russell and Terry Gilliam). You can imagine Pasolini-worshippers turning up to theatres to see *Pigsty* in 1969 or *The Canterbury Tales* in 1972, and wondering if their Freudo-Marxo-Poetico God was losing his marbles. Jean-Pierre Léaud getting freaky with pigs in a film about cannibalism? Eh?! Hugh Griffith humping on top of Charlie Chaplin's daughter in a movie stuffed with spotty, greasy, British non-actors?

✳

When you watch the films of Pier Paolo Pasolini again and again, some of the technical aspects and the flaws do rankle: the shaky, handheld camera,[14] the patchy sound, the endless shots of people walking, and too much Ninetto Davoli.

There is a *lot* of filler in Pier Paolo Pasolini's later films. Filler meaning, for example, shots of people walking in landscapes and towns. Now, the Pasolini sympathizers can point out the atmospherics, the mood, the Existential loneliness, the exquisitely-poised, ontological *ennui*, etc, of a shot of a guy walking across a volcano (*Pigsty*) or thru an anonymous, Middle Eastern town (*The Arabian Nights*). But Pasolini detractors can rightly criticize such images as pointless, redundant, or dramatically, poetically empty – the characters have already been established, the story is already in progress, the chief locales have been explored, so four shots of a guy getting from A to B are not necessary, and even harm the narrative flow.

---

[14] Pier Paolo Pasolini operated the *macchina* himself sometimes. Unfortunately, he's no Stanley Kubrick, Ridley Scott or Ken Russell. He can't hold a camera. (One of the reasons for his terrible camerawork might be that he's yelling instructions at his actors at the same time!)

Take a movie everybody has seen – *Jaws* (1975): do we need to watch Police Chief Brody driving for 15 minutes down to the dock where he joins the crew of the *Orca* boat? No – we cut straight to it. Do we need to see all fifteen hours of the connecting flights from the U.S.A. to the island off the coast of Costa Rica in *Jurassic Park* (1993) – plus four hours waiting in the terminal at Panama? No – we cut straight to the island. (An Ancient Greek text might say, 'And then he went to Thebes'. But that doesn't mean we need to see five lengthy shots of a guy walking to Thebes!).

Endless shots of people walking are a sure sign that a filmmaker is out of ideas. Yes, even a hyper-super-mega-genius like Pasolini. There's no juice in such shots (even isolated, Existential, metaphysical, ontological, outsider-ish juice). The filmmaker has admitted to the audience: *I have no idea how to dramatize the script or the story.* (This occurs even in *The Gospel According To Matthew*).

ANTI-CINEMA

When you consider all of the films of Pier Paolo Pasolini, sometimes it seems as if these movies *don't* want to be liked, or enjoyed (at least in the usual manner). As if, as with Carl-Theodor Dreyer, Robert Bresson and Andrei Tarkovsky, Pasolini wasn't going to make it easy for the viewer. And sometimes it can appear as if Pasolini's movies are being deliberately off-putting. Not 'offensive' or 'obscene', just plain difficult or obscure. A kind of anti-cinema, where expectations are wilfully, stubbornly scuppered. (Yes, there is definitely in Pasolini a delight in being difficult for the sake of it, as with Jean-Luc Godard).

For example, how would a Pier Paolo Pasolini movie play in a big cinema multiplex today? Reactions might run from laughter, scorn and ridicule to dismay and walk-outs. These are not movies that're going to preview well! They would die a death in the preview process, where unreleased movies are shown to invited audiences from the general public, getting a near-zero rating from the score cards. (Pasolini's personality, his financial contracts – and his reputation – would mean his films would be exempted from the preview process. Is a Pasolini movie going to be screened before an audience culled from shopping malls in San Diego who're then going to 'judge' his movie? I don't think so!).

They are not funny when they're meant to be funny, they are not scary when they're meant to be scary, they are not thrilling when they're meant to be thrilling, they are not dramatic when you expect/ hope them to be dramatic, they are not romantic when you think they might be romantic. They don't do what audiences would expect them to do. The technical aspects let Pier Paolo Pasolini's movies down, from the sound (the crude voice dubbing, the lack of sound effects (or 'immersion'), and the poor sound mixes),[15] to the picture (the too-shaky camerawork, and the sometimes indifferent staging).

There's an impossible-to-miss self-analysis in Pier Paolo Pasolini's cinema, a love-hate relationship with the material: as with the movies of Jean-Luc Godard, you can feel Pasolini's films arguing with themselves, simultaneously loving as well as distrusting the material, the themes, even individual shots. Like all artists, Pasolini wants to have it all ways: to evoke a scene of, say, extras in exotic costumes in a dusty, Mediterranean setting, but also to critique the subject and the very idea of making a movie in the first place.

This restlessness and dissatisfaction permeates not

---

[15] Oh, how I wish that Alfredo Bini or Franco Rossellini or Alberto Grimaldi, the principal producers of Pier Paolo Pasolini's movies, had said, OK, we will use some of the budget to buy some decent sound equipment. This time it's live sound for us! Direct sound! Sound recorded on the set! *Si, si*, no more crappy dubbing at Cinecittà for us! (But the maestro of course preferred to deal with the sound in post-production).

only Pier Paolo Pasolini's cinema but also his poetry, and his whole work. And his personality, too, as those who knew him attest. Pasolini, everybody agrees, was a very complicated person.

✵

The cinema of Pier Paolo Pasolini does not do other things that audiences expect from movies. They do not employ conventional dramaturgy, for example. They avoid the conventions of rising action and cause and effect. So the flow of the drama and the narrative from scene-to-scene of your average movie is negated. Pasolini's movies do not build and build with suspense or tension or drama. Many scenes are self-enclosed, with little relation to scenes before or after.

And when you couple that avoidance of conventional dramaturgy with the intense stylizations of Pier Paolo Pasolini's cinematic approach – the flattened, static, *tableau* approach, for instance, or the paucity of dialogue or exposition – it creates a cinema that can be tough-going for some viewers. You can't slide thru a Pasolini movie easily, quickly and cheaply (with no investment): you have to *work*. It's not easy-to-digest television, like *C.S.I.* or *Friends*.

Pier Paolo Pasolini wasn't interested in action, either, or staging impressive spectacles (the 1st A.D.s would organize a vast array of extras, animals and props, which would then be filmed with a single, wobbly, handheld shot from a single viewpoint).[16] Like Jean-Luc Godard, Pasolini was indifferent to action (Godard famously filmed action as quickly as possible; he just couldn't be bothered with it). Pasolini wasn't interested in the glamour of cinema, or in making people look gorgeous, like the Hollywood Dream Factory (tho' he would insist on very extravagant costumes and hats. Which would then be filmed somewhat casually – unlike Walerian Borowczyk, who has probably the most acute and sensual feeling for clothes in all cinema).

---

[16] No multiple cameras, either, or additional takes for safety, to make sure that a scene had been captured.

DOCUMENTARIES

Sam Rohdie noted that 'Pasolini's documentaries were feigned. His past was not real, but a fragment framed, cut out. Reality was mutilated to make it all the more beautiful' (1995, 109). Pasolini realized that his essay/documentary pieces were for a minority, intellectual audience (PP, 140).

Pier Paolo Pasolini's documentaries are niche, certainly, and they are let down by misguided concepts, some dubious ideology, and poor technical aspects. But with the right producer, or maybe the right commissions from television companies, I reckon that Pasolini might've been amongst the finest documentary filmmakers in cinema. He possessed all of the skills required to deliver some great material, except for the discipline and rigour to really make the material fly. Plus, with a major TV company behind him, he could have drawn on the resources necessary to complete the ambitious projects he wanted to make. (But he would also need a very strong TV producer who could say 'no' to his face).

Take the documentary made in Africa and Italy about staging an African version of Aeschylus' *Oresteia* – *Notes Towards an African Oresteia* (1970). The concept is full of ideological holes, and the execution is scrappy at best, and downright dreadful at worst.

So dump all of that material, and start again with a decent team of filmmakers and decent resources, and put the director himself in the picture (it's silly to squander a striking and well-known personality on camera like Pasolini, and have him hide behind a microphone back in Roma. Put Pasolini front and centre. And let's also see Pasolini directing his cast of amateurs in Africa).

Compare Pier Paolo Pasolini's documentaries with two geniuses of the medium in the same Euro-art arena: Werner Herzog and Jean-Luc Godard. Herzog has produced a striking and lively set of documentaries and film essays, often about exotic subjects in far-flung places (the Amazon, Africa, caves, etc). Like Pasolini,

Herzog often appears in his documentaries, exploring places and interviewing people. He is a far more sympathetic interviewer than Pasolini, who tended to dominate his interviewees, and to ask them rhetorical questions (as if he'd already decided what he wanted his documentary to say). Herzog's documentaries are quirky and very distinctive (Herzog's German-accented voice-overs identified them as thoroughly Herzogian).

Jean-Luc Godard, meanwhile, is a master of the film essay form – half of his fiction movies, for example, might be characterized as film essays. Godard produced several fascinating film essays about his feature films, which he called notes for films (and Godard can talk about cinema as few people can, including Pasolini. Godard is a formidable intellectual talent). And with *Histoire(s) du Cinéma,* Godard created an epic history of cinema (between 1989 and 1998). *Histories of Cinema* was a major work, and has generated a good deal of critical comment. As well as being a history of cinema, it was also a history of the age – and a history of Godard himself.

DOCUMENTARIES ABOUT PASOLINI

Pier Paolo Pasolini has fascinated TV documentary producers – there was a documentary of 1970 (filmed with Pasolini's co-operation), and *Who Says the Truth Shall Die* (Phil Bregstein, 1981). Several documentaries have appeared on *Salò – Fade To Black* (2001), *Salò: Yesterday and Today* (2002), *Enfants de Salò* (2006, French), *Pasolini Prossimo Nostro* (2006, Italian) and *The End of Salò* (2008). Pasolini's murder was explored in *Who Killed Pasolini?* (1995). A ficionalized account of Pasolini was released in 2014 (with Willem Dafoe as the great man).

PASOLINI.

Pasolini (Abel Ferrara, 2014) was a biographical portrait of the last days of Pier Paolo Pasolini. Starring Willem Dafoe, Maria de Medeiros, Ninetto Davoli, Adrianna Asti and Riccardo Scamarcio, produced by Thierry Lounas and Fabio Massimo Cacciatori for the production companies Urania Pictures/ Dublin Films/ Belgacom/ Canal Plus, and scripted by Maurizio Braucci, *Pasolini* was a curiously flat and unengaging take on an incendiary filmmaker and poet. For Pasolinians, there was not only nothing new here, and the opportunities for depicting a complex and compelling artist were squandered. *Pasolini* took a de-dramatized approach, flattening the aspects of this passionate artist into a series of boring images and boring dialogues.

We see: Pasolini working on the post-production of *Salò;* a snippet of Pasolini's home life (with his mother Susanna prominent (played by Pasolini regular Adriana Asti – she was Amore in *Accattone*)); an interview with a journalist; a visit from an effervescent actress;[17] and extracts from a novel that Pasolini was working on.

Pasolini was one of those works in which nothing much happens – either visually, narratively, dramatically, psychologically or philosophically. More like notes for a possible movie about Pier Paolo Pasolini (in the Godardian manner). It's scrappy. Bitty.

Time passes... *Pasolini* ends... a pointless group of images and sounds. Cinema at its worst.

Pasolini came alive a tad when Ninetto Davoli entered the frame – sort of playing himself (and shadowed by his former self, played by Riccardo Scamarcio), in an illustration of an unmade film idea from Pasolini about a spiritual journey/ religious skits, which included a visit to a gay and lesbian Sodom and Gomorrah (a festival where couples tup and the audience around them jeers and cheers. Presumably this is meant to be the 1973 unmade film project *Porno-Teo-Kolossal*). Not a patch on what Pasolini himself

---

[17] Is that meant to be Laura Betti? (Played by Maria de Medeiros).

would've done with a modern-day Sodom and Gomorrah scenario, of course.

Pasolini recreated the night in November, 1975, when the director was murdered after picking up a youth. This played out as expected, but without the political/ ideological/ blackmailing motives (instead, the three youths who round on Pasolini attack him partly for homophobic reasons, yelling insults as they kick him. That fudged the issue, avoiding an opportunity to explore the more controversial issues surrounding Pasolini's demise).

4

ASPECTS OF PASOLINI'S CINEMA

PIER PAOLO PASOLINI AND ITALIAN CINEMA

Pier Paolo Pasolini made his thirteen feature movies as a film director between 1961 and 1975, the years of a boom in the Italian film business, and of the European New Wave (but he had been working on co-written scripts thru the Fifties). This period of Italian cinema was marked by the regeneration of production after WW2, with movements such as the development of Neo-realism (embodied in productions such as *Rome: Open City*, Roberto Rossellini, 1945 and *Bicycle Thieves*, Vittorio de Sica, 1948). However, Neo-realist cinema was not popular in Italy itself, but overseas (especially North America). The significant filmmakers of this period were, with Rossellini and de Sica, Luchino Visconti and Alberto Lattuada. North American companies increasingly used Italian studios (such as Cinecittà): they followed the money, which couldn't be repatriated. When M.G.M. made *Quo Vadis* in Italy in 1950, other U.S. studios followed (and the Yanks visited Italy throughout the 1960s).

Actually, how 'Italian' is Italian cinema? Pasolini's and Fellini's later films, for example, were backed by North American companies (such as United Artists). It was the same with Visconti and Antonioni, as director Glauber Rocha of Brazil's New Cinema pointed out in the mid-1960s: 'Italy does not really have a national film industry, a truly Italian cinema, anymore' (in D. Georgakas, 17).

In the 1960s, Federico Fellini, Michelangelo Antonioni, Bernardo Bertolucci, Marco Bellocchio, Sergei Leone and the Tavianis were among the key film directors in Italy, as well as Pier Paolo Pasolini. The film stars included Marcello Mastroianni, Monica Vitti, Anna Magnani, Gina Lollobrigida, Sophia Loren, Vittorio Gassman, Totò and Silvana Mangano (Pasolini used Totò and Mangano the most). Among film producers of the period, such as Alberto Grimaldi and Alfredo Bini (who produced Pasolillni's films), two stand out in the Italian industry: Carlo Ponti[18] (married to Loren) and Dino de Laurentiis (married to Mangano); Pasolini worked with all of them).

The 1960s, according to Gian Brunetta,

> would prove to be the years of the greatest experimentation, freedom, and expressive riches. Not everything in the cauldron was made of gold, but the average qualitative level was the highest of all time. (171)

The Italian film industry reacted swiftly to any big hit movie, hurrying copies and sequels into production. Thus, successful movies such as *Spartacus* (1960), *Cleopatra* (1963), *Ben-Hur* (1959), and *Hercules* (1958) led to instant cash-ins. As Howard Hughes noted in *Cinema Italiano*:

> The story of Italian cinema is essentially a series of creative explosions, interspersed with fallow periods of audience exhaustion. If a film was popular, literally dozens of imitations would be made to cash-in at the domestic and international

---

[18] Carlo Ponti (1912-2007) is one of the legends of the Italian film industry. Ponti produced some 140 movies, including many film classics, such as *La Strada, Boccaccio '70, Doctor Zhivago, War and Peace, Closely Watched Trains, Cléo From 5 To 7*, and three Michelangelo Antonioni flicks, *The Passenger, Blow-Up* and *Zabriskie Point*.

box office. This intense technique often resulted in each fad enjoying rather limited longevity, as the glut quickly satisfied audience interest. (ix-xi)

Thus, there was a craze of musclemen movies with mythological or ancient world settings, inaugurated by *Hercules*[19] (1958),[20] which lasted from 1958 to 1964. The Spaghetti Western fad, sparked by the *Dollars* films starring Clint Eastwood, ran from 1965 to 1970 (but continued into the 1970s). The *James Bond*-inspired spy cycle ran from 1963 to 1967. Gothic horror flicks were popular from 1960 to 1965 (and again in the 1970s with the *gialli*). 1960 was a triumphant year for Italian cinema, with *Rocco and His Brothers* and *La Dolce Vita* becoming big critical and commercial successes. Pasolini's cinema had its own cash-ins (the 'trilogy of life' movies were obvious candidates for rip-offs, which were released rapidly following the success of *The Decameron*. Producers saw that they could deliver sex romps much cheaper, by leaving out the elaborate set-pieces with extras and animals).

Along with Germany, Spain, Holland and of course France, Italy has been one of the most significant film production territories in Europe. The number of productions made each year and the number of tickets sold (i.e., punters going to the cinema) is among the highest in Europe.

Pier Paolo Pasolini benefited from the boom years of Italian film production, when it was making more movies per year than Hollywood: 242 films were produced in 1962, for example, compared to 174 in North America. 245 films in Italy in 1966, compared to

---

[19] The Italian 1958 *Hercules* (the first one), starring Steve Reeves (Mr Universe) and helmed by Pietro Francisci, was so successful it inaugurated a series of Italian 'muscle-men', sword-and-sandal epics – some 180 films. *Hercules* cost $120,000 and made $20 million, and was released in 1959 thru Warners (producer Joe Levine had paid $120,000 for the rights). Its budget was less than 1% of that of Hollywood's *Ben-Hur* or *The Ten Commandments*, yet it made somewhere between 1/8th and 1/3rd as much (a producer's dream!). Levine launched *Hercules* with $1.1 million of advertizing, including on television ('the most aggressive campaign any film ever had', as William Goldman put it).
[20] The couple in *A Violent Life* go to see a *Hercules* movie at the cinema.

168 in the U.S.A. 237 productions in 1974, compared to 156 in America (the recession hit Hollywood badly in the early 1970s).

In the 1960s and the 1970s, the period when Pier Paolo Pasolini was active as a film director, Italy made more movies than any other European country, including France (which since then has become the premier country for production *and* consumption), and more people went to the cinema in Italy than in any other nation (this's if you exclude Russia from Europe – which most people did in the Cold War era).

So film culture is immensely significant in Italy (even though de-regulated, hyper-capitalist television in the Silvio Berlusconi era has over-shadowed it). And the star filmmakers, like Federico Fellini, Luchino Visconti, Bernardo Bertolucci, Michelangelo Antonioni and Pier Paolo Pasolini, have become well-known outside film circles. And Dino de Laurentiis is a legendary mogul whose movies (and those produced by his daughter Raffaella) have generated billions.[21]

Dino de Laurentiis (1919-2010) was probably the most well-known Italian producer of recent times, a formidable mogul who moved from Italian movies (*Il Bandito, Bitter Rice, Anna, Europa '51, La Lupa, La Strada*), to North American co-productions (*War and Peace, Ulysses*), to international movies (*Barabbas, Bandits In Rome, Serpico, Barbarella, Three Days of the Condor* and *The Valachi Papers*), and epics (*The Bible, Waterloo, The Bounty* and *Dune*). De Laurentiis produced all-out commercial ventures (such as *King Kong, Death Wish, Hurricane, Orca the Killer Whale, Flash Gordon, Conan the Barbarian, Year of the Dragon, Body of Evidence,* and *Hannibal*), but also movies by art maestros like Ingmar Bergman, Federico Fellini, Luchino Visconti, Michael Cimino, Milos Forman, David Lynch, Vittorio de Sica and Robert

---

[21] Jean-Luc Godard sent up Italian producers such as Carlo Ponti and Dino de Laurentiis (whom he's worked with), in his film *Passion* (1982), who always turn up with a beautiful woman on their arm. The producer in *Passion* yells: 'where's my money?', 'what have you done with my money?' It's one of the recurring phrases in the film business (usually yelled out, as of course it should be).

Altman (such as *Buffalo Bill, Desperate Hours, Face To Face, Lo Straniero,* and *Blue Velvet*). In North America in the 1980s, de Laurentiis founded D.E.G. (De Laurentiis Entertainment Group) in North Carolina, which flourished until it ended in 1988 (with, some said, debts of $200 million).

Dino de Laurentiis' career is truly remarkable – and long-running (he began producing during the German Occupation of Italy). He formed Real Cine in 1941 (when he was 23), produced *Il Bandito* (Alberto Lattuada, 1946), when he was 28, and married actress Silvana Mangano (who appeared in Pier Paolo Pasolini's *Theorem, The Decameron, The Witches* and *Oedipus Rex*, among others). With Carlo Ponti, de Laurentiis formed Ponti-De Laurentiis in 1950 (they owned the Farnesina Studios in Rome). De Laurentiis created Dinocittà outside Rome, where *The Bible, The Great War* and *Barabbas* were based. (Dinocittà has since become a movie theme park).

PASOLINI AND FELLINI

In the late 1950s, Pier Paolo Pasolini became part of Federico Fellini's court.[22] They had met at the Canova (Franco Rossi had brought them together). They took to wandering around Roma at night, with Pasolini introducing Fellini to some of the locations he drew inspiration from: Idroscalo, Tiburtino Terzo, Pietralata and Guidonia. The maestro had brought in Pasolini (and his partner, Sergio Citti) to help with some of his scripts (such as advising on the dialect in *Nights of Cabiria*[23] – dialect being one of Pasolini's passions). Pasolini wrote

---

[22] Totò parodied *La Dolce Vita* in *Totò, Peppino and La Dolce Vita* (1960).
[23] The settings of *Nights of Cabiria* – the outskirts of Roma, the scrubland and the caves – were employed several times in Pasolini's early films.

about 40 pages of the screenplay, according to Moraldo Rossi, but Fellini hardly used any of it.[24]

Federico Fellini later invited P.P. Pasolini to sit in on auditions at Cinecittà for projects such as *La Dolce Vita* (1960). Although some in the Fellini camp resented the maestro becoming so close to Pasolini, it was not a long-lasting friendship.[25] Fellini's wife Giulietta took 'an immediate dislike to the homosexual Pier Paolo as a corruptor of innocent young souls'),[26] and Fellini's regular screenwriter, Ennio Flaiano, refused to work with Pasolini on *La Dolce Vita*. Flaiano (known as a cynical, spiky writer) wrote a skit about it – "*La Dolce Vita* According To Pasolini" (which Fellini begged him not to publish).

Pier Paolo Pasolini had hoped that Federico Fellini (and his new company, Federiz, formed with the publisher Angelo Rizzoli), would back his first movie as director, *Accattone*[27] (Fellini and Rizzoli were also planning movies by Vittorio De Seta, Ermanno Olmi, Marco Ferreri and of course Fellini. But in the end, Fellini wasn't bothered about becoming a movie mogul – he only wanted to make his own films).

Tests for *Accattone* were shot (in September, 1960),[28] including two scenes: at via Fanfulla da Lodi, in the pine woods, and outside Castel Sant'Angelo. Pasolini later recalled meeting with Fellini to discuss them (after hearing nothing from the maestro): but it

---

24 Quoted in *Fellini On Fellini* 1995, 50.
25 It was a lively friendship, tho', according to Enzo Siciliano, 'a deep human attachment' (ES, 223).
26 Quoted in T. Kezich, 178.
27 *Accattone* announces its quirkiness from the outset: after those Renaissance-elegant opening titles, and the breezy, rarefied tones of J.S. Bach, what is the first shot of the movie? A pretty aerial view of the Eternal City? Oh no, this is not going to be a film featuring dignified professional actors spouting Shakespeare or Petrarch! Instead, it's a close-up of the ugly mug of Fulvio, joshing with the lads in their customary position: sitting outside the café in the side street. The final shot of *Accattone* is of Balilla, crossing himself as he looks down at the dying Accattone.
28 This was Pier Paolo Pasolini's first experience of being a film director, at least with his own material. His model was the 'absolutely simplicity of expression' in *The Passion of Joan of Arc*, directed by Carl-Theodor Dreyer. Another influential film for Pasolini was the 1950 *Francesco*, the portrait of St Francis and his followers directed by Roberto Rossellini using all non-professional actors (except for Aldo Fabrizi).

became apparent that Fellini and Rizzoli were not going to get behind *Accattone* (which in the event was produced by Alfredo Bini[29] – it was Bini who persuaded Pasolini to make *Accattone*).[30] According to Moraldo Rossi, Pasolini 'had staked everything on Fellini, but Fellini had dropped him'.[31] And from that point, Fellini and Pasolini fell out, sniping at each other's projects in the press.

PIER PAOLO PASOLINI'S COLLEAGUES

Critics typically talk about Pier Paolo Pasolini's movies in awed, auteurist terms, as if the director did *everything* in his movies. He didn't, though: he directed them, sometimes appeared in them in cameos, and wrote or co-wrote most of them (Pasolini did, however, believe in the *auteur* theory, unlike almost every filmmaker).[32] Thus, his films usually have the credit:

scritto e diretto da
or: *un film scritto e diretto da*

But one must always remember that Pier Paolo Pasolini was surrounded by some legends in Italian cinema – such as designers Dante Ferretti and Danilo Donati, DPs Giuseppe Rotunno and Tonino Delli Colli, producers Alfredo Bini and Alberto Grimaldi, and composer Ennio Morricone. And numerous others: by the 1960s, when Pasolini started to direct features, the Italian film industry boasted some of the finest, most

---

29 Mauro Bolognini saw photographs of the tests, and suggested the project to Bini.
30 E. Siciliano, 227.
31 Quoted in C. Constantin, 1995, 50.
32 Pasolini insisted that he 'always thought of a film as the work of an author, not only the script and the direction, but the choice of sets and locations, the characters, even the clothes. I choose everything – not to mention the music' (PP,32).

imaginative and skilled technicians and talents in the world. (Italian cinema was on a high, an up, a boom in this period).

The *auteur* credit, the 'un film de' credit, is dishonest and dumb. Who drew up all of the contracts (sometimes thousands for big movies)? Who oversaw the insurance, taxes, and liabilities? Who bought the cloth for the costumes? Who built the sets? Who booked the hotels? Who carried the lights up ten flights of stairs?[33] Who drove the actors to the locations? Who created the opticals for the titles? Who logged all of the rushes and takes? Who rented the vehicles? Who processed the exposed celluloid?[34] And who does 100s of other jobs in movie production?

Not the director.

This is a simplistic argument of who does what in movies, but *auteur* theory has also been disparaged on ideological, political, social, philosophical and cultural grounds.

The producers of Pier Paolo Pasolini's movies included Alfredo Bini, Alberto Grimaldi, Franco Rossellini (brother of Roberto Rossellini), Carlo Lizzani, Dino de Laurentiis, and Gian Vittorio Baldi. Bini produced the early works, Rossellini the middle period pictures (late 1960s), and Grimaldi the later ones.[35]

ALFREDO BINI (Dec 12, 1926-Oct 16, 2010)[36] is a hugely important figure[37] in the cinema of Pier Paolo Pasolini.[38] That he not only produced Pasolini's movies (and took a chance on him with his first film as director), but also supported the movies and stood behind them (when they attracted controversy), is also not to be

---

[33] No elevators in some of those old buildings.
[34] I could go on!
[35] The only problems he had with producers, Pasolini said, were *Pigsty* and *Medea*, which were flops.
[36] Pasolini was four years older than Bini.
[37] Occasionally you see snipes at Bini – but that goes with the territory of being a film producer. It doesn't detract from Bini's significance in Pasolini's film career.
[38] 'My contemporary from Gorizia | red-haired, hands in his pockets, | heavy as a paratrooper after mess-hall', as Pasolini characterized Bini in a poem in *Il padre salvaggio*.

under-estimated. Producing Pasolini's films wasn't the easiest gig in town, I would imagine, adding all sorts of unforeseen challenges that went beyond your run-of-the-mill producing duties. I bet you had to be on top of your game to keep up with Pasolini.

> Bini had confidence in me at a time when that was extremely hard: I knew nothing about the cinema, and he gave me *carte blanche* and let me work in peace. (PP, 138)

Alfredo Bini formed Arco Film in 1960, and the companies Finarco and Gerico Sound. Bini produced most of Pier Paolo Pasolini's earlier movies (such as *RoGoPaG, The Gospel According to St Matthew, Mamma Roma* and *Accattone* and, later, *Oedipus Rex*). Bini's other producer credits included films helmed by Mauro Bolognini (*The Mandrake*, 1965), *El Greco* (1966), a rival version of *Satyricon* to the Federico Fellini film (1969), *Simon Bolivar* (1969), *Gli Eroi* (*The Horse*, 1973), *Lancelot du Lac* (Robert Bresson, 1974), and adaptations of theatrical plays aimed at the video market. He was married to actress Rosanna Schiaffino.

ALBERTO GRIMALDI (Mch 28, 1925-Jan 23, 2021, born in Naples) produced Pasolini's last four films, from *Il Decamerone* to *Salò*. Grimaldi was a lawyer from Naples; he had formed Produzioni Europee Associate S.p.A. in Roma in 1961. He had made plenty of $$$$ by producing the *Fistful of Dollars* Spaghetti Westerns starring Clint Eastwood. Grimaldi went on to become a big cheese in the Italian film industry – producing several Federico Fellini films, for instance, plus *Last Tango In Paris, 1900, Burn!, Trastevere, Man of La Mancha* and *Bawdy Tales*. One of Grimaldi's last producing jobs was *Gangs of New York* (2002). Grimaldi had a distribution deal with United Artists (hence, the films were released thru U.A. in North America, including the Pasolini productions).

United Artists was investing, like other North American studios in the 1960s, in European productions (brokering deals with Dino de Laurentiis as well as Alberto Grimaldi and other Italian producers). United Artists wanted prestige pictures – 'more complex, larger-scale pictures' than Spaghetti Westerns (see below).

The films produced by Alberto Grimaldi often had erotic content – in the 1970s alone, there was *Last Tango In Paris*, the 'trilogy of life' films, *Salò, Novecento* and *Casanova* (dir. Federico Fellini, 1976). But that also reflects the era, when eroticism meant box office.

Many of Pasolini's later films were backed by Les Productions Artistes Associées along with Alberto Grimaldi's Produzioni Europee Associate (so they were Italian and French co-productions). Les Productions Artistes Associées had been founded in 1963 in Paris. Their movies included *Last Tango In Paris, Le Cage aux Folles, The Night Porter, 1900, Man of the East, The Story of Adele H., Roma, The Train, Burn!,* and *Moonraker* (the *James Bond* film).

UNITED ARTISTS. In the early Seventies, United Artists was known as one of the more adventurous of the Hollywood studios, and backed some of the more eccentric or left-of-centre productions. (U.A. was instrumental in forging the 'New Hollywood' cinema, for instance). From its early days, United Artists was known as a filmmaker-friendly studio, on the side of the filmmaker-as-artist. It was set up by Mary Pickford, Charlie Chaplin, Douglas Fairbanks and D.W. Griffith in 1919, where it was known as a company that would control marketing and distribution of the artists' products, rather than a conventional film studio (it didn't have sound stages and production facilities, didn't own cinemas, and didn't have a roster of stars).

By the 1960s, among United Artists' successes were the *Pink Panther* franchise (led by Blake Edwards and Peter Sellers), the Beatles films (*A Hard Day's Night* and *Help!*), and the ever-reliable *James Bond* franchise. (There were flops in the 1960s, however, such as the very costly picture *The Greatest Story Ever Told* (1965) – $20 million, and disappointments such as *Chitty Chitty*

Bang Bang (1968, cost: $10m), *Battle of Britain* (1969, cost: $12m) and *The Private Life of Sherlock Holmes* (1970, cost: $10m). These productions were part of the over-spending cycle of the late Sixties.)

In the 1970s, *Rocky* was an important franchise for U.A. – the Chartoff-Winkler movies were sequelized several times. Chartoff and Winkler made a *ton* of money from United Artists' *Rocky* series (the first *Rocky* movie cost $1.5 million and took $55.9 million in North American rentals alone – equivalent to $487m in 2005 dollars). Among Chartoff and Winkler's productions was the controversial movie *The Last Temptation of Christ* (1988), which they had set up with Paramount in the early 1980s.

And let's not forget editor NINO BARAGLI (1925-2013), who cut nearly all of Pier Paolo Pasolini's features. Thus, Baragli (three years younger than the maestro), is one of the most important figures in Pasolini's cinema, and in Italian cinema of recent times (yet some film critics don't even mention him). Baragli worked with all of the major Italian filmmakers, including Federico Fellini, Luchino Visconti, Sergio Leone, Bernardo Bertolucci, Damiano Damiani, Mauro Bolognini, Massimo Troisi, Alberto Lattuada, Tinto Brass and Roberto Benigni, and directors such as Gabriele Salvatores and Margarethe von Trotta (for many of those directors, Baragli worked on many of their projects).

Editing is always underrated by film critics, even critics you'd think would know better (partly because critics don't really know what editing is. I think film critics should spend a day or so with a film editor, to learn exactly what the job entails). Among Baragli's credits were important collaborations with Sergio Leone (the *Fistful* Spaghetti Westerns and *Once Upon a Time In America*), *Ginger and Fred* and *The Voice of the Moon* (Federico Fellini), and *Mediterraneo*.

Editing a Pier Paolo Pasolini production, though, meant working with intuitive, spontaneously-shot material, where eyelines didn't match, where inserts and close-ups were often not filmed (plus all of the other 'coverage' of a scene of a typical movie), where non-naturalistic and discontinuous images had to be welded together. Pasolini didn't arrive on set with a regular shot list, and didn't approach scenes in a conventional manner. Editing a Pasolini film would be a challenge, with different requirements from your average film or TV show. Luckily, Nino Baragli was a master editor – some critics have called him a genius.

As for costumes, in DANILO DONATI (1926-2001), Pier Paolo Pasolini had one of the great costume designers (and set designers) of recent times: Donati's feeling for costume is simply astonishing.[39] Solely in the realm of *hats* and *headgear*, Donati has few peers. If you want to study the history of costume in cinema, you have to include lengthy research into Danilo Donati, or the cinema of Federico Fellini and Luchino Visconti. (In many ways, in Pasolini's cinema, as with Vincente Minnelli, Walerian Borowczyk and Ken Russell, it's all about the clothes).

For Pier Paolo Pasolini, Danilo Donati designed *RoGoPaG, The Gospel According To Matthew, The Hawks and the Sparrows, Oedipus Rex, Pigsty, Salò* and the 'trilogy of life' movies. For Federico Fellini, Donati designed *Satyricon* (1969), *The Clowns* (1971), *Roma* (1972), *Armarcord* (1973), *Casanova* (1976), *Ginger and Fred* (1986) and *Intervista* (1987). As well as working for Visconti, Fellini and Pasolini, Donati also provided costumes for films such as *The Taming of the Shrew* (1967), *Romeo and Juiliet* (1968), *Bawdy Tales* (1973), *Caligula* (1979), *Flash Gordon* (1980), *Red Sonja* (1985), *Nostromo* (1996), *Life Is Beautiful* (1997) and *Pinocchio* (2002).

On a Pier Paolo Pasolini production, costume designers were often encouraged to go all-out, and not hold back from outrageous designs. A huge challenge were the ancient world and mediæval movies – especially the ones set in archaic societies. Not least

---

[39] Pier Paolo Pasolini praised Donati's genius with costume – 'he does all that, extremely well, with excellent taste and zest' (PP, 32).

among the challenges would be getting all of the costumes to those remote locations in Africa or Turkey (or even Southern Italia). No doubt quite a few costumes were manufactured near the set, using local workers (which would require a whole new way of working). For some of the historical productions, the wardrobe dept also had to clothe huge numbers of extras – and on budgets that were a fraction of their Hollywood equivalents. Yet each Pasolini movie has a look in costume design that's unique: a single frame, or a single still photograph from a Pasolini movie is instantly recognizable as coming from Danilo Donati. If there was a touring exhibition of costumes from Pasolini's movies, I would be first in line. (You can see some of Donati's costumes today at Cinecittà).

DANTE FERRETTI (b. 1943) is one of the superstars of production design in recent cinema. His list of credits is extraordinary by any standards. Ferretti worked with Pier Paolo Pasolini as production designer on *Medea, The Arabian Nights, The Decameron, The Canterbury Tales* and *Salò* (and as an assistant on earlier pictures, such as *The Gospel According To Matthew*). Ferretti also designed for Federico Fellini – *City of Women, And the Ship Sails On, The Voice of the Moon* and *Ginger and Fred*, and films such as *The Night Porter, Tales of Ordinary Madness, The Name of the Rose, Hamlet, Titus, The Adventures of Baron von Munchausen, Bram Stoker's Dracula, Sweeney Todd* and *Interview With a Vampire*; Ferretti worked with Martin Scorsese on *The Age of Innocence, The Aviator, Kundun, Bringing Out the Dead* and *Casino,* and with directors such as Tim Burton, Francis Coppola, Terry Gilliam, Jean-Jacques Annaud and Marco Ferreri.

Pier Paolo Pasolini would research the designs for his films from paintings, Ferretti said. Ferretti recalled that he was

> always a little intimidated by Pasolini. He was like a poet or a priest, and his approach to filmmaking was architectural: his shots were always like

geometrical *tableaux*, with the camera dead centre. (P. Ettedgui, 49)

TONINO DELLI COLLI (1923-2005) began, with *Accattone,* a long-running collaboration with Pier Paolo Pasolini that must rank as one of the finest in recent cinema – alongside Federico Fellini and Giuseppe Rotunno, Bernardo Bertolucci and Vittorio Storaro or Jean-Luc Godard and Raoul Coutard. Delli Colli (a year younger than Pasolini) was the cinematographer on eleven out of the maestro's thirteen feature films[40] (plus the episodes for anthology films). He was also DP for Federico Fellini, Roman Polanski, Jean-Jacques Annaud, Claude Chabrol and Sergio Leone (you can see Delli Colli at work with Fellini in *Interview*, 1987).[41] Delli Colli was known for subsuming his style into the material, and what the director wanted. He didn't impose his style on the movie, he served the movie. (He was described by Enzo Siciliano as short, Roman, nervous and given to uncontrollable rages, but was gentle with Pasolini.[42] From Delli Colli Pasolini learnt much of the art and practice of cinema).

> Come on, Tonino, come on,
> set it at fifty, don't be afraid
> of the light sinking – let's take
> this unnatural shot![43]

Tonino Delli Colli recalled: 'Our relations were perfect. [Pasolini] was an incredibly sweet and kind person, and he had respect for everyone on the set.' In terms of camera movement and style, Pier Paolo Pasolini preferred a simple visual approach: Pasolini was not interested in tricks, gimmicks or the 'magic' of cinema (even the greatest of filmmakers are full of tricks and gimmicks: Orson Welles, D.W. Griffith, F.W. Murnau, Jean Cocteau, Akira Kurosawa, Ingmar Bergman and

---
[40] And Tonino Delli Colli would've shot the other movies if it weren't for scheduling conflicts.
[41] He filmed the famous Spaghetti Westerns, for instance.
[42] Delli Colli was described by Gideon Bachmann as a 'small, wiry man'.
[43] Pasolini, *La Poesie*, 337.

Jean-Luc Godard. And Federico Fellini, of course, used every trick available).[44] Pasolini liked the 50 mil lens, Delli Colli said,[45] which gave a slightly compressed, squashed image, but approximated to the field of vision of the naked human eye.

GIUSEPPE ROTUNNO (1923-2021) is one of the great cinematographers of Italian cinema: he was DP on many classics, including the incredible *The Leopard* (1963), and worked for Federico Fellini (as his chief cameraman, from the late 1960s to the end of Fellini's life), Luchino Visconti,[46] Terry Gilliam (*Baron Munchausen*), Bob Fosse (*All That Jazz*) and John Huston (*The Bible*). Rotunno also lit films such as *Candy*, *The Secret of Santa Vittoria, Carnal Knowledge, Popeye, Red Sonja* and *Five Days One Summer.* Solely for his work for three Italian maestros – Fellini, Pasolini and Visconti – Rotunno should be regarded as one of the greats among photographers.

SERGIO CITTI (1933-2005) was a very important collaborator in the cinema of Pier Paolo Pasolini – he worked on the scripts, on the dialogue, and was an assistant director (as well as having a relationship with the maestro). Born in Rome, Citti was one of the longest-serving members of the Pasolini Movie Circus, following the master everywhere.

In 1970, Sergio Citti stepped up to become a film director: Pier Paolo Pasolini co-wrote Citti's first two films as director: *Ostia* (1970) and *Bawdy Tales* (1973). If anyone could step in to direct in Pasolini's absence, it would be Citti.

Sergio Citti's subsequent films included: *Beach House* (1977), *Happy Hobos* (1979), *Il Minestrone* (1981), *Mortacci* (1989, *We Free Kings* (1996), *Cartoni Animati* (1997), *Vipera* (2001) and *Fratella e Sorello* (2005). *Sogni e Bisogni* (1985) was a TV mini-series.

---

44 Sergio Citti, in the 1970 documentary on Pier Paolo Pasolini, insists that *he* didn't use zooms or dollies or other trickery on his movies, as Pasolini did.
45 Delli Colli said that Pasolini liked to use either long lenses or wide angle lenses.
46 Rotunno started out on Visconti productions such as *Senso* and *White Nights*.

SILVANA MANGANO. One of Pier Paolo Pasolini's favourite actresses was Dino de Laurentiis' wife Silvana Mangano (1930-89): she appeared in *Theorem, The Decameron, The Earth Seen From the Moon* (the episode in *The Witches*), and *Oedipus Rex*. As well as films helmed by Pasolini, she was in *Ulysses, Barabbas, Black Magic, Mambo, Tempest, Il Processo di Verona, Gold of Naples, Five Branded Women, Conversation Piece, Dune* and *Death In Venice* (many of those movies were produced by de Laurentiis). Like Sophia Loren, Gina Lollobrigida, Anna Magnani and Alida Valli, Mangano was an icon of Italian cinema; her face, which could melt the camera, was instantly recognizable (she was a hit aged nineteen in *Bitter Rice* (1949), walking in rice fields with her skirt up around her thighs).

LAURA BETTI (1927-2004) was another of Pier Paolo Pasolini's special actresses, appearing in many of his films (and providing the voice in others). Betti was one of his most important friends. The bond between Betti and Pasolini could be fiery, however – she would yell at him, hurling insults, and Elsa Morante, listening, would interject: 'If you two want to make love, stop doing it in words' (ES, 261). Betti was possessive over her friendship with Pasolini, pushing away anyone who threatened it (such as Maria Callas).

ALBERTO MORAVIA (1907-1990, born in Rome) was a favourite author with Italian filmmakers – most of his fiction was adapted into movies (including *The Conformist, La Romana, Agostino, Gli Indifferenti*, etc). Moravia also wrote films.

Novelist ELSA MORANTE (1912-85) was an valued advisor and encourager for Pier Paolo Pasolini, and influenced several of his film projects (such as advising on the music for *The Gospel According To Matthew* and others). Morante's husband, author Alberto Moravia, was a fellow colleague and traveller (he appeared in *Love Meetings* and went on trips with Morante and Pasolini, such as to India in 1960).

FRANCO CITTI

Apart from six Pier Paolo Pasolini movies, Franco Citti (1938-2016) has also appeared in mainly Italian movies – by Bernardo Bertolucci (*La Luna*), Sergio Citti, Sergio Pastore, Elio Petri, Franco Rossi, Antonio Bido, Antonio Avati, and two *Godfather* movies.

While Nino Davoli represented the lighter side of Pasolini's art, the Charlie Chaplin aspects which mocked existence, Franco Citti, from *Accattone* onwards, embodied the murky, egotistic, and degenerate sides of the Pasolini persona, with its tendency towards self-loathing, violence and depression. Citti played Pasolini's grandiose but doomed hero Oedipus (his finest role for the maestro, along with Accattone), a ruthless crook (in *The Decameron*), a fellow cannibal (in *Pigsty*), the Devil in *The Canterbury Tales,* an enigmatic demon (in *The Arabian Nights*), and an arrogant pimp (in *Mamma Roma*).

Franco Citti's characters operate on the wrong side of the law, are introspective and difficult, and see themselves as Existential rebels (who feel that the whole world is against them). They want an easy life (they think they deserve it), and they can't understand why everybody isn't falling over themselves to do their bidding. They are charismatic and independent (which makes them initially attractive), but they implode under pressure (and arrogance).

NINETTO DAVOLI

While actors such as Franco Citti might be associated with Pier Paolo Pasolini's cinema in its arty, handsome, dramatic mode, just as significant were actors such as Ninetto Davoli (b. 1948, Calabria).[47] With his toothy

---
[47] Davoli's parents were Calabrian peasants.

grin and frizzy hair, Davoli is terrific as hapless, lusty, rather dim youths on the make. Energetic, naïve, indefatigable, cowardly, Davoli is an unlikely leading man: he can never be the romantic lead, he is always the ordinary guy looking for the easiest way out.

Enzo Siciliano portrays Davoli as having a

> slight and skinny build, pimples on his face, kinky hair, and incredibly "merry" eyes... His voice was raucous, his physicality pliant and emaciated. His histrionics had a melancholy tinge and conveyed from the depths an inexpressible emotional anxiety. (284-5)

Ninetto Davoli was also Pier Paolo Pasolini's lover (from 1963, when Davoli was 15) – and they lived together for years after they'd ceased being lovers. So Davoli plays a special role in Pasolini's cinema on many levels[48] (he is also, like Franco Citti, a manifestation of the street kid from the Roman shanty towns, the kind of youth that Pasolini liked to hang out with).

Enzo Siciliano characterized the relationship of Pier Paolo Pasolini and Ninetto Davoli after the eroticism had gone as a male friendship of near-equals (tho' Pasolini was 26 years older). Pasolini wasn't a father figure to Davoli, Siciliano reckoned, and they were not dependent on each other. But Pasolini was in despair when Davoli wed (in January, 1973).

In the midst of filming *The Canterbury Tales* Ninetto Davoli told Pier Paolo Pasolini that he was getting married (during shooting in Bath in the West Country). According to Enzo Siciliano, Pasolini was distraught: 'Pier Paolo's despair was uncontainable. He wanted to die' (ES, 338). The high emotion behind the camera may have coloured the movie (Pasolini composed many poems about his relationship with Davoli).

In a 1965 poem, Pier Paolo Pasolini wrote:

---

[48] 'Pasolini deserves credit for foregrounding his relationship... with Davoli, who was not from the class in which the director's chic friends thought he should look for a boyfriend, and for his public frankness about this infatuation', commented Gary Indiana (91).

> Ninetto is a herald
> and overcoming (with a sweet laugh
> that blazes from his whole being
> as in a Muslim or a Hindu)

And that's exactly how Pasolini cast him in some films: in *Theorem*, he's the angelic messenger who visits the morose Milanese family; in *Oedipus the King*, he's the herald who guides Oedipus to the Sphinx.

However, altho' Pier Paolo Pasolini became infatuated with Ninetto Davoli and put him in quite a few films following *The Hawks and the Sparrows*,[49] he is a somewhat limited actor in terms of range (Davoli on screen tries the patience of even the most committed Pasolinian devotees). But Pasolini was quite enamoured of Davoli – especially when Davoli was teamed up with Totò (after *The Hawks and the Sparrows*, Pasolini cast Davoli in a series of films alongside Totò, including the episodes in *The Witches* and *Love and Anger*).

MAKING A FILM WITH PASOLINI

I imagine that Pier Paolo Pasolini, though a perfectionist in some areas of filmmaking, would not push his actors to numerous takes.[50] It seems as if Pasolini and the team are searching for the spontaneity of performances that *haven't* been rehearsed and blocked at length. There must be times when Pasolini would ask for many takes, but I bet in general he would shoot one or two takes then move on.

'I always shoot very short takes' (PP, 132). Pier Paolo Pasolini's cinema is constructed from short pieces of film – not for him lengthy takes where the camera and

---
[49] And a brief cameo in *The Gospel*.
[50] Sometimes Pasolini would ask for retakes with the camera still running – asking his actors to do the scene repeatedly without cutting.

the actors're hitting many marks, and seven minute takes run thru numerous beats. 'I never use the long take (or virtually never). I hate naturalness. I reconstruct everything' (ibid.). And he didn't shoot a single master shot to cover a scene – 'I never do a whole all in one take' (ibid.). However, there *are* many examples of lengthy takes in Pasolini's films (or lengthy by the standards of today's cinema).

Sometimes Pasolini would shoot a scene with both actors in shot, and ask them not to get too close, so that he wouldn't have to film a reverse angle. That way, a scene could be covered with a single shot (Pasolini like to move fast, and get shots done quickly).

Like George Lucas in the age of digital filmmaking (and the *Star Wars* prequels), Pier Paolo Pasolini spoke of shooting as 'collecting material': he was gathering content that he would shape later into a movie (in the editing room). Thus, there were opportunities for spontaneity and improvization from the non-professional actors, and later in post-production the best bits from the takes would be selected and put together.

While crews complain about being cold and wet on locations, I wonder if Pier Paolo Pasolini's crews moaned about the heat (Pasolini and co. filmed in hot, dry climes far more than in rainy, chilly regions). I bet a Pasolini shoot moved fast, too – I bet the crew didn't sit around on the grass, drinking and chatting and dancing to Euro-pop as depicted in *La Ricotta*, either. Instead, I bet it was one or two takes for each set up, then swiftly on to the next set up.

Filming a Pier Paolo Pasolini movie would provide many opportunities for cinematographic challenges for DPs – candlelight, firelight, magic hour, sunrise, sunset, plus lighting all sorts of existing locations, some of which would probably be miles from the nearest town, and with no power nearby (thus, many of the African and distant European locations in Pasolini's movies were filmed during daytime, using available light augmented by lamps. Because filming at night in remote locations is tough – and expensive).

Camera operators on a Pier Paolo Pasolini movie would need to be physically fit, too – there would be much clambering over rocks in hot sun to reach that perfect spot under an over-hanging cliff, or climbing Mount Etna[51] yet again in gales or heat. And Pasolini often preferred to have the cameras handheld, so the operators would be shouldering heavy cameras all day.[52] (On the plus side, most scenes would be filmed in one or two takes – no going to 12,457 takes like Jackie Chan or Michael Cimino for Pasolini!).

Pasolini was fond of staging scenes as *tableaux*. Carl-Theodor Dreyer often used the frontal, *tableau* style – in *Ordet* (1955), for instance.[53] Theo Angelopoulos took it up in films like *Ulysses' Gaze* (1995). Sergei Paradjanov was a master of the form (in *The Color of Pomegranates*, 1969). Walerian Borowczyk used it in all of his films. Werner Herzog exploited the *tableau* approach in movies such as *Aguirre, Wrath of God* (1972)[54] and *Heart of Glass* (1976 – in which he also hypnotized the cast!).

For the first features, Pier Paolo Pasolini and his DP Tonino Delli Colli filmed in black-and-white (Delli Colli, like many cinematographers, spoke nostalgically of b/w, and preferred it in many respects to colour film). By the Sixties, tho', colour film stock was cheaper, and distributors and television wanted colour (everybody wants colour except for filmmakers). Pasolini stuck with monochrome longer than necessary, perhaps (as did filmmakers like Federico Fellini and Ingmar Bergman), tho' the pressure of the marketplace prevailed, and from around 1966 onwards, his movies were in colour.

---

51 A favourite Pasolini location.

52 Thus, tripod shots were dispensed with – no need to carry a tripod if the shot's going to be handheld anyway.

53 Many of the compositions in *Ordet* are flattened, with the performers arranged in a tight, flat space at right angles to the camera. It's a frontal, *tableau* approach to composition that Carl-Theodor Dreyer favoured in other movies. You might say that action is staged this way in *Ordet* because it derives from a theatrical play, and the film set is a replica of a stage. No. That has nothing to do with it: this is how some filmmakers like to block their actors (Walerian Borowczyk was the same, and so was Sergei Paradjanov).

54 *Aguirre* employed stylized *tableaux*, scenes which were consciously staged as paintings or portraits.

Colour was more complicated for Pier Paolo Pasolini, and it took more planning. Pasolini's approach to colour films was to take out all of the colours he didn't want: there are too many colours in real life, Pasolini remarked. He said he chose to shoot *Oedipus Rex* in Morocco[55] 'because there are only a few main colours there – ochre, rose, brown, green, the blue of the sky' (PP, 63). That's one reason why some filmmakers preferred to film in the studio, where the settings could be controlled entirely.

The running times of Pier Paolo Pasolini's films as director tend to be in the 80-110 minute range (with *Accattone* and *The Gospel According To Matthew* and others going over slightly). One wonders what sort of movies Pasolini might've made in the era of the 1990s, 2000s and after, when movies (and not only prestige productions), ran to 140 and 150 minutes. We might've seen longer, perhaps more rambling pictures (Pasolini was headed that way, though, with the 'trilogy of life' movies).

Compared with his contemporaries, it's striking how much of Pier Paolo Pasolini's output is comical: his first three fiction features were dead serious, but for his fourth feature, *The Hawks and the Sparrows*, Pasolini and the team attempted a comedy (with mixed results). Short films of the period, such as in the anthologies *RoGoPaG* and *The Witches*, were also comedies. And large parts of the 'trilogy of life' pictures were humorous (or they tried to be). A good reason for making the 'trilogy of life' series was to tackle something upbeat and positive after the gloom and seriousness of *Pigsty, Medea* and *Theorem.*

However, contemporaries of Pasolini's such as Federico Fellini and Jacques Tati were far more skilled with comedy, and Pasolini's attempts at humour are often badly conceived and badly executed (excellent editing is absolutely foundational for screen comedy, and Pasolini's films really do lack that, even with

---

[55] *Edipo Re* was shot in Italy and Morocco (including San Petronio, Bologna).

cutting by the great editor Nino Baragli). Pasolini is also *way* too indulgent with his performers (with Totò and Ninetto Davoli in particular. Totò is a great screen clown, but you can see even him struggling with the material and the situations. Davoli, meanwhile, relies too much on charm, energy and enthusiasm. Pasolini's comedies hope to get by on Marx Brothers-type clowning around, but it doesn't work. Mel Brooks and the Zucker-Abrahams-Zucker team insisted that the performers or the director shouldn't try to be funny – it was the script, the situations and the characters that were funny. And that was what Pasolini's comedies lacked – amusing characters and situations).

Indeed, it's curious that Pier Paolo Pasolini persisted in attempting to direct (and write or co-write) movies in a comical mode, when they clearly were not working. Surely people in Pasolini's entourage pointed out to him that his so-called comedies were not funny – and worse, they might damage Pasolini's reputation as a world-class director? (Or did no one dare to voice their opinion to the director? Would *you* have the guts to tell Pasolini to his face that his comedies stank?[56]).

Well, anyway, the maestro kept going, from *The Hawks and the Sparrows* and the anthology movies of the mid-Sixties onwards, to the mediæval trilogy. (It's possible that nobody dared to suggest to the maestro that the comedies weren't amusing. And anyway, *The Decameron* had been a big hit in Italia in 1971, encouraging the production of further historical comedies).

One of the chief reasons why the comedy of the 'trilogy of life' films and others can seem laboured, or haphazard, or incomprehensible is due to that issue that irks so many TV broadcasters and film distributors: cultural translation. Humour is often difficult to translate not only into different languages but different cultures and societies. It's not only the language issue – it's the cultural and social context of the jokes. If you don't know what the joke is referring to or spoofing, it

---

[56] Not if you wanted to keep all of your fingers! Just kidding.

probably won't be funny. Thus, comedy stars can be huge in Asia (Stephen Chow Sing-chi, for example), but almost unknown in the Western world (Stephen Chow is *very* funny – *Royal Tramp, Fight Back To School, Shaolin Soccer, The Mad Monk*, etc – but nobody knows who Chow is in the West, and he's rarely celebrated).

Some of the producers of the films directed by Pier Paolo Pasolini. Alberto Grimaldi (left). Franco Rossellini (below), and Alfredo Bini (bottom).

Pasolini with Totò during The Hawks and the Sparrows (top).
And with Anna Magnani during Mamma Roma (above).

ACTORS AND ACTING

Like Tim Burton, Woody Allen and Ken Russell, Pier Paolo Pasolini preferred actors who just 'got it' straight away, without needing lots of discussion, coddling, encouragement, and analysis. No lengthy sessions of questions and answers between actors, producers and directors, and no arguments about the characterizations. 'I choose people for what they are and not for what they pretend to be', Pasolini remarked (PP, 49).

> In general, I choose actors because of what they are as human beings, not because of what they can do. Terence Stamp was offended by this because I never asked him to demonstrate his acting ability. It was like stealing from him, using his reality. I had a similar experience with Anna Magnani on 'Mamma Roma.' She also felt I was stealing from her. (1968)

Actors were given the screenplay, but Pasolini preferred to talk them through their roles. As with many directors (such as Ken Russell), it was in the chats before filming that Pasolini really did much of his directing. The scripts might be adjusted slightly during shooting, usually in response to what an actor was doing.

The trouble with the non-acting, Robert Bressonian approach to film performance is that it can too easily come over as wooden, uninspired or just plain *boring*. There are instances in the cinema of Pier Paolo Pasolini, as well as Robert Bresson, Michelangelo Antonioni and Carl-Theodor Dreyer (four of the key exponents of the non-performance performance style), where any heat/ juice/ drama/ tension/ suspense in a scene is deflated or negated. Yes, that may be one of the goals of Bresson, Antonioni, Dreyer and Pasolini, but there are trade-offs with every performance style. (More recent proponents of po-faced non-acting include Mamoru Oshii and Theo Angelopoulos).

✽

You have to admit that Pier Paolo Pasolini's appearances in his own movies were, like those of many other film directors, not especially special (quite a few film directors are convinced they can act). He was no Orson Welles or John Huston. But at least he didn't deliberately send his movies up, like Jean-Luc Godard did in his cameos in his own films.[1] And Pasolini is a significant presence in his documentaries, too – he had no problem appearing before the camera, interviewing people (or simply talk-talk-talking), or providing voiceovers (which sometimes sound like he is making it up on the spot).

SAINTS, SINNERS AND STRANGERS (OUTSIDERS)

Filmed like mediæval saints[2] (or martyrs) in the modern world, Pier Paolo Pasolini's characters – Accattone, Stracci, Zumurrud, Ninetto – were ancient souls, who didn't fit into contemporary society, as Sam Rohdie explained in his book on the *maître*: they were outsiders, eternally at odds with their society; they are useless in terms of economy and capitalist production; they are innocents in a corrupt land; they are otherworldly, and as such were revolutionary: 'their otherworldliness, essentially their uselessness, made of them revolutionary in *this* world' (123), but not because they existed within this world, but because they refused it, they didn't compromise with it.

And yet the Pasolinian sanctification of these subproletarian characters was æsthetic and artistic, not practical or even social: that is, it was a sacralization of the subproletariat that could only take place in cinema

---

[1] Jean-Luc Godard's best cameo is in *First Name: Carmen*, where he plays a director who commits himself to hospital because he can't – or won't – make movies anymore. And Godard's worst cameo is in *King Lear*, in which he sports a wig of electrical cables and plugs, chomps on a cigar permanently, and speaks out the side of his mouth like a would-be wise guy. It's *so* bad!

[2] In *Accattone*, they refer to themselves as saints. What they really mean is martyrs.

and poetry and similar arts. As Sam Rohdie commented, Pier Paolo Pasolini gave his characters

> a sacred halo, as if they were sanctified angels. He made them into Masaccio saints, Caravaggio apostles, a Mantegna Christ, a Piero della Francesca Madonna, the Christs of Pontormo and Rosso Fiorentino. (123-4)

THE POETRY OF CINEMA

> The cinema should always be the discovery of something. I believe that the cinema should be essentially poetic.
>
> Orson Welles[3]

Pier Paolo Pasolini was a poet: his aim was to be 'purely poetical and natural'.[4] Pasolini remarked that he was 'the least Catholic of all the Italians I know' and that his religion was 'probably only a form of psychological aberration with a tendency towards mysticism'. Pasolini said he saw the world in childlike, reverential ways (PP, 14).

Poetry was an early love of Pier Paolo Pasolini's – he started to write poems in the Friulan dialect, poems of the hermetic, Symbolist kind (he cited Stéphane Mallarmé, Giuseppe Ungaretti, Eugenio Montale and Rainer Maria Rilke as influences [1969, 15]). He began publishing his books of poetry in the mid-1940s (with *Poesie e Casarsa* in 1942 and *Poesie* in 1945).

Instead of one recognizable style, as with Robert Bresson or Orson Welles, underneath Pasolini's cinema was his own recognizable tone. 'You can always feel underneath my love for Dreyer, Mizoguchi and Chaplin – and some of Tati, etc, etc' (PP, 28). Of Dreyer,

---
[3] O. Welles, interview, in A. Sarris,1969.
[4] In A. Pavelin, 33.

Mizoguchi and Chaplin,[5] Pasolini said: 'all three see things from a point of view which is absolute, essential and in a certain way holy, reverential' (PP, 43). (Notice that Pasolini cites big, serious names in cinema, not commercial, exploitation directors such as Roger Corman or William Castle.) You can't cheat in style, Pasolini maintained, but you could cheat with the content (PP, 83).

'One sees, often, an *idea* of sensuality instead of sensuality, a *concept* of comedy', Gary Indiana commented (20). Pier Paolo Pasolini's films come across as essays or notes for movies that might be made. They are films of ideas, of possibilities for future projects. The comedies aren't funny, but they contain seeds that might be explored in further works.

Pier Paolo Pasolini defends himself in this respect by insisting that his films are not finished works: rather, they are questions. 'My films are not supposed to have a finished sense, they always end with a question. I always intend them to remain suspended' (PP, 56-57).

> I've never wanted to make a conclusive statement. I've always posed various problems and left them open to consideration. (1971)

'I don't want to be paternalistic, or pedagogical, or engage in propaganda, or be an apostle', Pasolini insisted in 1970 (yet part of his personality couldn't help being a teacher).

Jean-Luc Godard was greatly admired by Pier Paolo Pasolini – to the point where some of Pasolini's films are infused with the spirit of Godard (such as *Pigsty, Theorem* and *Salò, or The 120 Days of Sodom*). Most committed filmmakers in the 1960s in Europa were inspired by Godard's films: Godard's 1960s movies remain one of the most extraordinary groups of works in cinema history.

---

[5] Charlie Chaplin and silent movie comedy was a touchstone for Pasolini, according to Sam Rohdie; Chaplin is *hommaged* in many Pasolini movies. But what did Chaplin himself think of the often very strange tributes to him in Pasolini's films?

And so many filmmakers have tried to put some Jean-Luc Godard on the screen as well as Pier Paolo Pasolini: Francis Coppola, George Lucas, Oliver Stone, Martin Scorsese, Luc Besson, Jean-Jacques Beineix, Bernardo Bertolucci, Terence Malick, Donald Cammell, Abel Ferrara, Rainer Werner Fassbinder, Wim Wenders, Peter Greenaway, and Robert Altman. But not even cinema giants like Coppola or Pasolini have managed it as successfully as the maestro himself. As they say, Godard is still the Man.

Pier Paolo Pasolini said he wasn't much fond of North American cinema (PP, 136), and the American films he did like were directed by Europeans who had moved to the U.S.A. (such as Fritz Lang and Ernest Lubitsch). Among American directors Pasolini has cited John Ford and Orson Welles.

Though he regarded himself as 'born from the Resistance' and a Marxist, Pier Paolo Pasolini was inevitably drawn to what he called 'irrational' and 'decadent' literature.

Pier Paolo Pasolini's form of cinema was (like that of Andrei Tarkovsky or Walerian Borowczyk) the 'cinema of the image', one of André Bazin's two definitions of cinema (the other was the 'cinema of reality').[6] Pasolini had more in common with Soviet silent cinema than with Italian Neo-realism, with Dziga Vertov and Sergei Eisenstein rather than Roberto Rossellini.[7]

Pier Paolo Pasolini used the formal aspects of cinema (quotation, pastiche, parody, analogy, repetition, rhyme) to foreground its construction, its writing, to make the viewer aware of the process of fictionality. Terence Stamp (*Theorem*) said Pasolini made films in a particular way which could be called 'using the camera to write poetry'.[8]

> To watch Pasolini's films [commented Sam Rohdie] is to watch a parable, a type of non-fictional fiction,

---
6 A. Bazin, 1960, 9f, 23f.
7 S. Rohdie, 1995, 3.
8 M. Cousins, *Scene By Scene*, Laurence King, 2002, 83.

evidently made up and false, yet whose falsity is there to express a truth. (1995, 3)

Orson Welles made the same distinction: like Pier Paolo Pasolini, Welles advocated a theatrical, abstract, expressive kind of cinema. Welles' take on the realism vs. artificiality debate was simple: his films might be 'unreal', might be 'theatrical' and 'baroque', but they were 'truthful'.[9] Welles' goal was to make something that wasn't necessarily 'real', but was 'true'. It could be unreal, stylized and theatrical, but it had to be true to life.

'Cinema represents reality with reality; it is metonymic and not metaphoric' (PP, 38). Yes but exactly what 'reality' is, and what 'reality' is in cinema, is difficult to define, Pier Paolo Pasolini admitted. The first question to ask when people use terms like 'reality' or 'realism' is: *whose reality? Whose realism?*

Alain Robbe-Grillet's comments (made at the time of 1962's *Last Year At Marienbad*) summarize the position of Pier Paolo Pasolini neatly:

> I don't think either the cinema or the novel is for explaining the world. Some people believe there's a certain definite reality and all that a work of art has to do is pursue it and try to describe it... I don't think believe a work of art has reference to anything outside itself. In a film there's no reality except that of the film, no time except that of the film... The only reality is the film's, and as for the criterion of that reality, for the author it's his vision, what he feels. For the spectator, the only test is whether he accepts.[10]

For Pier Paolo Pasolini, cinema was not an image but 'an audio-visual technique in which the word and the sound have the same importance as the image' (PP, 146). Pasolini said that it was easy to see, by looking at a page, if a text was in poetry or prose, but in cinema it was more difficult. A cinema of poetry could be

---

[9] 'In my case, everything has to be real', Pier Paolo Pasolini insisted, 'even if only by analogy' (PP, 90).
[10] A. Robbe-Grillet, *The Observer*, Nov 18, 1962.

produced by particular techniques. For Pasolini, certain sounds could get closer quicker to the mystery of reality than written poetry.

> Even a sound image, say thunder booming in a clouded sky, is somehow infinitely more mysterious than even the most poetic description a writer could give of it. A writer has to find oniricity through a highly refined linguistic operation, while the cinema is much nearer to sounds physically, it doesn't need any elaboration. All it needs is to produce a clouded sky with thunder and straight away you are close to the mystery and ambiguity of reality. (PP, 150)

For Pier Paolo Pasolini, cinema was 'substantially and naturally poetic', because it was dream-like,[11] and because things in themselves were 'profoundly poetic':

> a tree photographed is poetic, a human face photographed is poetic because physicity is poetic in itself, because it is an apparition, because it is full of mystery, because it is full of ambiguity, because it is full of polyvalent meaning, because even a tree is a sign of a linguistic system. But who talks through a tree? God, or reality itself. Therefore the tree as a sign puts us in communication with a mysterious speaker. (PP, 153)

Even the most banal films could contain the poetry of cinema, Pier Paolo Pasolini said, but the cinema of poetry proper was a cinema 'which adopts a particular technique just as a poet adopts a particular technique when he writes verse' (PP, 153). In short: 'to make a film is to be a poet'.

Pier Paolo Pasolini believed in the notion of the author of a film. He said he was the author not only of the script[12] and the direction, but of everything else (such as the choice of sets, locations, characters and

---

[11] 'Cinema is already a dream' (PP, 150)

[12] Many of Pasolini's scripts didn't alter much during production. And the filmmakers shot pretty much what was in the script. For *The Hawks and the Sparrows*, a sequence was filmed but cut (for running time). For *Accattone*, a scene was cut because the film was too long.

costumes [PP, 32]). True, Pasolini's stamp is all over his movies, but he could not have made them without a large group of collaborators, such as regular actors like Ninetto Davoli, Silvana Mangano, Laura Betti, and Franco Citti, and production crew such as Nino Baragli (editor), Tonio Delli Colli (DP), Umberto Angelucci (assistant director), Ennio Morricone (music), Dante Ferretti (production designer), Alfredo Bini, Franco Rossellini, and Alberto Grimaldi (producers).

Once again, let's not forget the actors: no matter how well a script is written, or the concept of the film is conceived, it is actors on set who have to express it all. So Pasolini *did not* do everything himself! (But his reputation persists even today in overshadowing everybody else).

In Pier Paolo Pasolini's poetics of cinema, reality and cinema commingle, as a system of signs.

> The cinema is a language which expresses reality with reality. So the question is: what is the difference between the cinema and reality? Practically none.

(Though in postmodern theory, the difference is practically everything). To express people, Pier Paolo Pasolini used people; to express trees, Pasolini used real trees, as he found them in reality. In a interview in the *New York Times* (1968), Pasolini stated:

> the cinema forced me to remain always at the level of reality, right inside reality: When I make a film I'm always in reality, among the trees and among the people; there's no symbolic or conventional filter between me and reality as there is in literature. The cinema is an explosion of my love for reality. I have never conceived of making a film that would be a work of a group, I've always thought of a film as a work of an author, not only the script and the direction but the choices of sets and locations, the characters, even the clothes. I choose everything, not to mention the music. (PP, 29)

No veils or no distantiation between the filmmaker and reality – and no metaphors either.

> Reality doesn't need metaphors to express itself...
> In the cinema it is as though reality expressed itself with itself, without metaphors, and without anything insipid and conventional and symbolic. (ib., 38)

However, despite Pier Paolo Pasolini's penchant for realistic, non-metaphorical or non-symbolic cinema, he did not like naturalism. He aimed for realism, not naturalism. 'I believe deeply in reality, in realism, but I can't stand naturalism', he asserted (PP, 39).

Pier Paolo Pasolini repositioned himself *vis-à-vis* the Neo-realism tradition (in Italian cinema) and the films of Roberto Rossellini, saying that the naturalistic, credulous and crepuscular everyday reality of Neo-realist cinema was not his style. The detachment, warmth and irony of Neo-realism were 'characteristics which I do not have', commented Pasolini (PP, 109). Maybe – but Pasolini's cinema, and not only his early works, exhibit many of the elements of Neo-realist cinema. In the late 1960s, Pasolini said he did not go to the cinema anymore for entertainment, unless he could be sure the film was going to be worth seeing (PP, 136).

PASOLINI AND PAINTING

Pier Paolo Pasolini is known as a Mannerist (the same accusations have been made of Bernardo Bertolucci, Walerian Borowczyk and Peter Greenaway). Sometimes critics also use the term 'Baroque' (yes, even film critics, God bless them!, don't know their art history as well as they should). Yet altho' the Mannerist artists – Pontormo, Michelangelo, Rosso, Mantegna – were cited often by the maestro, he also revered the Early Renaissance artists (Giotto, Duccio, Piero, Masaccio, Angelico, etc).

Pier Paolo Pasolini was something of a 'Renaissance' man, in the sense of being happy to work in a number of disciplines: poetry, painting, criticism/essays, short stories, novels, films, reportage and theatre. He was 'Renaissance' in another sense, taking much of his inspiration from (mainly Italian) Renaissance art (in the deployment of religious imagery in *The Gospel According To Matthew*, for example).

The two favoured periods of painting in Pier Paolo Pasolini's cinema were the Early Renaissance (Giotto di Bondone, Duccio Buoninsegna, Masaccio and Piero della Francesca), and the High Renaissance, Mannerism and Baroque (Michelangelo Buonarroti, Jacopo Pontormo, Sebastiano del Piombo, Giovanni Battista Rosso and Andrea del Sarto). Pasolini spoke of being deeply influenced by the Early Renaissance masters like Giotto and Masaccio – to the point where, in cinema, he automatically composed shots using their visual techniques (where 'man stands at the center of every perspective', as Pasolini put it). Even moving shots were like the lens was moving over a painting. 'I always conceive the background of a painting, like a stage set, and for this reason I always attack it frontally' (and even tho' he sometimes fought against the Renaissance pictorial approach, he could never lose it completely, because it was so deeply embedded in his psyche). Books of art were used on the set to help with setting up shots.

STYLE

One can cheat in everything except style.

Pier Paolo Pasolini

Pier Paolo Pasolini said he didn't have a cinematic style of his own, like Charlie Chaplin or Jean-Luc Godard: his style was made up of many influences and inspirations; he was a *pasticheur*, he said (among the filmmakers that Pasolini cited were Jacques Tati, Carl Theodor Dreyer, Kenji Mizoguchi, Chaplin and Godard). The dream in *Wild Strawberries* (1957) was admired by Pasolini – 'remarkable, it comes very close to what dreams are really like' (PP, 150). Anyway, what counts, Pasolini insisted, wasn't the form or even the content, but the violence and intensity of the work, 'the passion I put into things' (PP, 28). Tsui Hark, a dragon emperor among film directors, said a similar thing: sometimes, it's not the characters, or the stories, or the themes that interest a filmmaker, but the *attitude* of the piece. In 2011, Tsui said (in *Twitch*):

> The best thing actually to do is write according to what you feel. If you feel your heart would take you to the point where you would want to express something to do with the story or the film. Sometimes it's not the story; sometimes it's the way you tell the story. Sometimes it's the attitude you have with the story. The attitude is something you build and you accumulate for a long time for no reason and no logic, it's there. When you write that way, you might want to make it that way.

Pier Paolo Pasolini's cinema is full of conventional and clichéd elements. Some are so obvious that they're seldom remarked upon, as if Pasolini is somehow exempt from being treated like any other filmmaker, as if he soars above narrative conventions (in the legend that is Pasolini the Poet, Pasolini the Saint). He doesn't: the motif of the death of the hero is a good example: films like *Accattone, Mamma Roma, Pigsty, Theorem* as well as the tragedies close with the demise of the main characters.

*

Not known as a technically brilliant filmmaker, or rather, a filmmaker for whom technique was an end in itself, or something that had to be got absolutely right, as with F.W. Murnau, Andrei Tarkovsky or Alfred Hitchcock, Pier Paolo Pasolini could nevertheless orchestrate the technical arsenal of cinema to do anything he wanted. But Pasolini is the opposite of a technical film director, the polar opposite of someone like Jackie Chan or Stanley Kubrick, who would shoot take after take until they got what they were looking for.[13] But for directors like Pasolini and Jean-Luc Godard, that approach to filmmaking would be ridiculous, wasteful, and pointless (Godard, like Werner Herzog, preferred to shoot one or two takes. No more were necessary).

Pier Paolo Pasolini did share one thing with perfectionists like Jackie Chan, Michael Cimino, Fritz Lang and George Lucas of course: total control. I bet there was no question as to who was the top guy on set in a Pasolini movie. Pasolini regarded cinema as the work of one man, an author. Terry Gilliam commented that in Italy the director is treated like a maestro (*à la* Luchino Visconti and Federico Fellini). Consequently, when Gilliam was shooting *The Adventures of Baron Munchausen* in Roma in 1988, one of the things he couldn't get used to was that production crew were reluctant to offer suggestions, and Gilliam preferred to work as a team.

---

[13] The final shot of *The Shining*, the slow tracking shot towards the hotel wall and the 1920s photograph, took ages to film. Stanley Kubrick wanted it to be as fluid as possible. The camera crew tried changing the dolly cart; they put it on a track; they took it off the track; they loaded it with more weight; they put more people on it (in V. LoBrutto, 1997, 444).

The idea of re-shooting that tracking shot again and again, until it was as smooth and perfect as possible, just wouldn't occur on a Pier Paolo Pasolini set! (Or a Jean-Luc Godard set!). Forget it!

PASOLINI: THEMES AND ISSUES

Consider the works of Pier Paolo Pasolini in print, theatre, TV or cinema (and in numerous interviews), and a host of concerns and themes will pop out time after time:

- Politics is part of pretty much everything that Pasolini did or said in the public arena.
- Communism – Pasolini was in constant dialogue with Communism, and with the Partito Comunista Italiano (which he voted for and was once a member[14]).
- Pasolini celebrated peasants, the under-class, and never lost his reverence for them.
- Southern Italy and its peasants were very important for Pasolini (he linked the area and its inhabitants to the Third World).
- The love of the Friulian dialect is part of Pasolini's exaltation of all things sub-proletarian and working class.
- The progress of Italy towards being a modern, capitalist nation was a recurring concern for Pasolini (in particular how modern technology would affect his beloved peasant class).
- For Pasolini, consumerism[15] was nothing less than 'a real anthropological cataclysm', and 'pure degradation'.
- Pasolini venerated his mother, and had a very ambiguous relationship with his father.
- Pasolini had a vision/ theory of cinema as poetry, as a means of mythicizing life.
- Pasolini was searching for the epic and the mythological in everyday life (and said he saw it everywhere).
- Sexuality – altho' many commentators always draw attention to Pasolini's homosexuality, it actually plays a much smaller role in his works than the Pasolini Legend would suggest.

✶

---

[14] He had been thrown out of the Communist Party following the sex scandal in 1949.
[15] Pasolini said he detested consumerism 'in a complete physical sense'.

Nothing is resolved to a point of bliss or unity in the cinema of Pier Paolo Pasolini: his art is one of eternal strife and dissatisfaction. There is a conflict between opposites, and the oppositions are instantly familiar:

Male	Female
Men	Women
Masculine	Feminine
Father	Mother
Present	Past
Youth	Age
Realism	Fantasy
Reality	Poetry
Heterosexuality	Homosexuality
North (Europe/ Italy)	South (Europe/ Italy)
Bologna	Rome
Italy	Third World
Europe	Asia/ Africa
Christianity	Communism
Capitalism	Marxism
Wealth	Poverty
Bourgeoisie	Proletariat

PRE-MODERN, PRE-INDUSTRIAL, PRE-CAPITALIST

Pier Paolo Pasolini enshrined pre-industrial Italy, the Italy of his youth, which he reckoned was being eroded in the modern era, with its advanced (North American/ Western) capitalism, its technology, its science. By the 1960s, much of the world that Pasolini yearned for was rapidly disappearing underneath concrete and tenements (it was a similar story of suburbanization all over the developed world).[16] Pasolini neglects to recognize that young people in the Western world embraced all things

---

[16] Yet if you visit Italy today it can still feel archaic.

American with incredible fervour. They *wanted* America, even more than America or the Americans did! (As director Elio Petri remarked, America had already been colonizing Italy culturally from the 1930s – via Hollywood cinema).

In short: after the war, *teenagers in Europe wanted all things American.*

They *yearned* for the U.S.A. following World War Two. The choice was: America or Europe? Dreary, war-torn, impoverished Europe or glitzy, out-size America? Pop acts in Britain such as the Beatles and the Rolling Stones opted for the Great American Dream. The coolest youth culture was American. The clothes. The music. The movies. The cars. The places. The language…

As Paul McCartney put it, Route 66 and the American South in the blues music that he and John Lennon loved sounded so much more glamourous than dear, old England:

> We know about the Cast-Iron Shore and the East Lancs Motorway but they never sounded as good to us, because we were in awe of the Americans. Even their Birmingham, Alabama, sounded better than our Birmingham.[17]

Let's remember that after WWII much of Italy was in pieces and it received around $1.2 billion in aid (from the Marshall Plan and other initiatives) from the U.S.A. (only France and Britain received more U.S. assistance). Like it or not, Italy and America were intimately linked politically and ideologically as well as economically and socially in the postwar era.

Anyway, these yearnings of Pier Paolo Pasolini's for earlier times which were thought to be better (even if they actually weren't), occur in many artists. Fifty years before Pier Paolo Pasolini, for instance, D.H. Lawrence (1885-1930) had spoken with incredible fury of the ugly, industrial Midlands, and how his England ('England, My England') was being destroyed by modern social and industrial forces (the Midlands is far

---
17 B. Miles. *Paul McCartney*, Secker & Warburg, London, 1997, 201.

worse today than in Lorenzo's time). And before Lawrence, Thomas Hardy had decried the advances of the modern era and the Industrial Revolution.

And so it goes, back and back, so that artists and writers can never reach that Eden, that Paradise, when all was better, richer, deeper, purer, juicier. No it wasn't. This is age talking, this is growing up to become an adult talking. Because if you are an eighteen year-old today, in the 21st century, I bet you could be having a *fantastic time*! But in thirty years, you'd look back and think, darn, things were cooler thirty years ago!

You can't win, because you can't turn back time. You can't be 17 again. What? Did Pier Paolo Pasolini want to return to the 1920s, the decade of his birth? Or – why hold back? – why not go back to the 1810s (pre-industrialization)? Or the 1580s, the height of Pasolini's beloved Renaissance era? Or, hell, why not go back to the Roman Empire?!

Truth is, Pier Paolo Pasolini's comparisons of then and now, of the 1930s with the 1960s, are simply more of his dualistic worldview, his penchant for oppositions, for automatically and violently slamming two eras, two political views, two artforms, two whatevers together. That's how Pasolini made art, by setting something up he could kick against (whether it was capitalism, or consumerism, or technology, or fascism, or old age, or poverty, or concrete jungles). With Pasolini, it's always 'us and them', 'me and that', 'I and those'.

Pier Paolo Pasolini knew that his mythical, ancient past didn't exist, and probably had never existed. But, as with God, or belief, or religion, an Eden was necessary for his existence.[18] He needed to believe that primitive cultures were more in touch with nature, or more 'authentic', or more substantial as communities, even if they weren't, even if nothing like his idealized, utopian communities ever existed.

The *idea* of the ancient world – and the Third World

---

[18] One of the recurring motifs in the 'trilogy of life' movies (and in other Pasolini movies) is the notion of miracles. Many times characters are speaking in awed tones of a *miracolo*. And in Fellini's cinema.

– is thus vital to Pier Paolo Pasolini's project: it might never have had any 'reality', outside of essays, and discussions, and films, and poems (the past as cultural imaginary), but that didn't matter. Because it was useful for Pasolini to have an invented, mythical past with which to accuse the present day (for falling short of his ideals, his utopia). The utopian, idealized past was also a realm, as Sam Rohdie pointed out (1995, 110), in which Pasolini could play and explore, and in which he was in control.

Pier Paolo Pasolini's utopias were not to be found in the real, contemporary world, which was too capitalist, too bourgeois, too consumerist and too superficial for him. Instead, he looked to exotic climes (to Southern Italia), to the Third World (particularly to Africa, the Middle East and India), and to the distant past (of the ancient world). The notion of *ancestors*, then, is crucial – Pasolini explored the idea of people living today who had ancestors going back to the ancient world.

The exaltation of peasant, primitive societies in Pier Paolo Pasolini's philosophy has a right-wing, regressive and racist component, as Sam Rohdie noted: this nostalgia for archaic, pre-modern societies (communities which Pasolini claimed to have found in Africa and the Middle East), chimes with the writings of Claude Lévi-Strauss, with D.H. Lawrence and Gustave Flaubert, with Marguerite Duras' novels of the Orient, and, most problematically with racist and Nazi theorists such as Ernest Renan and Arthur de Gobineau.

Pier Paolo Pasolini might've known what was wrong with contemporary society in the West, but he didn't know how to put it right, or how to make his utopian visions come to fruition. Of course. It's much easier to attack, to identify targets and hit them, than it is to build a whole new world. (No artist of recent times has come up with a complete, complex, and convincing vision of how a utopia/ paradise/ new world would work).

Artists complain about modern society, and in TV

and films super-villains are always destroying the world (or trying to). But *no one* has any idea at all what to put in its place. (We could get into a really fascinating topic here – the formation of alternative communities or societies in the modern era. For example, communities that have been developed along women-only, or feminist and lesbian lines (several female communes/communities have been founded in the U.S.A.). Many would-be utopias tend to be very small, and often last only as long as the lifetimes of the original founders. When the creators die, or leave, alternative communities often go into decline and break up).

PASOLINI AND AMERICA

Pier Paolo Pasolini remained a European film director, and didn't leave for North America like some of his contemporaries. Nor did he venture into co-productions with North American companies. And he tended to cast from European (mainly Italian) actors, and didn't use North American actors, like many of his contemporaries. He also didn't take up North American subjects: his movies stay in Italy, or they venture into the Middle East, Africa, Britain or India (whereas a filmmaker such as Jean-Luc Godard has explored probably the most passionate love-hate relationship with the U.S.A. in all of cinema). Pasolini's films are Italian, made by and for Italians, even when their subjects are Ancient Greek or Arabian. However, thru producer Alberto Grimaldi and his distribution deals with United Artists, Pasolini was linked to the North American movie business (and some of his movies were financed with U.$. dollars; this occurred throughout the Italian film industry).

Pier Paolo Pasolini visited Gotham in October, 1966, for a retrospective of his cinema organized by Richard Roud, an important showcase for Pasolini's work in the New World. Pasolini loved N.Y.C. (it was his first trip to the U.S.A.).

> I'm in love with New York. I have a passion beyond words for it. Like Romeo and Juliet – love at first sight. It is the most beautiful city in the world. I love the huge mingling of enormous amounts of people, races. The mixture of cruelty and innocence. New York is a piece of mythical reality, as beautiful as the Sahara Desert.

ON EROTICISM AND VOYEURISM

A significant ingredient in the cinema of Pier Paolo Pasolini is the emphasis on voyeurism: every movie contains sequences of people looking and being looked at. And, like the cinema of Tsui Hark, Alfred Hitchcock or Orson Welles, Pasolini is a master at orchestrating the network of looks and camera angles: consider the angles and the viewpoints that Pasolini and the DPs select, for instance, or how editor Nino Baragli cuts those shots together.

It's not only the erotic aspect of voyeurism and scopophilia that Pier Paolo Pasolini's cinema activates – power and the relationship of power between the observer and the object are more to the point than sex. 'Desire' is a better term than sex or eroticism – 'desire' with all its philosophical associations with the Lacanian lack, with loss, with distance, with Kristevan abjection, with Foucauldian power. Yes – *distance* – the looking and looked-at-ness in Pasolini's cinema emphasizes the sadness and loss evoked by the distance between people. Looking is not pleasurable in Pasolini's work – the observers are not getting off on looking: rather, looking reminds them of their own loneliness, their separateness from everything. Pasolini made a remark about sex in cinema that resonates here, how seeing sex emphasizes sadness and distance.

As for sex, titillation, nudity – well, Pier Paolo Pasolini didn't use *those* particular ingredients the same way anyone else did, either. Sex and nudity are some of the tried and tested and above all *cheap* means of getting an audience's attention (maintaining it is something else). Hence so much of exploitation cinema, *mondo* cinema, cult cinema, and European (art) cinema, has used the genres of horror, fantasy and thriller (all cheap genres to produce), and included plenty of naked bodies. Or any scenario where characters can disrobe and get freaky. Sex and nudity are simply easier to market than, say, abstract concepts like Ludwig Wittgenstein's philosophy of language or the notion of pessimism in the philosophy of Arthur Schopenhauer.

So if Pier Paolo Pasolini wasn't going (to be persuaded) to use stars in his movies, a producer might think, at least we'll have some T. and A. to be able to market the picture – something for the film poster and the trailers (in the way that producers Joe Levine and Carlo Ponti asked Jean-Luc Godard to shoot some nude scenes featuring Brigitte Bardot in *Contempt*.[19] As Levine told Godard, the 1963 movie 'didn't have enough ass in it'. So Godard, Raoul Coutard and co. duly filmed B.B. naked[20]).

But Pier Paolo Pasolini wouldn't do that! Yes, there *would* be naked bodies and people Doing The Deed in his movies, but the sex would be either desperate or off-the-wall, or the bodies wouldn't be slinky, European vixens and handsome, buff men.

---

[19] Joe Levine and Carlo Ponti, wanted Brigitte Bardot to be seen nude in *Le Mépris*. Levine demanded reshoots of Bardot nude, and Godard drew up a budget which he thought Levine might not pay, being twice what it should be. But Levine OK-ed it and the scenes were filmed: Bardot nude with Michel Piccoli, Bardot nude on different coloured rugs, Bardot running by a lake, and Bardot with Jack Palance (dressing after sex, tho' this wasn't used).

[20] That must've been a tough day of filming: 'OK, Brigitte, now you take your clothes off, *bien?*'

HANDHELD CAMERA

Sometimes, the over-use of handheld camera can be irritating in the films of Pier Paolo Pasolini. So much effort has clearly gone into the production design, the costume design, the props, the art direction, the casting, the hair and make-up, the lighting and the visuals of Pasolini's films, it seems wasteful or irresponsible (at first) that all that hard work should be captured with a shaky camera (a *very* shaky camera at times – there are many ways of doing a handheld shot!). But the viewer soon gets used to it, and the handheld camera becomes a cinematic device that Pasolini and the camera operators employed repeatedly to achieve a sense of poetic immediacy and urgency to their narratives.[21] The handheld camera becomes a tool of someone totally confident about capturing the action in front of the lens. (One can't imagine studio executives in a Hollywood studio being satisfied with that kind of loose, improvized camerawork if they had been financing Pasolini's films. Of course, self-consciously shaky camerawork has become fashionable in TV and movies since the 1990s, but it's fake, simulating *cinéma verité*, and is never as haphazard as the handheld camerawork in Pasolini's movies).[22] (You can see Pasolini at work filming *Salò*, where it seems that he operated the *macchina* himself sometimes, and you can see that he is wobbling the camera at times).

Other *auteurs* employed handheld camerawork far more than usual – Walerian Borowczyk comes to mind, and also Ken Russell (which Russell often operated himself – his camerawork is instantly recognizable). In their movies, the handheld camera isn't used to evoke a 'documentary' approach, or to emulate an actor's

---

[21] Enzo Siciliano has rationalized the shaky camerawork by saying that it expresses 'the sign of his hand, the visual possibility of his retina. Style tries to be life, life in its entirety' (240).

[22] The actors are always in focus and framed nicely and well-lit, for a start. The framing is traditional, even if the camerawork seems shaky. And the self-conscious, wobbly camerawork is always integrated into familiar editing patterns and dramatic structures. Not so with Pasolini's cinema.

movement or viewpoint, it is a whole stylistic manner bound entirely to the material and the drama.[23]

SOUND

One reason given for the tradition of dubbing in Italian cinema is the lack of decent equipment following WWII (and the absence of it during the war). Yes, true, you could use that excuse at the start of the 1960s, but not by the end of the 1960s, when so many hit movies had been filmed in Italy. And movies that shot in Cinecittà, such as 1963's *Cleopatra,* used direct sound (when Italy was the biggest film production centre in Europa). Besides, the cost of a Nagra tape recorder, a couple of mics, a boom and some electrical cables isn't really *that* much (even provincial film schools have them).

There are other reasons, however: one is that Italian sound stages could be noisy (and were not constructed to the same sound-proofed standards of state-of-the-art studios. Cinecittà, for instance, might possess the largest stage in Europe, but it had only had one indoor restroom). Another reason is that the casts of Italian movies often comprised actors who spoke different languages. A key reason is probably the cinema distributors and exhibitors, who wouldn't want to pay the extra costs for sound editing and mixing (with looping, actors can sit in a studio and dub their lines in a few hours). Also, apparently, Benito Mussolini (a big influence on Italian cinema) didn't want to hear foreign languages in movies, so they were dubbed in Italian.

For overseas versions of his films, Pier Paolo Pasolini said he preferred subtitles rather than dubbing (PP, 40). Jean-Luc Godard preferred dubbing to subtitling for foreign prints – he thought it was more

---
[23] And also for speed – Borowczyk liked to use the handheld camera to start shooting quickly once everything was ready.

honest. As Godard noted in *Histoire(s) du Cinéma*,[24] postwar Italian cinema was filmed without sound – instead, the great Italian poetry (Ovid, Dante) replaced the sound.

And not only is the sound added afterwards in all Italian cinema after WWII, it's often a completely new cast. As in any industry which relies on voices, like radio, or TV commercials, or feature animation, producers and directors will have their favourite voice actors (often they're also the actors who dub Hollywood movies for Italian distributors). Pasolini would have likely certain voice actors in mind when he was casting their screen counterparts, for example.

Pier Paolo Pasolini followed the example of Federico Fellini in the use of sound. For Fellini, direct sound wasn't a big deal, and he didn't think highly of the fetishization of it in North American movies. In short, Fellini much preferred to add the sound on after shooting. It was also because Fellini liked to talk to his actors during takes (or, as U.S. director Elia Kazan observed on a visit to a Fellini set: he 'yelled at the actors'). So a take on a Fellini film often had the maestro telling his actors what to do. Famously, Fellini had his performers simply recite numbers if they didn't know the text.

The point is, when you are replacing the entire soundtrack to a movie, and not using any live sound recorded on set at all, there is an enormous *potential* for exploring some really interesting things in sound and music and dialogue. Unfortunately, the films directed by Pier Paolo Pasolini don't often take advantage of that (compared to the king of post-synchronized soundtracks, Orson Welles. And even when some of Welles' experiments were spoilt by technical faults, as in *Othello* or *Macbeth*, and interference from studios or producers, the results are still fascinating). The truth is, Pasolini as a film director is far less compelling in the realms of sound compared to some other filmmakers

---
24 Pier Paolo Pasolini appears in *Histoire(s) du Cinéma*, with Jean-Luc Godard intercutting a photograph of the maestro with a painting by Piero della Francesca (from *The Legend of the True Cross*).

(even tho' he thought of cinema not as simply an image, but as an audio-visual experience). Part of this is attributable to the poor technical facilities in sound in Italian cinema.

Pier Paolo Pasolini preferred to dub voices on later: he reckoned that dubbing 'while altering a character, also makes it more mysterious; it enlarges and enriches it. I'm against filming in sync' (PP, 39). It was part of Pasolini's penchant for pastiche and anti-naturalism: 'I believe deeply in reality, in realism, but I can't stand naturalism' (ibid.).

It was also because many of the actors in Pier Paolo Pasolini's films were non-professionals, and weren't used to the rigours of acting, such as remembering cues and dialogue (so their voices were replaced by professional actors back in Roma). And Pasolini also liked to direct actors during takes (like Federico Fellini), from behind the camera (again, this is also partly due to using non-professionals, who needed more guidance than professional actors).

Often even the professional actors in a Pier Paolo Pasolini movie didn't dub their own voices.[25] Pasolini liked this – and he liked to have two non-professional actors create a character: one to perform it on set, and one in the dubbing theatre.[26] In fact, Pasolini would travel to parts of Italy to hire actors who weren't Roman or part of the film business, because he was after unaffected, untrained, working class voices, or a particular regional accent. (Thus, the performances in Italian cinema are actually a double act: the actor *and* the voice actor).

---

[25] The voice dubbing actors in *The Gospel* include Enrico Maria Salerno, Cesare Barnetti, Gianni Bonagura, Pino Locchi and Emanuela Rossi.

[26] Pier Paolo Pasolini also said that he wasn't interested in actors who depended on their voices (PP, 40).

MUSIC

Too many film critics had (and still have) little idea about the music that Pier Paolo Pasolini included in his movies – particularly what is now known as 'world music'. After several decades of 'world music' circulating in the media and popular culture, we can spot particular sounds and musics, we are used to hearing those sounds – but critical accounts of the 1960s tended to flounder (but musical appreciation is often way down the list for film critics, and they also don't have the intellectual capabilities to assess it. Also music can be fiendishly challenging to *really* describe (try describing the physical sound of a piano). Hence, critics talk about everything else – the musicians, the singers, the lyrics, the celebrities, the fashions, the concerts; anything but the actual music).

Notice that the classical music composers that Pasolini liked to use in his films tended to be German/Austrian – Bach, Mozart, Webern, Orff, etc – rather than Italian. Pasolini did employ Antonio Vivaldi, but often neglected the big names of Italy, such as Verdi, Rossini, Puccini, Monteverdi, etc.

Sometimes the music in a Pier Paolo Pasolini-directed movie is allowed to burble along, without editing, punctuation or dramatic significance: altho' Pasolini is often described as a genius with putting music in movies, occasionally the underscore meanders thru scenes at a low volume for too long (this usually occurs with existing recordings). And his films do that with genius composers such as Vivaldi, Bach and Mozart (for musos, this is sacrilege, demeaning, a crime against music, turning music into muzak).

Also, the music is often mixed far too low – this may be due to the unsatisfying sound mixes on the home entertainment releases of movies. (Sometimes movies are remixed for DVD and video releases, but often they're not: the sound mixes of the films directed by Pier Paolo Pasolini, stemming from 1961-1975, will probably all be the original mono mixes).

There are times in Pasolini's movies when you wish that some effort had been undertaken during pre-production (1) to select the *final* pieces of music for a film, and (2) to clear the rights to use the music. Adding the music later often doesn't work in sections featuring singing and dancing. There are wonderful scenes captured in the historical movies (*Medea, Oedipus Rex, The Arabian Nights*, etc) of players playing and singers singing which have completely different music dubbed over them.

PASOLINI, BOROWCZYK AND JARMAN

The cinema of Walerian Borowczyk (1923-2006) has many affinities with that of Pier Paolo Pasolini: both come from the same highly intellectual, highly educated, European backgrounds which valorize *avant garde* art, philosophy (Existentialism), Surrealism, de Sade, etc. Both were mavericks, who worked on the fringes of commercial cinema. Both produced controversial, Euro-art movies which included plenty of eroticism and nudity as well as politically provocative subject matter. Borowczyk's debut feature, *Goto: Island of Love*, was seen as an allegory about a Communist state, echoing Borowczyk's own experience of growing up in Poland. It amused Borowczyk, for example, that *Goto: Island of Love* was banned in fascist Spain as well as Eastern Bloc nations. In the truly remarkable *Immoral Tales* (1974), Borowczyk attacked European fascism in the 20th century, with his take on the 'Countess Dracula' myth – in which Countess Báthory collects and slays a group of virgins in order to bathe in their blood (*Erzsébet Báthory* was set in Eastern Europe in 1610, and starred Pablo Picasso's daughter Paloma in her only film role). With its scenes of mass degradation and nudity, of naked victims being herded and controlled like concentration camp inmates, *Immoral Tales* chimes closely with *Salò*.

Derek Jarman (1942-1994) was one of a number of filmmakers who cited Pier Paolo Pasolini as an inspiration. Jarman worked with Ken Russell in the early 1970s (on *The Devils* and *Savage Messiah*). Jarman came to critics' attention with the gay film *Sebastiane* (1976), a totally Pasolinian piece. Jarman wanted the film to be like Pasolini, but it turned out (or was sold or consumed) as gay soft porn (though it wasn't). Jarman spoke of a 'romance in the camera' that he saw 'all over the Pasolini films – something vulnerable, an archaic smile. I see it in our films, nowhere else. This is all I really want to film' (1991, 143).

Attempting a film in the manner of Pier Paolo Pasolini on one's first feature was very ambitious (Derek Jarman had already made many short Super-8 films by 1976). But Pasolini is by far the greater artist than Jarman in every respect. None of Jarman's films come close to even Pasolini's middling efforts. There is simply a welter more life, more humour, more emotion, more imagination and more invention in Pasolini's cinema than in Jarman's cinema. Take the use of non-actors, which both directors liked to do a lot: Pasolini could compose a poetry of unusual faces and characters from the simplest means, while in Jarman's pictures the non-actors drift about aimlessly. Pasolini had a genius for choosing fascinating people and orchestrating them within sequences, and putting them in amongst his professional actors which's pretty much unique in cinema. Absolutely no other filmmaker employs extras like Pasolini. By contrast, too often the non-professional actors in Jarman's movies are dull people doing dull things.

Pasolini making documentaries in Africa (top) and India (above).

Filming The Arabian Nights in Isafahan (left).
Filming Salò (below).

Pasolini's books and films on display in Rome's biggest bookstore

PART TWO

SALO, OR THE 120 DAYS OF SODOM

One should never hope for anything. Hope is a thing invented by politicians to keep the electorate happy.

Pier Paolo Pasolini (1975)

1

SALO, O LE 120 GIORANTE DI SODOMA

SALO, OR THE 120 DAYS OF SODOM

> My friend, sensual pleasure was always the dearest of my possessions. I have worshipped it all my life and I wish to embrace it to my end.
>
> Marquis de Sade, *Dialogue entre un Prêtre et un Moribond* (1782)

INTRO.

...A man lies on his back and forces a girl to piss over him...

...A man shits on the floor (in front of 30 people), then orders a girl to eat his fæces...

...A man fucks a young woman from behind while another guy in turn does him...

...A youth is staked to the ground and has his tongue cut out...

It can only be *Salò, o Le 120 Giornate di Sodoma*,[1] the last feature movie directed by Pier Paolo Pasolini.[2]

---
[1] The film's title brings together Italy and France, fascism and de Sade.
[2] Before his death on the night of Nov 1-2, 1975.

Salò, o Le 120 Giornate di Sodoma (= *Salò, or The 120 Days of Sodom*, 1975) had some high power credits: it was *un film scritto e diretto da* Pier Paolo Pasolini from the Marquis de Sade's 1785 novel *The 120 Days of Sodom*, with assistance with the screenplay from Sergio Citti and Pupi Avati, produced by Alberto Grimaldi, Alberto De Stefanis and Antonio Girasante for Produzioni Europee Associate S.p.A. (Roma) and Les Productions Artistes Associés S.A. (Paris), Ennio Morricone was music advisor,[3] Dante Ferretti was production designer, Enzo Ocone was supervising editor, Nino Baragli was editor, Danilo Donati was costume designer (Vanni Castellani was wardrobe assistant, and Sartoria Farani created some costumes), make-up by Alfredo Tiberi, hair by Giuseppina Bovino, wigs and special make-up by Carboni-Roccohetti, special make-up by Sergio Chiusi, Umberto Angelucci was A.D., sound[4] was by Domenico Pasquadibisceglie and Giorgio Loviscek, and Tonino Delli Colli was DP (in short, a very strong and very talented group of filmmakers, many of whom had worked with the maestro for years, and some of them right back to his first film, *Accattone*, in 1961).

Principal photography ended on May 16, 1975. *Salò* was completed by the end of October, 1975. The film is in the standard 35mm ratio of 1:1.85. Technicolor. (The movie, as usual in Italian cinema, was entirely looped). Released November 22, 1975 – it premiered in Paris (Italian release: Dec 23,[5] 1975). 118 minutes.[6]

The *Salò, or The 120 Days of Sodom* project did not originate with Pier Paolo Pasolini: Sergio Citti had

---

[3] The music in *Salò, or The 120 Days of Sodom* includes a piano version of 'These Foolish Things', Mikhail Glinka (*Nocturne In F Minor*), and Frédéric Chopin (*Prelude 28: 17* and *Valse* 34: 2). Pasolini had planned to use *Carmina Burana* by Carl Orff – 'typical fascist music', as he called the now very famous music.

[4] The sound mixes were in mono.

[5] Released at Yuletide, it's the Ultimate Non-Christmas or Anti-Christmas Movie!

[6] Running times on the home format releases range from 1h 51m to 1h 56m. (Some of the variations are due to the speed up of 4% for P.A.L. systems).

developed the idea, and Pasolini helped him with the screenplay. Pasolini became more interested in the concept as they co-wrote it, while Citti lost interest and moved onto other projects (by this time, Citti was forging his own career as a film director; he had recently directed *Ostia*, 1970 and *Bawdy Tales*, 1973).

Among *Salò*'s cast it's likely you will not recognize a single actor, unless you have seen other Pier Paolo Pasolini movies, or other Italian movies and TV of the era. With many of his films, Pasolini cast at least one known face among the cast (such as Anna Magnani, Totò, Jean-Pierre Léaud and Terence Stamp) – possibly at the behest of his producers/ backers. Here, none.[7] Instead, *Salò, or The 120 Days of Sodom* is sold with two names:

PASOLINI
DE SADE

(Indeed, Pier Paolo Pasolini taking on de Sade would be enough to bring a few punters into a cinema in Italy in 1975).[8]

Salò, or The 120 Days of Sodom's cast included Paolo Bonacelli[9] (Blangis), Giorgio Cataldi (the Bishop), Umberto Palo Quintavalle (Curval), Aldo Valletti (Durcet), Caterina Boratto (Signora Castelli, the narrator), Elsa De Girgio (Signora Maggi) and Hélène Surgère (Signora Vaccari). However, there are two name actors in *Salò, o Le 120 Giornate di Sodoma* in the voice dubbing: Bonacelli was dubbed by Michel Piccoli and Laura Betti dubbed Hélène Surgère. In Italy,

---

[7] One reason is probably the kind of things the cast are asked to do in *Salò:* Marlon Brando might bugger Maria Schneider in *Last Tango In Paris* (yes, while keeping his clothes on!), but would he want another guy kneeling over him and taking *him*? Well, 1,000s of actors and actresses wouldn't want to do that!

[8] Gideon Bachmann: 'The Marquis de Sade couldn't have found a better interpreter. Pasolini was making a film against fascism, maybe, but he was also making a film that showed how deeply anchored in our souls cruelty and destructiveness really are.'

[9] Paolo Bonacelli appeared in *Caligula* (1979), a film which seems partly inspired by the erotica of the 'trilogy of life' series. Incidentally, several others from Pasolini's team worked on *Caligula*, including Danilo Donati and Nino Baragli.

Giancarlo Vigorelli dubbed Bonacelli, Marco Bellocchio dubbed Aldo Vitlletti, Giorgio Caproni dubbed Giorgio Cataldi and Aurelio Roncaglia dubbed Umberto Quintavalle. Some of the actors were friends of the director (such as Valletti and Betti).

It's odd that Laura Betti, one of Pasolini's favourite actresses, wasn't cast as one of the four matriarchs in *Salò, o Le 120 Giornate di Sodoma*; however, she was appearing in *1900*, filmed at the same time, nearby. Betti did, tho', supply the voice of Hélène Surgère (playing Signora Vaccari – which she would've played had she appeared in *Salò*. Surgère tells several stories in the first half of *Salò*, so Betti's contribution as her voice was considerable). Franco Citti might've played one of the collaborators.

Other actors in *Salò, or The 120 Days of Sodom* included: Ezio Manni as the Collaborator; Inès Pellegrini as the Slave Girl; Sergio Fascetti; Bruno Musso as Carlo Porro; Antonio Orlando as Tonino; Claudio Cicchetti; Franco Merli; Umberto Chessari; Lamberto Book (Gobbi); Gaspare di Jenno as Rino; Giuliana Melis; Faridah Malik as Fatimah; Graziella Aniceto; Renata Moar; Dorit Henke; Antiniska Nemour; Benedetta Gaetani; and Olga Andreis as Eva. Some of the characters take their names from the actors playing them (such as Franco, Claudio and Sergio).

If you've seen the later Pier Paolo Pasolini movies, you will recognize Franco Merli and Ines Pellegrini in amongst the large cast – they were Nuredin and Zumurrud in *The Arabian Nights*. And for once Ninetto Davoli *isn't* cavorting thru this movie with his trademark permanent, goofy grin! (Anyway, who would Davoli play in *Salò*? Not one of the victims, and seeing Davoli as one of the soldiers or collaborators would be uncomfortable[10]).

As to the locations of *Salò, or The 120 Days of Sodom*, the scene where the candidates are chosen is Villa Feltrinelli (the former home of Benito Mussolini

---

[10] Apparently, Davoli was going to play one of the collaborators, Claudio.

– it's now a hotel); the bridge where prisoners try to escape is on Via Gardeletta, at Gardeletta. The main mansion is Villa Aldini, Via dell'Osservanza 35, Bologna (for the exteriors). Some interiors were filmed in the Villa Gonzaga-Zani in Villimpenta, and Villa Riesenfeld, Pontemerlano, near Mantua (it was abandoned, and adapted by the production). Villa Mirra at Cavriana, near Mantua, was also used. The round-up was staged in a public park near Bologna. The courtyard and interiors were filmed at Cinecittà Studios.

Salò, o Le 120 Giornate di Sodoma was not filmed in secret, miles from anywhere; it was produced at Cinecittà in Roma and on location in Mantua. And it had people photographing and filming it (U.S. journalist Gideon Bachmann[11] kept a diary of the production, and was also involved with a filmed record (some of the footage has appeared in documentaries about *Salò*. The documentary cameras covered the final week of photography, the torture scenes in the finale, filmed at Cinecittà).)

The film was dubbed at Alberto Grimaldi's Produzioni Europee Associate studios in Viale Oceano Pacifico in Rome (also the production office for the movie), during July, 1975.

Pier Paolo Pasolini was directly involved in the sound mixing for the French version of *Salò, or The 120 Days of Sodom* (he went to Paris to oversee the French dub in Oct, 1975). Apparently, Pasolini considered the French version to be the 'official' one.[12]

Several versions of the film exist. *Salò, or The 120 Days of Sodom* originally ran 145 minutes, but Pier Paolo Pasolini took out 25 minutes for story pacing reasons (some versions have been released by Gaumont/ Columbia, Criterion Collection, British Film Institute and others). There are slight differences of running times, the odd scene, and elements such as the quotation

---

[11] Gideon Bachmann had been making a film about Pasolini during 1975; it was planned to be a biographical portrait as well as about artists and art. It remained unfinished, altho' interviews had been filmed, plus the last week of principal photography of *Salò, or The 120 Days of Sodom* at Cinecittà.

[12] I'm not sure why.

of a poem by Gottfried Benn lasting 25s.

※

Like *Apocalypse Now, Cleopatra, Heaven's Gate* and *Basic Instinct*, *Salò, o Le 120 Giornate di Sodoma* was one of those movies about which people have asked: just what went on during filming? Did actors really eat shit on film? Was the sex simulated or real? Did anybody get paid?

Salò is one of those films that will *never* be broadcast on a major television network in many parts of the world (even at four in the morning), unless maybe the Roman Empire or the Third Reich is resurrected. *Salò* is problematic in pretty much every way.

If there really was a Fascist, Sadeian Holiday Camp[13] as depicted in *Salò, or The 120 Days of Sodom* – let's call it Hotel Sodom or Hotel De Sade – where orgies were the first and the only item on the daily schedule, it would be popular with a certain section of the global population. (It would be built in Las Vegas, of course. In fact, the Fifth Level of Hell already has an outlet branch on the Vegas Strip – you take the elevators down from street level next to the M.G.M. Grand. More people than you'd think are willing to pay the high price of entry – your soul[14]).

Salò, or The 120 Days of Sodom doesn't come out of nowhere – this is Pier Paolo Pasolini we're talking about! Consider the tortures and horrors that're performed for the libertines in *Salò*. Well, Pasolini-sensei had already filmed similar scenes of archaic, violent rituals in movies such as *Medea* and *Porcile*, where victims're killed and eaten, or have their blood strewn over field crops. Pasolini's movies are fond of ceremonies conducted in a slow, arcane (and somewhat chilly) manner. If the rites feature sensational elements – like cannibalism or slaughter – all the better! (By the way, Italian cinema in the 1970s was still churning out horror and *gialli* movies, which contained plenty of graphic violence.)

---

13 A Hogwarts boarding school for pervs and psychos.
14 But you do get two free drinks per soul – three if it's a party of ten.

Salò, or The 120 Days of Sodom isn't interested in staging grand scenes, or humanizing or characterizing the victims. It's anti-grand, anti-arty, anti-emotional, anti-operatic. (If it were turned into a Broadway theatre musical (!), *Salò, or The 120 Days of Sodom* – a sort of *Hair* meets *Sweeney Todd* meets Grand Guignol – it would be really boring, because all of the emo-psycho-spirito-socio ingredients and the amazing potential for theatrical wackola would be ditched by the Stern Schoolmistress of a Stage Director).

✳

Salò, or The 120 Days of Sodom is a film-text that can (and has) been interpreted in many ways: the sex-death-violence-nudity aspects are merely the flashy top level that grabs the attention. Power (the abuses of power) is a far more pertinent layer to *Salò* than sex or nudity. Consumerism, the degradation of neo-capitalism and commodification, are absolutely fundamental issues in this movie (as Pasolini explained in interviews). The violent treatment of the body in political systems is key, too. Another layer is the lament over the destruction of Ye Olde Italie.

Salò, or The 120 Days of Sodom is also an attack on the apparent 'freedom' of consumerism, the illusion of 'progression' of capitalism, and the over-reliance on the individual pursuing their own goals of a better standard of living (degrading the emphasis on community and the socialist projects of Communism). The 'me' society, the 'greed is good' society.

The script for *Salò, or The 120 Days of Sodom* was precisely worked out: Pier Paolo Pasolini wanted the actors to speak the lines as written, even though the entire movie was looped. It's customary for Italian movies to have dialogue changed during dubbing, or rewritten, but for *Salò, or The 120 Days of Sodom* the script was retained. Also, the screenplay was filmed as written, though inevitably some scenes were shot but cut out (and some footage was stolen in Oct, 1975).

THE MARQUIS DE SADE.

God of the Surrealists, of French intellectuals and bohemians, and Grand Vizier of pornographers, wannabe trendies and avant gardists, Donatien-Alphonse-François de Sade, a.k.a. the Marquis de Sade (1740-1814), is the controversial author of 4 novels, short stories, plays, dialogues, letters, journals and pamphlets (including *Justine, Philosophy of the Bedroom, The Story of Juliette* and *Les Cent Vingt Journés de Sodome*). De Sade's was a notorious life, leading to a number of spells in prison (prostitutes, attempts on his life, run-ins with the police, accused of poisoning Marseilles hookers, etc).[15] He apparently indulged in some of the sadomasochistic practices described in his fiction (some of which led to his imprisonment); that's part of the Sadeian myth and legend, of course.[16]

The Marquis de Sade has been exalted to the status of Major Philosopher for many Euro-intellectuals, taking his place alongside Friedrich Nietzsche, Sigmund Freud, Karl Marx and Jean-Paul Sartre.

And the Marquis de Sade himself has been the subject of many movies and famous plays, including the plays *Marat/ Sade, Sade, Divine Marquis, Lost Cherry Orchard* and *Quills,* horror flicks from Jess Franco (*Justine, Eugenie*) and Hammer horror, such as *The Skull* (with the Marquis as a villain or monster), to lit'ry, arty fare such as *De Sade* (1969), *Justine de Sade* (1972), *Cruel Passion* (1977), and the play and film *Quills* (2000). Richard Matheson, Peter Brook, Tobe Hooper, Luis Buñuel, Philip Kaufman, Jan Svankmajer and others have taken on de Sade as a person or character, and he's been played by Klaus Kinski, Christopher Lee, Geoffrey Rush, Keir Dullea, Patrick Magee, Robert Englund and Daniel Auteuil.

The Marquis de Sade has been a high profile and much-loathed target for feminists. Andrea Dworkin

---
[15] According to Gérard Zwang, 'it is because of excessive imprisonment and vindictive and cowardly censorship that Sade has been put on a pedestal and consecrated a martyr, great philosopher, major writer and specialist in eroticism' (quoted in B. Groult, 69).

[16] We want to believe that notorious writers are *really* notorious! And not just like everybody else after all.

decimated de Sade in her 1983 book *Pornography*. 'The commercialized sex movement's theoreticians have unearthed the Marquis de Sade and undertaken to deify him', noted Benoîte Groult in "Les Portiers de Nuit" (69).

Benoîte Groult summarizes the work of Georges Bataille, the Marquis de Sade and Henry Miller as 'monstrous selfishness, morbid scatology, and the most classic of sado-anal regressions'. It's grim stuff for Groult: 'there is not the slightest trace of a kiss in the works of these morticians, not the slightest tenderness'.[17]

The 120 Days of Sodom (*Les Cent Vingt Journés de Sodome*, 1785) was written in the Bastille prison. in Paris[18] It concerns four aristocrats (they are described as libertines/ perpetrators/ collaborators/ lusty fuckers) who form a cabal devoted to sexual pleasure; three of their wives join the interrelated group, as well as one of their daughters, and four women who procure their victims (as well as recount stories). There are also four decaying, elderly women. And eight boys and girls, all teenagers, and eight youths (16 victims), also described by de Sade as 'lusty fuckers'.[19] (In the film version, the four tycoons are representatives of modern, Italian society: a Duke, a Judge (magistrate), a Businessman and a Bishop.[20] They embody institutions such as wealth/ privilege, the bourgeoisie, capitalism, the law, and religion).

The victims are interchangeable, but so is everybody else. There are four categories of participants in *Salò, or The 120 Days of Sodom:* 1. libertines; 2. courtesans (and storytellers); 3. accomplices; and 4. victims. (It's a condensation of social roles rather like a mediæval tale, where you have kings/ queens,

---

17 As for giving pleasure, forget it! There's no mention of the clitoris, for instance, 'since the 'heroes' give no thought to wasting their time by arousing female pleasure'.

18 It was rediscovered in 1904. It had been rescued by a guard during the revolution.

19 See M. Crosland, 2000.

20 The libertines were not proletarian or peasant class, Pasolini explained, they were cultured, they could quote from French philosophers.

merchants, artisans, soldiers and peasants). The number four in the film also extended to the soldiers aiding the operation, the four daughters lined up for marriage, and so on.

Incest is a much bigger issue in the Marquis de Sade's laugh riot novel of 1785 than in the 1975 movie (incest, like anal sex, seems to really titillate French pornographers). Thus, that each of the libertines has had sexual relations with their daughters is a given, but the film adaptation doesn't make much of that. (However, the aristos offer their daughters to each other in an early scene, which is a correspondence with de Sade's incest theme).

It is not only the sexual perversions explored in *Les Cent Vingt Journés de Sodome* that interested Pier Paolo Pasolini, but other aspects of the Marquis de Sade's story: for instance, that the four procuresses also tell tales (storytelling is an important ingredient in Pasolini's cinema – the 'trilogy of life' films had been founded on it, and even Jesus in *The Gospel According To Matthew* is a storyteller,[21] and the *Scriptures* themselves are also stories. Notice how the libertines demand imaginative tales with full details, and aren't satisfied unless their demands are met (the first story in *Salò, o Le 120 Giornate di Sodoma* is interrupted to make this clear): like film producers, they command the storytellers to deliver the goods, to arouse them. Porn must be titillating, and telling a good anecdote becomes more important than whatever the story is about – sex, adventures in distant galaxies, or lawnmowers).

The stories told by the ladies tend to be about under-age sex (to add to the shock value), and about lewd acts with old men, with an emphasis on anal sex, defecating, urination and the buttocks (however, they are heterosexual stories, although they're about child abuse).

According to the storytellers, the tales are actually memories, things that happened to them when they

---

[21] Philip Pullman describes Jesus as one of the greatest storytellers in history.

encountered pervy, old guys when they were pre-teens or teens. The stories are Sadeian skits, sketches told in the style of the Marquis de Sade's prose: the women remember being young girls who were preyed upon by old men; following defecation or the caressing of the all-important ass, the stories end with ejaculation. Thus, the tales adhere to the standard format of pornography: some scene-setting, the first meeting, the undressing, the foreplay and groping, intercourse and the orgasm.

The unreality and high fantasy of the scenario in the *120 Days of Sodom* novel by the Marquis de Sade – a group of aristos who cut themselves off from the rest of the world to indulge their desires – would also appeal to Pier Paolo Pasolini.[22] The aristocrats are like artists, but very rich, who have the funds and resources to recreate a world to their own liking (a position very few filmmakers have enjoyed!).

The 120 Days of Sodom was written while the Marquis de Sade was in prison. It is set shortly before 1715. As Margaret Crosland describes in her excellent *De Sade Reader*, *The 120 Days of Sodom* came directly out of de Sade's experience of being behind bars:

> If his physical life was empty, his head was full of ideas. He now began to write the blackest of his books; blackest because no ray of light, no memory of what might have been happy or 'good' ever gleams through it. Sade conceived and wrote it (part of it, at least) as though the 'normal' world did not exist, and he may well have thought that even if it did, he might never see it again. (2000, 31)

That Pier Paolo Pasolini would take on the Marquis de Sade seems somewhat inevitable – de Sade being a perfect author for Pasolini (and for filmmakers like Jean-Luc Godard, Rainer Maria Fassbinder, Walerian Borowczyk and Luis Buñuel). And that Pasolini would do so in his own highly unusual manner is also to be expected (following the 'trilogia di vita' movies, it was certain

---

[22] 'Rendering Sade's decadent Salon as a sort of homicidal boarding school' (Gary Indiana, 56).

that Pasolini and the team would deliver a unique take on de Sade's text. And they did. From the comedy and conservatism of the 'trilogy of life' movies, Pasolini and co. bounce back in the other direction, just as they did after the earnest ambience of *Medea* and *Pigsty* into the comedy of *The Decameron*). That the author was very controversial, and spent a good deal of his life in prison, or living in notoriety, added to the spice for Pasolini (he feels an immediate empathy with the underdog, with masochists, with those who've been persecuted. An author set against society (like, say, Jean Genet or Arthur Rimbaud) is the ideal material for Pasolini to adapt (and yet Pasolini also adapted works from conservative, very traditional authors, such as Ancient Greek mythology, Sophocles, Giovanni Boccaccio, Geoffrey Chaucer and the *Bible*).

The Marquis de Sade also possessed the childish urge to shock society, which Pier Paolo Pasolini also never grew out of (nor did the Surrealists and so many other avant gardists – and a good many filmmakers, too!). There is undoubtedly an urge to upset audiences in the *Salò, or The 120 Days of Sodom* film, a conscious effort to find *something* that will angrify someone in the audience.

After the Marquis de Sade, the fiction of Henry Miller, Jean Genet,[23] Georges Bataille and even William Burroughs seems a mere postscript. This extract from *The 120 Days of Sodom* is typical:

> Curval, who had not been experiencing such an onslaught, blasphemed with joy. He quivered in excitement, opened his legs wide and prepared himself. At that moment the youthful sperm of the charming boy he was masturbating dripped down to the enormous tip of his frenzied instrument. This warm sperm which drenched him, the repeated shuddering of the duke who was beginning to discharge also, everything led him on, everything brought on his climax and floods of foaming sperm

---

[23] Bruce Kawin and Gerald Mast in *A Short History of the Movies* link the four pillars of society represented by the four fascists to themes in the plays of Jean Genet (338).

flooded Durcet's arse.[24]

We talk all the time about Pier Paolo Pasolini in relation to *Salò, or The 120 Days of Sodom,* but of course we have to remember that he co-wrote the picture with Pupi Avati and Sergio Citti (and in this movie, the script is the foundation of the entire enterprise). And also, it was Citti who developed the project initially, before handing it to Pasolini. In additon, it was the Divine Marquis, bless his twisted mind, that came up with the scenario: four aristos who gather a host of victims for 120 days of naughtiness and nastiness in a mansion.

Si, si – Salò, o Le 120 Giornate di Sodoma is the fiction of Marquis de Sade by way of Georges Bataille and Jean-Luc Godard, but if you know those authors, and also writers such as Arthur Rimbaud, William Burroughs and Henry Miller, you'll know that the movie *Salò* isn't a patch on any of them. Burroughs in *The Naked Lunch*, Miller in *Tropic of Cancer*, and Bataille in *The Story of O* had not only already explored the same territory of coercion, power, excess and extremism in terms of politics and sex (sexual politics and political sex),[25] they had also done it better, quicker, and *way* more radically and polemically.[26] (There is, however, an added jolt in *seeing* this kind of material on a movie screen, compared to reading it in a novel. One imagines that de Sade himself would be delighted).

PASOLINI ON SET.

There are several documentaries about *Salò, or The 120 Days of Sodom,* including *Fade To Black* (2001), with Mark Kermode, *Salò: Yesterday and Today* (2002), *Pasolini Prossimo Nostro* (2006, Italian), *Enfants de*

---

[24] Quoted in M. Crosland, 2000, 37.

[25] *Salò, o Le 120 Giornate di Sodoma* is very much a film of the mid-1970s, when (second wave) feminists and intellectuals spoke of the 'politics of sex', and 'sexual politics', the era when the issues of gender, sex and eroticism were politicized.

[26] De Sade is one of the key forerunners of the 'no limits' modernist tradition: Henry Miller, Pauline Réage, Jean de Berg, Emmanuelle Arsan, Géorges Bataille, William Burroughs, D.H. Lawrence, Anaïs Nin, etc.

Salò (2006, French) and *The End of Salò* (2008).

In the video documentaries, you can see the Italian maestro at work at Cinecittà Studios making the film (some of the footage was filmed by Gideon Bachmann and co.). The 2002 documentary (*Salò: Yesterday and Today*) contains among the fullest footage of Pasolini working on set of any of his productions as director. The 2006 documentary (*Pasolini Prossimo Nostro*), directed by Giuseppe Bertolucci, comprises mainly on-set photographs, plus some of the same footage as the 2002 documentary, and several audio-only interviews with Pasolini, plus extracts from a filmed interview at the time of *Salò*.

In the documentaries, Pier Paolo Pasolini is clearly the leader on set, and everybody defers to him (i.e., he's the director-as-king in the Italian system). He often operates the *macchina fotografica* himself (here is definitely where some of the shaky camerawork in Pasolini's cinema originates!). And he is constantly directing the actors during the takes (he implores them, more screaming!,[27] or move over there, or he cues them). Thus, the production (live) sound of a Pasolini movie would consist primarily of the director talking to the actors (that would be the same in silent cinema), plus camera noise, plus wind noise, plus the mandatory jets and cars (which always appear out of nowhere as soon as you turn on a camera. Try it: go outdoors with a camera and try to film a quiet, emotional scene, and World War Three will break out and the sky will be full of B52-H bombers so you can't hear a thing).

Altho' *Salò, o Le 120 Giornate di Sodoma* isn't a bunch of laughs, and altho' it comes across as a deadly serious work, the filming of *Salò*, as the actors attest, was often filled with laughter as one of the teenage cast made a joke. If you only consider the movie, you'd think that *Salò, or The 120 Days of Sodom* was wall-to-wall horror and boredom for everyone concerned. But it wasn't: the shooting was something else – there was rehearsal, plenty of discussion, and the atmosphere on

---

[27] Alas, none of those screams make the final cut – they're all dubbed.

set was informal.

Salò, o Le 120 Giornate di Sodoma was filmed mainly in the studio for obvious reasons. Material as tricky as this to stage (plus a young and amateur cast) required the controllable and more comfortable environment of Cinecittà, Pasolini's home-from-home, and the adapted buildings in Mantua.

Pier Paolo Pasolini wanted the actors to stick to the script in *Salò, or The 120 Days of Sodom*. He was after takes which repeated the action, so it meshed. It wasn't a question, this time, of shooting material until the filmmakers had enough to create a movie (Pasolini's usual method).

REFERENCES, ALLUSIONS.

Salò, or The 120 Days of Sodom is a movie in which a list of intellectual writers and philosophers are part of the opening credits[28] (predominantly French literati such as Simone de Beauvoir, Philippe Sollers, Roland Barthes, Pierre Klossowski and Maurice Blanchot). The references in the 'Essential Bibliography' to left-wing writers and intellectuals makes the movie feel like an essay, a PhD thesis, perhaps. (Did you bring your notebook? Start writing those names down! There will be a test in tomorrow's class!).

The 'Essential Bibliography' of *Salò* includes:
- Roland Barthes: "Sade, Fourier, Loyola",
- Maurice Blanchot: "Lautréamont et Sade",
- Simone de Beauvoir: "Faut-il-brûler Sade",
- Pierre Klossowski: "Sade mon prochain, le philosophe scélérat",
- Philippe Sollers: "L'écriture et l'experience des limites".

Wait a minute – a film which opens with a list of philosophers and intellectuals? Are you kidding!? Talk about pretentious! Except we know that Pier Paolo Pasolini wasn't 'pretending'. Oh no, Pasolini was the real deal: that list of Euro-eggheads isn't put there to raise a laugh! Pasolini means it, *man*. (But the film

---

[28] Accompanied by some *ersatz* jazz composed by Ennio Morricone.

doesn't mean it, always – the citations and hi-falutin' allusions are also derided. And anyway, in a film this savage in its satire or comedy or whatever it is, nothing is to be taken straight).

There are allusions to poets and poetry in *Salò, or The 120 Days of Sodom*: Dante Alighieri, Italy's national poet, inevitably (the four sections of the movie are titled: 'Ante-Inferno', 'Circle of Manias' ('Girone delle Manie'), 'Circle of Shit' ('Girone della Merda') and 'Circle of Blood' ('Girone del Sangue')). Thus, *Salò* might be as close as Pasolini got to filming *The Divine Comedy*. Other references include Charles Baudelaire, St Paul and Gottfried Benn. Plus Friedrich Nietzsche and J.-K. Huysmans (of course). Many modernist paintings decorate the walls of the villa (some are in the Italian Futurist style, others are Cubist, including Fernand Léger).

There are religious/ Catholic allusions in *Salò, or The 120 Days of Sodom*, too – inevitably for a Pasolini project: the first young woman to be led into the interview room and stripped is of course called Eva (Olga Andreis). As they sit in a bathtub covered in fæces, one of the young women cries out, 'Lord, why hast thou forsaken us?' (As you do – I mean, that's what *you* would yell out if you were sitting in a tub covered in filth, wouldn't you?). The allusion to the Crucifixion, in this particular context, makes a striking contrast with Pasolini's most celebrated film, *The Gospel According To Matthew*.[29]

Characters aren't addressed by name, but by title or formal address – 'Signore', etc. The libertines aren't named (as they are in the Marquis de Sade's text). It's what they embody, socially and politically, that's more important – a Duke, a Banker, a Bishop, and a Judge. (However, some of the victims are named during the round-up, and sometimes the victims speak each other's

---

[29] Eve Tushnet called *Salò, or The 120 Days of Sodom* 'even more uncompromisingly Christian than Pasolini's 1964 *The Gospel According To Saint Matthew*. *Salò* depicts a world of Christian anthropology without Christian eschatology – a world where human beings are made in the image of God, and there's no hope' (*America* magazine, Aug 23, 2019).

names).[30]

The male victims include Franco Merli, Claudio Chiccetti, Carlo Porro, Tonino, Sergio Fascetti, Umberto Chessari, Rino and Lamberto Gobbi. The female victims include: Giuliana Melis, Fatimah, Eva, Dorit Henke, Benedetta Gaetini, Renata, Graziella and Antinska Nemour. The collaborators include: Bruno, Ezio, Claudio Troccoli and Fabrizio Menichini. The daughters include: Susanna Radaelli, Tatiana Mogilansky, Liana Acquaviva and Giuliana Orlandi. The storytellers include: Signora Vaccari, Signora Maggi and Signora Castelli. The studs include: Efisio Etzi, Guido Galletti, Rinaldo Missaglia and Giuseppe Patruno.

The libertines are often portrayed as polite (though black-hearted); they sit about drinking coffee and spirits, they discuss their rules, and they comment on how their 120 days of orgies is unfolding. But they also lose it – some of them whip the victims in frenzy, or scream when the rules are broken or when a victim refuses to do something.

THE POLITICS OF *SALO.*

Salò, or The 120 Days of Sodom's set in the short-lived fascist state of Salò (= Italian Social Republic) in Northern Italy (the caption says 1944-45).[31] Pier Paolo Pasolini said it was about fascism and capitalism in the 1930s and 1940s. In *Salò* desire is unbridled, the lust for sex, death and torture is unfettered by social constraints.[32] Nothing impinges from outside on the activities inside the *palazzo*. The aristocrats seem to be free to do whatever they wish (they announce that they are operating without legal restraint).[33]

---

[30] As the brief exchange between the libertines and the victims in the round-up shows, some of the aristos have had their eye on particular youths in the region.

[31] The sound of planes is mixed behind the action throughout the movie, the cheapest and easiest way of suggesting that the military conflict continues in the outside world.

[32] 'Pasolini's film is not about sex but the death of sex', noted Naomi Greene, very obviously.

[33] The aristocrats are kings who're being waited on and pleasured: they don't lift a finger. Instead, it's their four wives who act as brothel madames and pimps, preparing the victims for the delectation of their masters.

Salò is a town in Northern Italy on the Riviera Bresciana, and the name of the last republic of Benito Mussolini (following his rescue by the Nazis from the Abruzzi), between 1943 and 1945. Salò is thus employed as a shorthand term for both Italian fascism and German fascism (and European fascism). A journalist, Mussolini (1883-1945) became the leader of the fascist movement in Italy following WWI. King Victor Emmanuel appointed Mussolini Prime Minister; by 1928, Mussolini had aligned Italian politics with fascism, disbanded opposing political parties, and attempted to emulate Germany (Mussolini was in love with the corporate appearance of fascist power at the same time as ruthlessly suppressing any opposition. Mussolini's regime also had an impact on the Italian film business).

It's also the North of Italy as the realm of the father, for Pier Paolo Pasolini personally – Bologna and the North was his father's world – Carlo Alberto Pasolini (he gives one of the characters his father's name; and other names have personal resonances, such as Sergio. There are references to Bologna, Milano, etc).

One of the reasons that Pier Paolo Pasolini said he set the story in WW2 and in Northern Italy was because it was a time and place he knew. It was far enough away from the present to make it convincing, but without it being too fairy tale-ish or allegorical had it been set in the Marquis de Sade's era.

In other words, keeping it real, as they say – for the same reason that other historical movies plump for an earlier era that's not too far from the present day. (Also, thousands of movies go back to the 1920s-1940s, a favourite era for all the obvious reasons. Francis Coppola, Steven Spielberg, George Lucas, Woody Allen, Alan Rudolph and Brian de Palma are some well-known examples among North American directors. Many European *auteurs* also revisit that period).

But the story, Pier Paolo Pasolini also insisted, could be set in any era – humans are cruel, and cruelty has been part of human history since forever. The 1975 film was about oppression, about those who exploit and those who are exploited, and about the disturbing links between oppression and submission. So it could've been set in Ancient Rome or contemporary New York.

'Power is anarchy,[34] says Pier Paolo Pasolini – power would like to abolish history and overcome nature. History and nature can be abolished and overcome through sex,' is how Enzo Siciliano sums up the theme of *Salò* (ES, 387).

For Pasolini, it seems that the theme of domination and submission was uppermost, and more significant than any of the other themes, such as sex, or exploitation, or consumerism, or the decline of modern Italy, or even political fascism. As the maestro explained to Gideon Bachmann:

> The common phenomenon is the instinct of submission, which in man is as strong, undoubtedly, as that of domination. Throughout history there have been stratifications of a social nature based on this dialectic. What we call the class struggle today is only one form of it; it was neither de Sade nor Marx, and certainly not myself, who have invented the tensions between the oppressor and the oppressed; these are as old as agriculture and perhaps as old as hunting. Most likely all our social organization, our pecking order as you might say, is based on it.

As Pasolini noted: 'where de Sade says God, I say Power; he was against the power over man's beliefs, I am against the power over man's body.' This puts *Salò, or The 120 Days of Sodom* into the same critical field as the philosophical debates about the body and slavery that you find in the writing of Michel Foucault[35] or 1970s second wave feminism. In *Salò*, the body is the site of the exploration of the issues of power, domination and submission.

Louis Valentin: Can love exist without sado-

---
34 'We fascists are the only true anarchists', Blangis boasts.
35 *Salò* is virtually an illustration of Foucault's writings on power and sexuality.

masochistic relations?
Pier Paolo Pasolini: It is inconceivable. But who started it? Sade or Masoch? It's the old story of the chicken and the egg. The equilibrium of these two forces is the result of human equilibrium. (1970)

When Pier Paolo Pasolini discussed *Salò, or The 120 Days of Sodom*, he talked about power and its abuses, about the impact of political power on the body, about consumerism as the new fascism,[36] and lamented the passing of the old Italy, the old Rome, as it was overwhelmed by postwar affluence, the media, and capitalist consumption.

'In this film', Pasolini noted in "The Lost Pasolini Interview",

> sex is nothing but an allegory of the commodification of bodies at the hands of power. I think that consumerism manipulates and violates bodies as much as Nazism did. My film represents this sinister coincidence between Nazism and consumerism.

And for Pasolini, capitalist consumerism was more insidious than fascism:

> I consider consumerism a worse fascism than the classical one, because clerical-fascism did not transform Italians. It did not get into them. It was totalitarian but not totalizing. (2012)

Director Elio Petri described Italian society as 'the kind of society that absorbs everything and turns it back into consumerism... All is absorbed into consumerism' (D. Georgakas, 56).

For Geoffrey Nowell-Smith, Pasolini's films ran out of proposing cinematic and social alternatives to the onslaught of consumerism and capitalism which he reckoned was destroying Italian society:

---

[36] For Pasolini, what Adolf Hitler did with bodies in WWII – turn them into things, then destroy them – was what the consumer culture was doing to his beloved Italy.

> The problem was that by the end of his life he had run out of imaginative alternatives to the modernity he increasingly hated. The peasantry, with its closeness to the soil and the seasons and the rituals of death and resurgence, had disappeared as a class throughout the western world. (In N. Power, 2017)

For Lorenzo Chiesa (writing in "Pasolini and the Ugliness of Bodies"), the degradations brought about by capitalist-consumerism affected everyone:

> Pasolini now believes that the hedonistic consumerism and sexual promiscuity imposed by the techno-fascist power of late-capitalism necessarily entails an anthropological genocide which is concomitant with a degeneration of *all* bodies.[37]

As Gary Indiana noted, there have been plenty of movies more explicit, more violent and repulsive than *Salò, or The 120 Days of Sodom* since 1975 (90). True, but few films have been as angry or as extreme ideologically as *Salò, or The 120 Days of Sodom*. There are details and images that might be more explicit in movies after 1975, but no one can deny that when Pier Paolo Pasolini is angry, he is truly scary. (One reason is that *Salò* is rooted in contemporary politics and in recent history; it's fantastical but its horrors cannot be dismissed as fantasy, as so many movies can be).

Ninetto Davoli saw *Salò, or The 120 Days of Sodom* as Pier Paolo Pasolini's reaction to a new era of cynicism, where you couldn't make fairy tales like the 'trilogy of life' movies anymore. *Salò, or The 120 Days of Sodom* for Davoli was consciously angry, intended to show Pasolini's critics what he *really* thought of life in modern Italy. It wasn't a 'negative' rejection of the mediæval trilogy, it was a concerted attempt to do something very different, to move in a very different direction.

Repudiating the 'trilogy of life' movies, Pier Paolo Pasolini veered towards the extreme in the other direction: a movie which would determinedly and

---
37 In L. Polezzi, 2007, 107.

ruthlessly avoid/ usurp/ subvert pleasure: *Salò*. A film of death to counter the 'trilogy of life' films, perhaps. A pleasure*less* movie, a movie where desire is negated by excess and torture. A movie in which joy would consist in witnessing people utterly without joy.[38] A movie as a jackboot in the face. As Pasolini put aside other movie projects (such as *St Paul*) in order to take up *Salò*, 'his vitality and joy had taken on a deep shadow of mourning', as Enzo Siciliano put it (ES, 366).

In an interview, Rosi Braidotti drew attention to the bogus nature of 'difference', and how it has its roots in fascism:

> I think the notion of "difference" is a concept rooted in European fascism, having been colonized and taken over by hierarchical and exclusionary ways of thinking. Fascism, however, does not come from nothing. In the European history of philosophy, "difference" is central insofar as it has *always* functioned by dualistic oppositions, which create sub-categories of otherness, or "difference-from". Because in this history, "difference" has been predicated on relations of domination and exclusion, to be "different-from" came to mean "less than", to be *worth* less than.[39]

Salò, or The 120 Days of Sodom is also a movie of social rituals, but perverted and deranged: the early rituals, like the joint signing of the document to inaugurate the grand scheme of debauchery, are conducted in a polite, refined manner (the black rulebook is later waved in front of naughty victims who dare to defy the laws the four aristos have composed). But the ceremonies rapidly become truly grotesque once the orgiastic terrors begin. There's a parody of a wedding ceremony, for instance (when Duke Blangis goes nuts and launches himself at the group of naked

---

[38] Gary Indiana notes that none of the libertines appears to enjoy their sex acts, which they do in the Marquis de Sade's text: 'these men exhibit a much more dour and grimly dutiful reaction to their own orgiastic agenda, as if monotonously running through a checklist of obligatory outrages' (53).

[39] Quoted in N. Schor, 1994, 45.

youths, groping and slathering over them).[40] The guests (the victims) carry white lillies. After their nuptials, Renata and Sergio are ordered to do the deed while the libertines watch, then they're raped. A second wedding feast has shit and more shit and only shit on the menu (yummy!),[41] served by naked maidens on a silver platter, evoking the *Monty Python* sketch about spam, spam, spam (meanwhile, the bride is a boy dressed in white. He looks quite darling).

The social rituals are empty, utterly devoid of their former value or meaning. They are also performed by people who have no relation to them, who are play-acting (it takes Brechtian alienation to an extreme).

The victims are not given much characterization, beyond their presence as an actor or an extra (i.e., their naked body). The 1975 movie isn't much interested in who they are or where they came from (tho' when such information can help to titillate the libertines, it is included, such as Renata losing her mom). Another filmmaking team, for example, would've made more of the round-up, and more of the victims.

Take an equivalent Hollywood example. Producers Gerald R. Molen and Branko Lustig, director Steven Spielberg and company, for instance, expanded the liquidation of the ghetto sequence in *Schindler's List* (1993) from the scene in Steve Zaillian's screenplay. The sequence in *Schindler's List* is staggering in its ferocity, its brilliant staging, its masterful editing by Michael Kahn, and its acute, hallucinatory sense of detail. You can see Spielberg and the team thinking in both a broad and a detailed manner, moving from the big view to the close-up view. And you can see the filmmakers improvising and adding to the scene as they developed new ideas, or hear another testimony from a Holocaust survivor. Zaillian said Spielberg kept coming

---

[40] You can see the actors quaking as Paolo Bonacelli (as Blangis) gets closer and closer to them, as they wait their turn to be groped and slobbered over.

[41] The fæces were produced with broken cookies mixed with chocolate, marmalade, olive oil, and condensed milk. *Mmmm!* (If there was merchandizing for *Salò*, like *Star Wars* robots or Reese's Pieces with *E.T.*, edible fæces would be sold).

up with visual ideas.[42]

Salò, or The 120 Days of Sodom is a movie that announces to the audience: *I am going to hit you in the face, then I'm going to do it again, and again, until you are bruised and bleeding. Then I'm going to beat you some more.*[43]

And yet... it's only a movie!

SALO AS 'NAZI CHIC'.

You could say that *Salò, o Le 120 Giornate di Sodoma* is part of a group of movies of the early-to-mid-1970s period which romanticized the National Socialists in Germany, giving them a kind of 'Nazi chic': *Cabaret, The Damned, The Conformist* and *The Night Porter*. Thus was historical fascism reduced to a-historical fashion, the emptying-out of history in postmodern surfaces. (Sidenote: these 'Nazi chic' movies heavily influenced punk rock and post-punk bands, for instance – Joy Division, New Order, Gary Numan, the New Romantics, the 'Blitz' kids and Siouxsie and the Banshees.[44] In punk and New Wave fashions of the late '70s/ early '80s, youths wore swastikas in order to shock, and played around with the imagery of fascism, military clothing and the Third Reich. David Bowie was the most well-known advocate of all things Germanic and decadent; Bowie led the Christopher Isherwood/ *Cabaret* lifestyle to the max in Berlin *circa* 1976-77).

Salò, or The 120 Days of Sodom had to be set in the twilight era of Nazism and the war – the audience needed to know that this would soon be over. It would've been

---

42 *Steven Spielberg Interviews*, University of Mississippi Press, Jackson, 2000, 1982.

43 '*Salò* is not meant to entertain us. Entertainment is a privilege to be enjoyed only by the power mongers in the film', as Renée Brack noted in a 2010 online essay. A recent book on horror cinema (2013) also took this view: *Salò* 'belongs to that select group of works for which issues of entertainment fall into irrelevance, and viewing becomes a question of endurance' (K. Newman, 186).

44 The Bromley Contingent used to adore *Cabaret* (mega-camp Joel Grey and diva Liza Minnelli); they were living the *Goodbye to Berlin* life, according to Berlin, who loved the decadent, Teutonic ambience so much he changed his name to Berlin (J. Savage. *England's Dreaming: Sex Pistols and Punk Rock*, Faber, London, 1991, 184).

'an intolerable movie' had it been set in the heyday of Nazism, Pasolini said (2012).

SALO, THE HOLOCAUST AND JEAN-LUC GODARD.

It should be noted that *Salò, or The 120 Days of Sodom* isn't *meant* to be a bundle of laughs. Like *The Devils* (1971) or *Schindler's List* (1993), this production seems to be intended as a difficult and uncomfortable film experience.[45] This is, after all, Pier Paolo Pasolini's movie about the Holocaust, about the extremes that humanity will go to in the pursuit of power, pleasure and coercion. *Salò* is unequivocal in its condemnation of the aristocrats and tycoons who stage their 120 days in Sodom and Gomorrah, 20th century-style. But it also, far more problematically, explores the collusion of the victims in this madness (and also the audience's collaboration – this movie doesn't exist without viewers. Everyone's implicated).

Salò, or The 120 Days of Sodom, for all its flaws, does raise fascinating issues about modern history: like, how could a number of Germans exterminate six million people? (Was it 50,000 or maybe 100,000 soldiers and officials running this killing operation? It depends how you look at it: it required hundreds of thousands of collaborators, perhaps millions). *Salò* evokes the every-day mechanics of the Holocaust, how it was actually achieved day-by-day, with its depictions of soldiers with guns herding the eighteen victims, its convoys of trucks and cars. (Documentaries such as *Shoah* (1985) and fiction films such as *Conspiracy* (2001) have explored the mechanics of the Holocaust).[46]

Meanwhile, Jean-Luc Godard has made the Holo-

---

[45] 'What is depicted in *Salò* is done without alibi, without comfort or saving grace' (Sam Rohdie, 41).

[46] In a 1963 interview, Jean-Luc Godard mused on the possibility of making a documentary about the concentration camps which would focus on the actual organization and means of dispensing with humans on a mass scale. Such a film, which would ask questions like 'how to load ten tons of arms and legs on to a three-ton lorry?' or 'How to burn a hundred women with petrol enough for ten?', would be 'intolerable', Godard admitted, adding: 'the really horrible thing about such scenes would not be their horror but their very ordinary everydayness' (1986, 198).

caust and World War Two one of his primary topics in his later cinematic and video works. For Godard, the Holocaust *must* be discussed in films, even tho' it's seen as the Ultimate Taboo Subject. The Holocaust and the concentration camps have long absorbed Godard (he relates part of his fascination to his father), cropping up in later works such as *Éloge de L'Amour* (2001) and *Histoire(s) du Cinéma*, his 1998 history of cinema (in amongst the rush of images in *Histoire(s) du Cinéma*, the footage of the concentration camps overwhelms everything else). The death camps were an event beyond history or above history or rupturing history. An event that couldn't be encompassed. Hence Godard's attacks on those who've tried to depict the Holocaust on film (such as *Schindler's List, Night and Fog* and *Shoah*.[47] No, not even *Shoah* was good enough for Godard).[48]

But the Holocaust should have been filmed, Jean-Luc Godard insisted, and it still must be put on screen. (Godard made similar remarks of the terrorist attacks of 9/11, criticizing French broadcasters for showing the Twin Towers collapsing, but not the people falling to their deaths.)

Cinema should have shown the concentration camps, but no one wanted to see them: this was one of Jean-Luc Godard's recurring issues in his later work. His view was that if the Holocaust had been filmed, and had been *seen*, it might've helped to avert later catastrophes: but 'it started again, so to speak, Vietnam, Algeria – it's not finished – Biafra, Afghanistan, Palestine', Godard remarked in 1995.[49]

---

[47] There are hints that Godard would take on the Holocaust in his earlier films – the women who're tattooed with numbers in *Alphaville*, a conversation in *Masculin Féminin*, and the investigator character in *Une Femme Mariée*.

[48] Jean-Luc Godard regarded *Shoah* (Claude Lanzmann, 1985) as a failure (even though he later called it 'a very great film'). And *Shoah* is of course one of the very few works about the Holocaust that many critics agree is a worthy attempt at depicting the impossible. But no, not even *Shoah* was good enough for Godard. He attacked Lanzmann in articles, too (such as in 1998). It's as if no film has got the concentration camps right for Godard, not even films such as *Night and Fog* directed by Alain Resnais.

[49] In a speech in Frankfurt, when Godard accepted the Theodor Adorno prize (in R. Brody, 564).

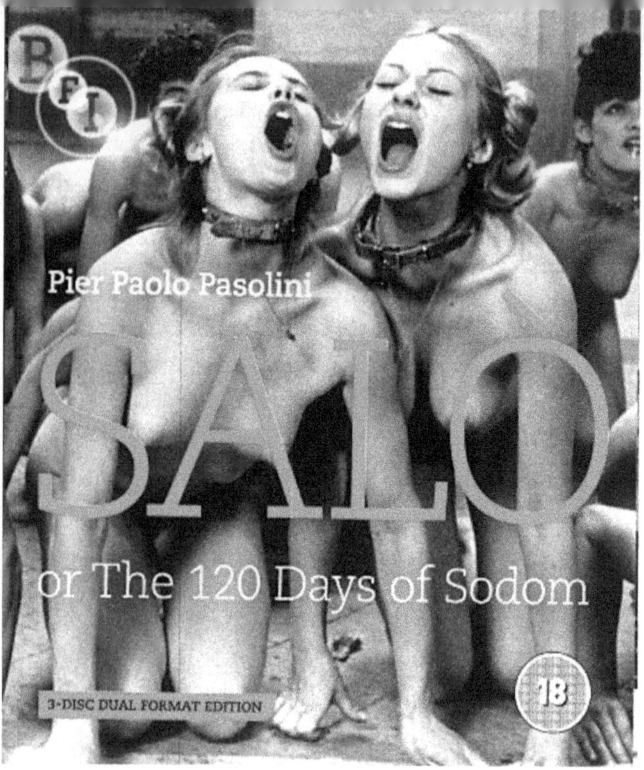

Salò (1975).
This page and over.

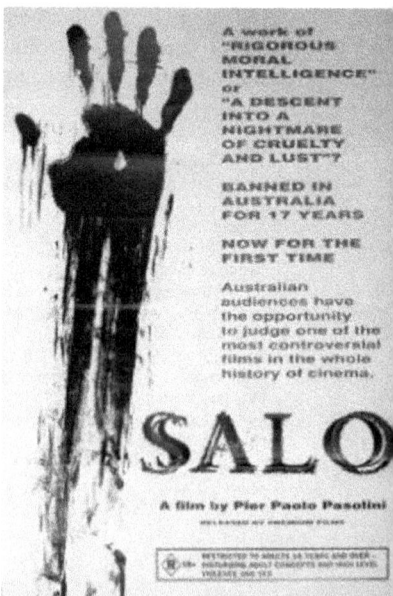

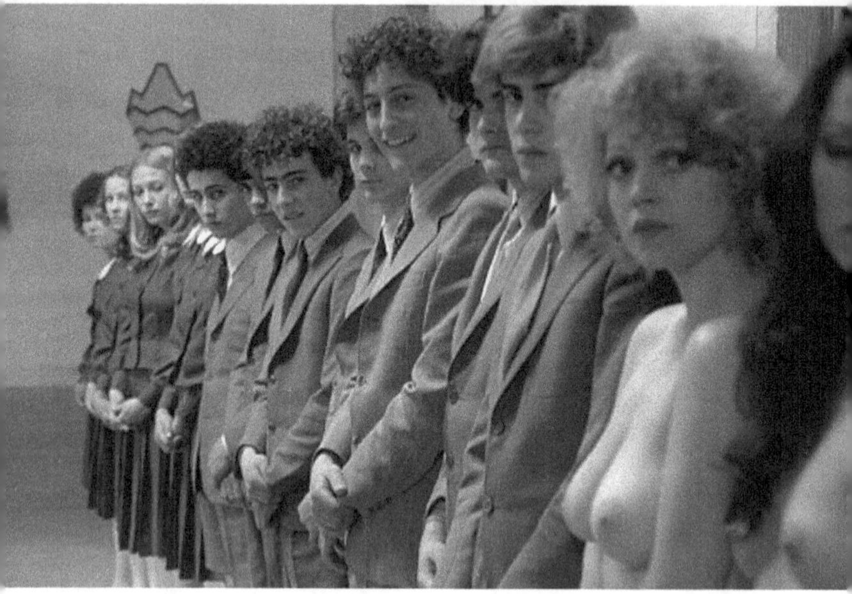

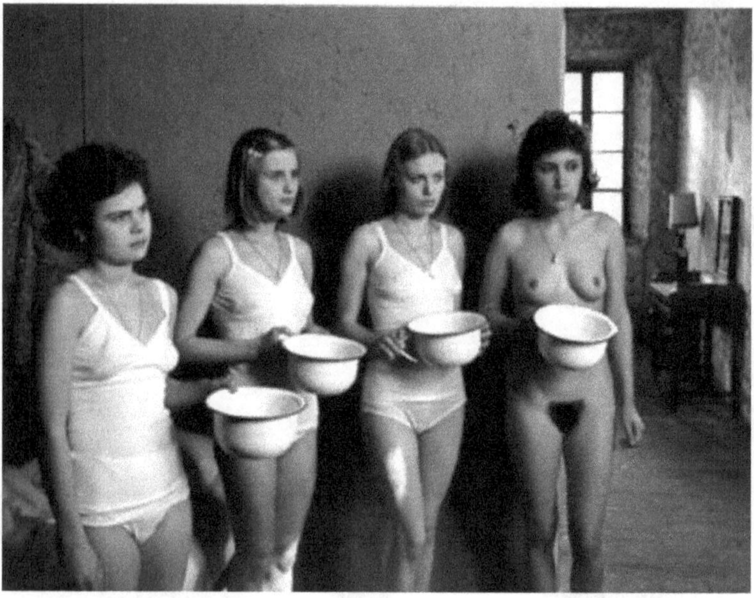

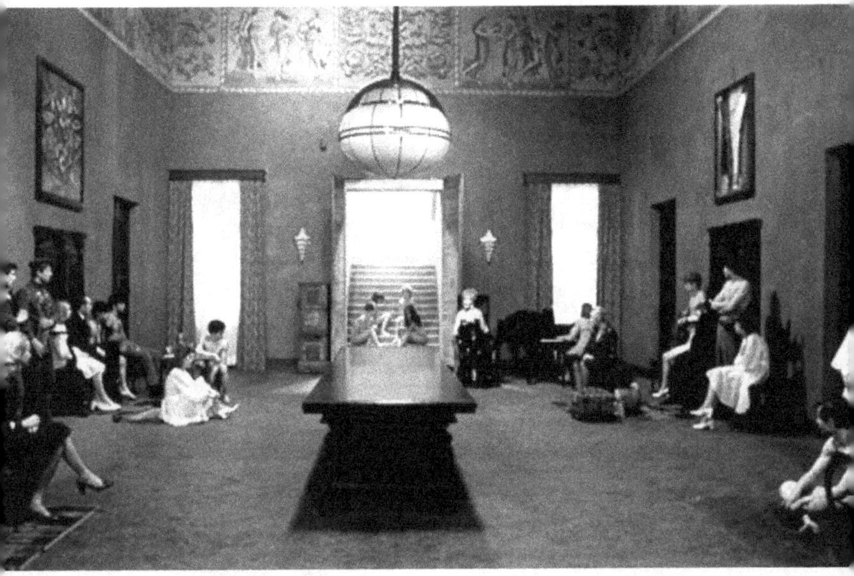

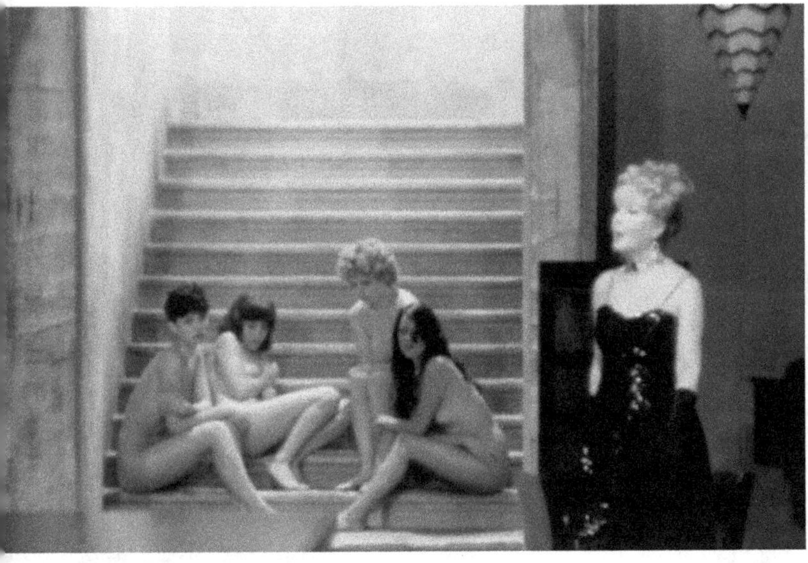

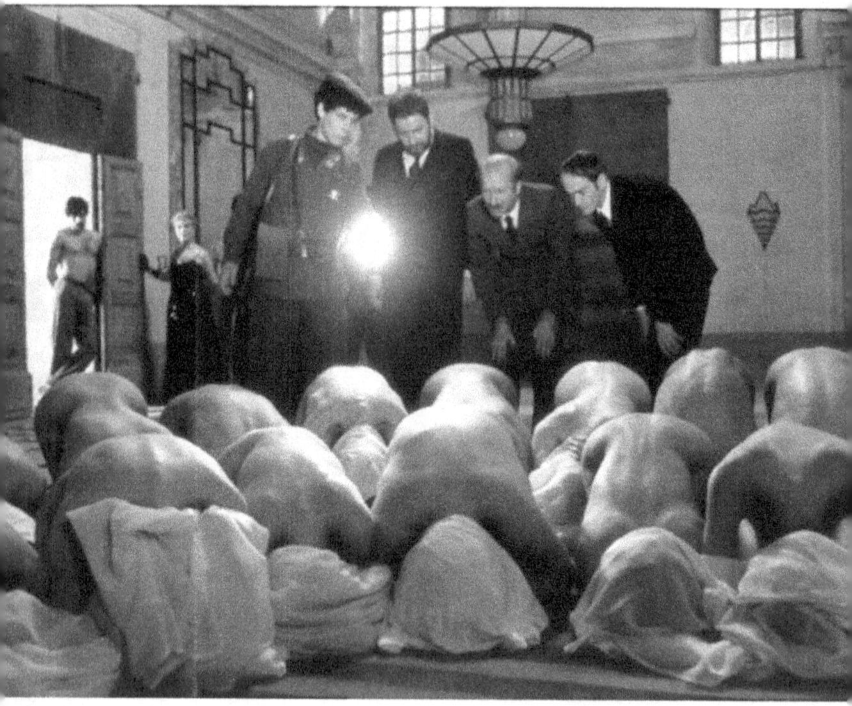

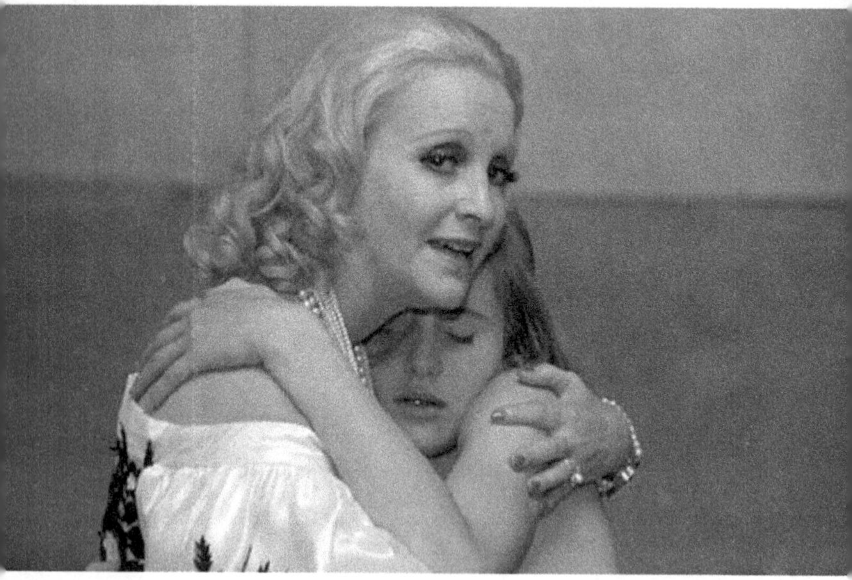

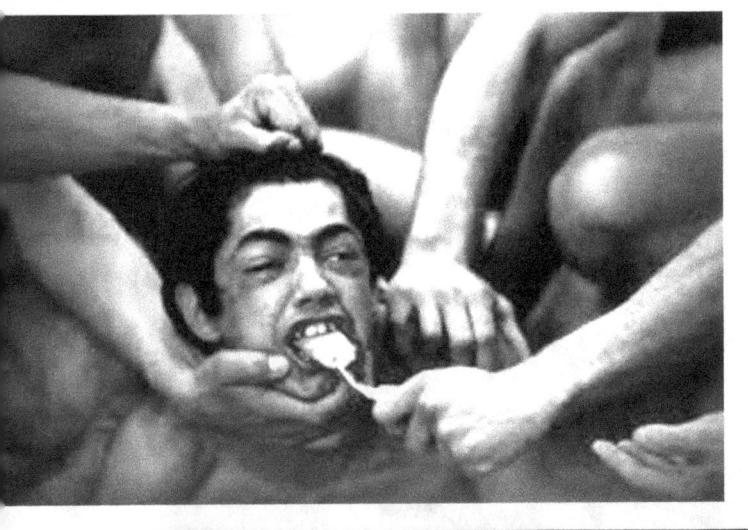

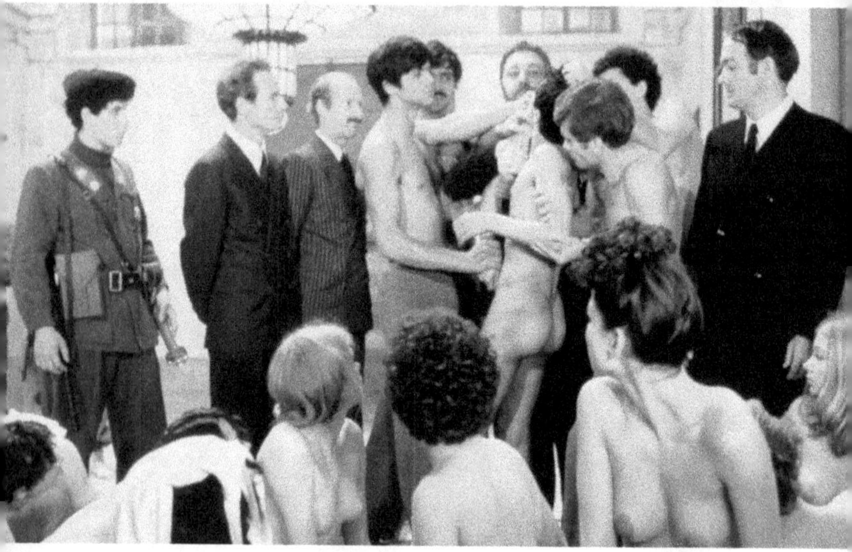

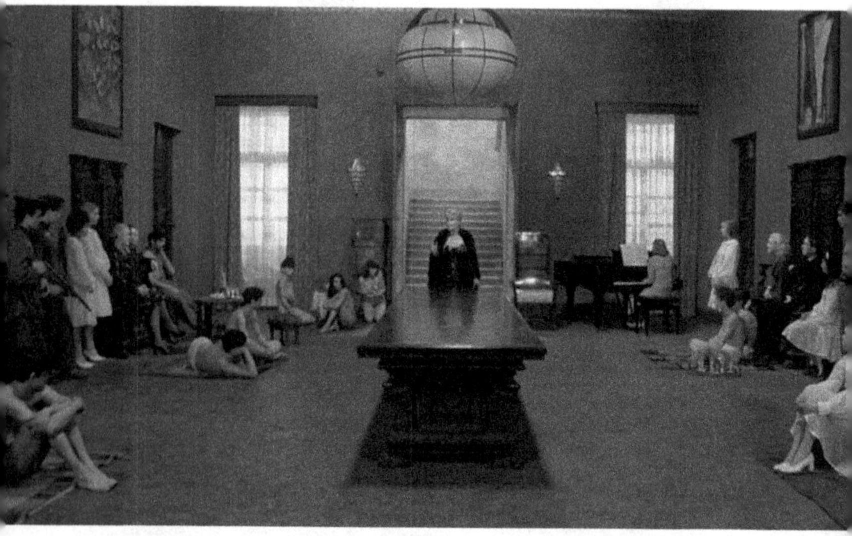

inspires some interesting reflections.

Filming Salò (this page and over).

ORAL-ANAL/ FREUDIAN-MARXIST.

Salò, or The 120 Days of Sodom is not the easiest film to watch – if you watch it, that is, from the same perspective as other movies. (But there are many ways of consuming movies, and many perspectives). Anyway, taking it straight on, *Salò, o Le 120 Giornate di Sodoma* contains images of brutality, degradation, torture, slavery, rape, murder and a range of sexual 'perversions': flagellation, urination,[1] and coprophilia. There's also sodomy, interracial sex and lesbian sex in there for good measure (as if it's trying to cover all bases). Women are buggered then hung up; captives have their tongues cut off and their eyeballs gouged out; victims are scalped; their skin's burnt with candles; they're covered in filth and left in a tub; they are forced to eat turds; they are sodomized in front of a banquet, and so on.

Among the first acts we witness in *Salò, or The 120 Days of Sodom* centre around homosexuality, under-age sex and the penis – one of the perpetrators is masturbated by a victim, and the storyteller spins a long yarn of being preyed upon by an old man as a pre-teen (of course, he had a huge ••••). One of the aristos, seemingly already turned on, drags a *ragazzo* impatiently out of the red room, and, when that backfires, he takes a girl.

Salò, or The 120 Days of Sodom is truly an anal film, a film obsessed with the anus, buttocks, sodomy, defecation, fæces, coprophilia, waste matter and urination (the 'civilization du cul', as Jean-Luc Godard put it in *Weekend*, a key filmic forerunner of Pasolini *e* de Sade). There are so many images of people presenting their asses, people defecating, people eating fæces, sodomy, and lots of talk about *derrières* and *merde*. *Salò* must rank among the most anally-fixated of movies (it shares an anal obsession with other European art films of the era, such as *Last Tango in Paris* (1972),[2]

---
[1] Hauled into the lavatory, a girl is told to urinate while a perpetrator watches.
[2] Pier Paolo Pasolini had disliked *Last Tango In Paris*: he thought that Bertolucci had sold out to commercialism.

Blow Out (1973), *Weekend* (1967), and the cinema of Walerian Borowcyzk).[3]

The 'Circle of Shit' section of *Salò, or The 120 Days of Sodom* is filled with stories of anal and fæcal sexuality: the storyteller (Signora Maggi) talks about a dying man from her youth who wanted to kiss the Almighty Ass for one last time (Maggi bent over and obliged – and shat too for good measure). The story's covered in a single, lengthy handheld shot, as the storyteller dances with the Bishop around the red room (countering the view that Pasolini only filmed in short takes. It's a *very* lengthy shot).

The obsessive anality of *Salò, or The 120 Days of Sodom* ties it in with European intellectual culture which made anal/ excremental discourse prominent: Georges Bataille and *The Story of the Eye*, James Joyce (*Ulysses*), D.H. Lawrence (*Lady Chatterley's Lover* with its talk of burning out the 'deepest, oldest shames' using anal sex), John Cowper Powys (in *A Glastonbury Romance*), Salvador Dali (in his painting *A Young Virgin Sodomized By Her Own Chastity*), Surrealist artist Hans Bellmer (multiple penetrations of orifices in his dolls), Paul Verlaine and Arthur Rimbaud (in their 'Sonnet To the Asshole', for instance), Pauline Réage (*The Story of O*), and most of William Burroughs' fiction (which far-outclasses Pasolini's cinema, including *Salò*, for outrageous homoeroticism and anal fetishism, and combining sex and death, as well as delivering an apocalyptic scream against many aspects of Western civilization).

Relentlessly polemical, with its Freudian-Marxist-poetic attack on contemporary, Western capitalist society and morality (an easy target for a veteran iconoclast like Pier Paolo Pasolini), *Salò, or The 120 Days of Sodom* is grim stuff (that is, if you view it solemnly and reverentially). In an interview at the time of *Salò*, Pasolini admitted that he no longer believed in

---

[3] Walerian Borowczyk's films have many affinities with those of Pier Paolo Pasolini – Borowczyk attacked 20th century fascism, for instance, in *Immoral Tales*, and bourgeois sensibilities with his controversial *The Beast*.

revolution, but acted as if he did.[4]

The style of filmmaking in *Salò, o Le 120 Giornate di Sodoma* is not to everyone's taste, either. The subject matter – a group of degenerate aristocrats abusing attractive youngsters in an Italian *palazzo* – would be 'difficult' enough for many audiences – but the cinematic treatment by Pasolini, Delli Colli, Ferretti, Baragli *et al* – geometrical, painterly *tableaux*, few close-ups, art cinema techniques, sudden eruptions of violence, and no main sympathetic characters to identify with – would likely also put off many viewers. In addition, there's a sly, ambiguous attitude towards the material, a cool, implacable distantiation which further complicates matters. The film refuses to condemn the libertines and their acts, or to offer a firm, moral stance to guide viewers. (*Salò* has 'niche' and 'minority' written all over it, in terms of audiences and markets. *Salò* would never open on 3,500 screens around the world, like a blockbuster movie!).

And yet *Salò, or The 120 Days of Sodom* is also completely silly, and knows it is. It's a black comedy, but with no laughs (and no jokes).[5] It's 'offensive' not in the degradations and excesses that it depicts (and wallows in, to a degree), but in its smug assumption that this is polemical, radical cinema. It's 'offensive' because it's so stupidly reductionist. It's 'offensive' because it assumes a patronizing attitude towards its audience, which starts with the condescending citation of intellectual authors in the credits. (Sam Rohdie suggests viewing *Salò* as burlesque, as a silent movie comedy. Rohdie is one of the few film critics who depart from taking *Salò, or The 120 Days of Sodom* straight).

✢

The first moment of nudity in the 1975 movie is, typically for a Pier Paolo Pasolini movie, not female but male: two youths, Sergio and Franco (one of them is Franco Merli) are ordered to undress in front of the

---

[4] Even Marxists are consumerists, according to Pasolini: 'all those who consider themselves either Marxists or Communists are consumerists, too' (2012).
[5] 'A comedy masquerading as Theatre of Cruelty' (Gary Indiana, 54).

group of visiting aristos, who've come to inspect them, and select their victims. However, female nudity follows soon after (from poor Eva, who's brought in to see the four libertines and stripped by one of the madames).

Franco Merli, by the way, is the object of many of the degradations in *Salò, or The 120 Days of Sodom* – maybe Pasolini and company thought he could handle them, because he had already survived the lengthy, globe-trotting production of *The Arabian Nights* the year before. Thus, Merli is the first of the victims to be undressed; he is the winner of the Best Ass Contest – and has a gun pointed at his head and fired; and he undergoes tortures in the courtyard sequence (having his tongue cut out. Merli is also placed at the front of several other scenes, such as the wedding processions).

The infractions perpetrated by the victims are punished immediately (or noted in the black book). It doesn't matter so much what the misdemeanours are, but that the rules laid down by the libertines have been broken.

The aristos like to stick to their rules (once the rules have been invented, they have to be adhered to), and the rulebook is waved around several times. Regardless of what the rules are, *Salò, or The 120 Days of Sodom* sends up the notion of religiously, stubbornly following them. Occasionally, the perpetrators adjust their rules (such as the collection of excrement).

Let's not forget, though, that in the 'trilogy of life' movies of 1971-1974, a common scenario had sexual play being punished – there were authority figures like knights, kings and priests, and religious institutions such as the Catholic Church. Persecution complexes were everywhere in the 'life' trilogy films, with 'sin' and 'guilt' leading to some excessive punishments. In one scene in *The Canterbury Tales*, participants in homosexual acts were condemned to public execution (in a Cathedral cloisters). So *Salò* sort of continues that social and moral set-up, but exaggerates the stakes, and also links the regime to fascism and World War Two and contemporary Italy.

By the start of the second act of *Salò, or The 120 Days of Sodom* (some 30-35 minutes into the piece), the movie has staged several acts of sexual degradation and exploitation. After this, there is repetition and variation. But the points have already been made. The rest of *Salò* is essentially redundant (indeed, it might be even more powerful if it were cut down 30 minutes: thus, the round-up, the set-up, and the inspection scenes could be curtailed to 7 minutes instead of 20 minutes, leaving time for a single story from Signora Castelli, then a few tortures. That's all it needs. It doesn't need to run to 1h 56m. And if it had been another half-an-hour longer, before the film was trimmed down, it would've been even tougher to sit through).

The scenes of the perpetrators in the ante rooms dressing up or of the storytellers primping themselves before mirrors remind us that this is an act, a performance. (Mirrors are a minor motif in *Salò, or The 120 Days of Sodom* – one of the libertines masturbates before a mirror, for instance – mirror motifs chime with the themes of voyeurism exploited in the final scenes). And notice how the storytellers descend the staircase at the other end of the red room, just like actors walking down to the stage, before they begin their stories, or like Ginger and Fred on a shiny staircase in a musical movie of the 1930s (they also dance a little, and sing. Folks, we're still waiting for *Salò: The Musical* to open on Broadway!).

In one scene the victims're led into the white room on leashes, barking, like a pack of dogs. Remaining on all-fours, they are fed by the libertines, and treated like animals (begging, barking, eating food off the floor). It's another instance of the in-your-face literalism in *Salò, or The 120 Days of Sodom* (but it's also a brilliant scene).

Late in the piece, the libertines stage a Best Ass Contest (oh so *very* de Sadeian! oh so *very* French! – it's Jean-Luc Godard's 'civilization of the ass'): by flashlight, they inspect the butts of the surviving victims one by one, and the captives crouch in foetal poses on the floor (there is a good deal of discussion about asses and anuses in *Salò, or The 120 Days of Sodom*. The 'lusty fuckers', in true de Sade-style, also ponder on which is the best asshole, male or female).

And what's the Prize for the Best Ass? Instant death, of course! ('Cept this time, it's a tease, and the pistol doesn't fire at the victim.[6] The framing of the scene, featuring poor Franco Merli, seems designed to echo the famous photograph of the execution of Viet Cong prisoner Nguyen Van Lem in the Vietnam War).

✳

In *Salò, or The 120 Days of Sodom*, the film techniques are part of the scheme of representation that the story is an everyday occurrence, a matter-of-fact approach which avoids histrionics, rhetoric, and excessive emotion. So the camera stays back and uses 50mm lenses, with simple mid-shots and long shots, and the staging is again often in a *tableau*-style. The handheld shots that characterize Pasolini's later style are replaced by the camera on a tripod. It's the normalcy of cruelty, the everydayness of it, the inevitability of it: this is what humans do. They can't help themselves.

Salò, or The 120 Days of Sodom isn't telling us or showing us stuff we don't already know.

We know about World War Two.

We know about the Holocaust.

We know about fascism.

We know that humans are extraordinarily cruel.

Do we need to be told or shown that in a movie? Not really – we don't give a darn.

Salò, or The 120 Days of Sodom comes across as one of those pictures of the era when the filmmakers decided, hell, we are going to go *all out*! In films of this era, you can see Ken Russell doing this with *The Devils*, Jean-Luc Godard with *Weekend*, Sam Peckinpah with *The Wild Bunch* and *Straw Dogs*, Walerian Borowczyk with *The Beast* and *Immoral Tales*, and Bernardo Bertolucci with *Last Tango In Paris*. No holds barred, nothing held back – *no limits*. (It's one of Werner Herzog's mantras: 'I

---

6 This was added to de Sade's novel.

don't believe in limits').

That the horrors in *Salò, or The 120 Days of Sodom* are perpetrated on a group of young Italians is significant: altho' the source may be French (the Marquis de Sade), and the 'official' voice dub may be French (according to Pasolini), and European fascism might be one of the themes, there is no question that *Salò* is set in modern Italy and is about modern Italy and attacking modern Italy. And the victims are modern, Italian kids.[7]

Pier Paolo Pasolini enshrined (nay, idealized) the notion of youth, and the young, vital body: *Salò* is thus a disturbing exploration of the corruption of the young. Nobody can miss the fact that the perpetrators are all middle-aged, and that the victims are all young. Forget fascism or the Nazis, this is also a movie about the eternal issue of youth versus age, the younger generation versus the older generation. It's about the Sins of the Fathers (with the sins this time being highly exaggerated).

The actors playing the victims were born after the war, but the middle-aged actors grew up in the shadow of WWII. Young people in modern Italy were one of Pasolini's preoccupations: he wanted to make them aware of their epoch, of where they stood in history. *Salò* is a message to the youth of modern Italy. Yet, ironically, *Salò* is precisely the sort of niche, arty film that would have a limited audience in 1975, as it would today, and the youth of Italia would not see it. Instead, in 1975, young Italians went to see Hollywood hits such as *One Flew Over the Cuckoo's Nest*, *The Rocky Horror Picture Show*, *Shampoo*, *Dog Day Afternoon* and the behemoth *Jaws*, and all the usual Italian comedies, action-adventures, dramas, *gialli*, costumers, and plenty of thrillers. There were many movies to see in Italy in 1975, and *Salò* would be way down the list. Consider

---

[7] Alberto Moravia saw in *Accattone* a link between Pier Paolo Pasolini's 'peasant utopia' (the utopia of the peasants in the past), and his 'homosexual utopia' (in the present day). The peasant world was the youth of the world in the past, Moravia pondered, while the homosexual world is the youth of today.

the question from a boy to a girl: 'Do you want to see *Salò* tonight, Anna, or *Shampoo*?'.[8]

STAGING, STYLE AND STORYTELLING.

The stories of the Signoras, like madames who preside over a brothel (or like whores who aren't getting paid), are at the narrative centre of *Salò, or The 120 Days of Sodom*; the 1975 picture keeps returning to the scene of Signoras Castelli or Maggi telling stories to the group of aristos and sex slaves who sit around the sides of the enormous 'Hall of Orgies' (which Dante Ferretti and co. have art-directed (and Tonino Delli Colli has lit) in faded reds, the colour of aged, dried blood,[9] of passionless, vampiric sex, of an abattoir). The other main set is a white space, with a marble floor (and a couple of huge, ominous doors at the far end – the Gates of Hell). The rooms're furnished sparsely with large mirrors, Art Deco lamps, and choice examples of age-brown wooden chairs. An enormous staircase and a second stairway also feature, plus several bedrooms and ante-rooms. Paintings by Lyonel Feininger, Oscar Kokoschka and Marcel Duchamp line the walls of the side rooms. The villa[10] might've been confiscated from 'some rich Jew', Pasolini explained – hence the paintings and the *objets d'art* (the villa with its art is a setting boasting wealth, heritage, old money, and high culture).

Altho' *Salò, or The 120 Days of Sodom* is regarded as a political rant in the form of a historical movie, it draws on the cinematic devices of horror cinema and pornographic cinema. These are both cinemas, incidentally, which focus on the human body, and they are both forms which aim for a visceral response from viewers.

The nightmares of the acts portrayed in *Salò, or The 120 Days of Sodom* aren't obscured by shadows or fancy

---

[8] And if it was still playing in 1976, *Salò* would be over-shadowed by the hits of 1976, such as *Rocky, King Kong* and *Logan's Run*.
[9] Recalling the dried blood colours of Mark Rothko's late paintings, including the famous murals of the Tate Gallery and Harvard.
[10] Bachmann saw the design as 'the typically Italian "Imperial" Bauhaus style'.

lighting: this is a horror movie that takes place in the light. The stylized lighting by Tonino Delli Colli and the camera team is often bright and all-over, illuminating the whole set. The shadowless, reflected light, from above, reveals the horrors in a clear, matter-of-fact manner. (Other filmmakers might've been tempted to plump for the flickering, shadowy, intricate lighting of Gothic and horror scenarios – which, of course, Italian cinema is famous for). The cinematic approach of *Salò, or The 120 Days of Sodom* results in the 'elimination of feeling, of psychology, of drama, of human interaction, of natural physical functions, and of social values' (G. Bachmann).

Pier Paolo Pasolini said he was 'proceeding more carefully' in filming *Salò, or The 120 Days of Sodom*, taking a more considered approach: 'to make this film with emotion and stylistic flair would make it only banal' (G. Bachmann). As DP Toninio Delli Colli recalled, Pasolini was after a 'crystaline' mood to the film, and originally he wanted to shoot in black-and-white (the producers persuaded him otherwise. Producers, studios, distributors and exhibitors always want colour).

✻

Each libertine is surrounded by a small group of armed collaborators and several naked victims sitting/lying on the floor. Castelli, Maggi and co. (the storytellers) speak of their sexual adventures, of people they've had, of guys who had kids masturbate them, of being groped by old men, of men who loved to eat fæces, of men who worshipped asses, of men who liked women to urinate in their mouths, of men who liked girls to defecate in their mouths then kick them out of a window. *Salò, or The 120 Days of Sodom*'s like a fable or legend, with a storyteller (appropriately, a prostitute) recounting erotic tales (to piano accompaniment, including many classical piano pieces, and some popular tunes. The pianist[11] gamely plinks and plonks throughout the

---

[11] It's Sonia Saviange who plays the piano in *Salò, or The 120 Days of Sodom*.

movie, until she can't stand anymore, and throws herself out of a window. Yet the piano player was one of the four older women hired by the libertines at the beginning of the story).

And it's also typical that the star role of the storyteller should be played by Caterina Boratto with studied indifference, not with the gusto and energy you might expect: it's as if Boratto's Castelli knows she's tiptoe-ing on the edge of a volcano: there's an atmosphere of violence just beneath the surface, which might erupt at any moment, but she steels herself to ignore it. (The madame politely listens to the recommendations of the perpetrators, and adjusts her stories accordingly.)

It's also typical of Pier Paolo Pasolini and the team to stage these scenes with an eerie, forced calm: nobody dares to titter, let alone laugh (yet there is plenty of laughter – the jeering laughter of the libertines' lackeys, and occasionally the libertines). No one is allowed to weep. And a girl who can't take it any more and flees is dragged back by a bunch of guys. When the girl Renata who lost her mom can't stop the tears, the Duke finds it especially alluring: she's the one he singles out to eat his filth off the floor.

(Force is always present in *Salò, or The 120 Days of Sodom;* there are youths with guns always ready to add the element of physical coercion lest any of the captives misbehave. Escapees are machine-gunned down by German soldiers[12] – the scene on the bridge in Marzabott where former political subversive Tonna Ferruca escapes might've come from any World War II action movie – *The Guns of Navarone*, say, or *The Dirty Dozen*. That is, it's a piece of generic, World War II filmmaking, but it does the job of reminding the audience that in war-time everybody is potentially a victim).

Time doesn't pass in *Salò, or The 120 Days of Sodom* – it remains perpetually an over-cast day, and, anyway, the exterior world isn't shown much after the arrival at the villa. It could be days, or it could be

---
[12] The round-up occurs in the landscape of the Po Valley.

months (a spell in Hell is eternal, after all). When it's supposed to be night, the scenes're filmed day-for-night (as usual in Pier Paolo Pasolini's cinema), but a day-for-night which doesn't do much to hide that it's day-for-night (again, as usual). Originally, the idea was to take 3 of the 120 days in Sodom from the novel by the Marquis de Sade and film them.

Some scenes in *Salò, or The 120 Days of Sodom* balance the degradations of the victims with scenes of total banality. For example, the artistos are depicted as gentlemanly connoisseurs of outrages, discussing matters over coffee or wine, in a civilized manner, in one of the fancy ante-rooms, as if they're resting after a game of golf (tho' we don't see the victims in similar relaxed moments – they don't have a rec room, only their own dorms). The oddest of the modest scenes featuring the libertines is the one where they are getting dressed for the wedding in women's clothing, carefully primping themselves in front of mirrors.

To get around film censorship, of not showing that dreaded item, the erect p•n•s, *Salò, or The 120 Days of Sodom* invents stand-ins (most usually, as ever in all cinema, guns. Guns for penises... *Yawn*). In one hilarious scene, a clothed, wooden dummy is carried into the red room, so that the girls can be taught how to masturbate men (Giuliana Melis is the victim who's berated for not doing it correctly).[13] If this was *The Rocky Horror Picture Show* or a Walerian Borowczyk romp, it would be an amusing scene. In Pier Paolo Pasolini's hands, it's yet another solemn *tableau* of brutality and coercion, even tho' the company laughs. (Yet the phallus is everywhere in this picture: *Salò* is also about the phallus's relation to aggression, narcissism, and power-gaming. The phallus, that is, as analyzed in second wave feminism and 1970s biopolitical commentary).

Unable to depict the p•n•s by film censorship, the solution in *Salò, or The 120 Days of Sodom* is typical of Pasolini's rebellious sensibilities: if he can't show the

---

[13] Presumably to get around censorship laws.

actual p•n•s, or an erection, he'll ask the special make-up guys at Cinecittà to kit out the actors with prosthetic peckers. And there's a dummy instead of the real thing. And the madames' stories mention genitals often (of course the men's members are large).

❋

The colour design of *Salò, or The 120 Days of Sodom* inevitably employs red as its signature hue. Dante Ferretti and the production design team use red throughout the sets.[14] The other two colours are the ones of alchemy, duality and numerous political movements, including fascism and Communism: black and white (there are numerous all-white and all-black costumes, provided by regular Pasolini designer, Danilo Donati). Often the victims're clad in sacrificial white (or they're in white underwear). The libertines're in black suits or dark suits. The collaborators're put in grey, military uniforms (so we have black, grey and white, with grey as a midway point – the collaborators are somewhere between the bosses and the slaves, and they are partly victims, too). No need to add anything about the symbolism of the colours black, white and red in *Salò:* as with everything else in the picture, it is all very obvious and clear.

In this film where the body is foregrounded to such an intense degree (almost overpowering for some viewers),[15] the hair, make-up and costume departments were essential: Danilo Donati was costume designer, Vanni Castellani was wardrobe assistant, and Sartoria Farani designed some costumes; make-up was by Alfredo Tiberi; hair was by Giuseppina Bovino; with wigs and special make-up by Sergio Chiusi and Carboni-Roccohetti).

The Grand Guignol visual effects in *Salò, or The 120 Days of Sodom* are both deliberately cheesy *and* slick, as if sending up the Italian horror genre (Dario

---

[14] Red also evokes royalty and wealth, and links to Catholic power (such as cardinal's robes), and Ancient Roman architecture (such as Pompeii).

[15] It's the naked human body that's the true star of *Salò*, as Gary Indiana notes (28).

Argento, Mario Bava, Lucio Fulci, Umberto Lenzi, Antonio Margheriti *et al*), as well as drawing on it. There's no doubt that *Salò* is part of the cultural shift towards increasingly graphic portrayals of violence, death and gore on screen (from the 1960s onwards), in addition to the more explicit images of sexuality in films of the era. The *gialli* and horror films were a big deal in the Italian film business in the 1970s (i.e., horror/ thriller films were making money).

Italian cinema has a tradition of flamboyant, operatic violence and death, as it does in painting, in art, in opera. Look at a famous horror movie made in Italia in the same year as *Salò*, *Deep Red* (Dario Argento, 1975). If you think the punishments in *Salò* are extreme, have a terrified peep through your fingers at the works of Argento, Bava, Lenzi, Fulci and Margheriti![16]

Scalping, eyeball-gouging, stabbing, hanging and all the rest are staples of the Grand Guignol tradition in horror cinema (and they are still staples in the horror genre the world over today). With the participants in *Salò* mostly naked, and in daylight, the practical effects teams and the special make-up artists have to go that much farther to make it all convincing (because there are even fewer places to hide the tricks).

An element of *Salò, or The 120 Days of Sodom* is thus the spectacle of cinema, of cinema as a visual effects medium: the 1975 film foregrounds the fascination that audiences have had with the self-conscious theatricality of the horror genre since the days of the Grand Guignol performances in Paris.

There's no doubt, tho', that the 53 year-old film director was staging the extreme events in *Salò, or The 120 Days of Sodom* with a veteran's eye for Shocks and Startles (this is Pier Paolo Pasolini's horror movie). How, for example, the first victim (Benedetta – Benedetta Gaetani) who tried to flee is revealed behind some doors, which are opened with a stagey flourish; the body is slumped below an altar and a painting of the Virgin

---

[16] Dario Argento, bless him, has spent years exploring the fiendishly nasty ways in which victims can be dispatched in his movies.

Mary. (Benedetta's death is the first one among the victims: dramatically, it's crucial, to show how high the stakes are, and that the perpetrators will be willing to punish the victims with execution).

Disregarding the ideological, political, social, cultural, psychological and philosophical issues evoked in *Salò, o Le 120 Giornate di Sodoma* (which threaten to swamp the movie), one can admire the assurance of the staging, blocking and presentation of the drama.

To encourage actors to perform some of the acts in *Salò, or The 120 Days of Sodom* you'd have to be an accomplished director, or a director who inspires trust, or a director who paid his actors millions.[17] Many of the victims in *Salò* are either young actors or non-professionals. They are required to perform much of the movie naked, and to indulge in some stuff they'd likely never done before in life or on celluloid, and things they'd never do in any other production (!). The requirement for full nudity in many scenes would automatically put off many actors.

The pre-production on a movie like this is essential for the actors – they need to know what they're going to be asked to do, to think about it, and to prepare for it. It's not only the nudity (which can be a big challenge for young actors), it's also all of the other acts. Discussing all of that beforehand is very important. *However*, when the actors were *on set*, and actually *doing* those things, it's something else. *Talking about* stripping off is one thing, but really *doing it* in front of thirty actors and forty crew members is something else.

As with the 1970s films of Walerian Borowczyk, I would imagine that many of the actors only appeared in *Salò, or The 120 Days of Sodom* and nothing else (this seems to be the case with many of the performers – *Salò* is their only significant credit). Not that *Salò* put them off acting (tho' it might've!), just that they were not actors in the first place, and did *Salò* for a laugh (!), or because they needed the money (tho' I bet that wasn't

---

[17] One of the toughest jobs on *Salò, or The 120 Days of Sodom* would be that of the assistant director – Umberto Angelucci. Fiorella Infascelli was second A.D.

great), or they were intrigued by the theme of the movie, or they were keen to work with a cultural legend like Pier Paolo Pasolini (so you could have it printed on a Tee shirt: 'I survived *Salò!*').[18] And *Salò* is very likely one of those movies where some of the actors and the crew wanted to kill the director. (Not really, just kidding!).

Certainly *Salò, or The 120 Days of Sodom* is a tough gig all-round – for the filmmakers, for the actors, for the audience, for everyone involved. It's bleak. It's harsh. It takes no prisoners – it slaughters them.

But Pier Paolo Pasolini is not the only star here – a challenging production such as this requires a dedicated team with veterans in many of the key posts. *Salò, o Le 120 Giornate di Sodoma* was possible partly because of the wonderful group of artistic talents that had been built up around Pasolini over many years, headed up by film producer Alberto Grimaldi. These were the filmmakers who'd survived clambering up Mount Etna in freezing gales, or baking in the heat of the deserts of Africa. (The actors got to do things they'd never done before or since in a Pasolini picture – yes, but so did the crew. Working on a Pasolini movie wasn't like shooting a boring TV commercial for life insurance in Rome).

✦

Salò, or The 120 Days of Sodom seems 'in its vehemence and negativity, its utterly black humour, a repudiation of everything cloying and pretentious in Pasolini's other work', as Gary Indiana put it (11).

Salò, or The 120 Days of Sodom is conceived and delivered as an anti-movie, an anti-drama, an anti-art project. It goes as far as Pier Paolo Pasolini and the production team could go in producing something that went *against everything*. Whatever is enshrined by convention, by tradition, by expectation in cinema and drama, is self-consciously negated. (As Groucho Marx

---

18 And of course film crews have had Tee shirts like that produced for movies that proved especially difficult. During *Blade Runner*, for example – the famous Tee shirt wars, when director Ridley Scott had made disparaging remarks in a British interview about U.S. film crews. Scott said that crews in Blighty were polite, and called the director 'guvnor': the Yanks at Warners responded with Tee shirts that read 'yes guvnor my ass'.

put it, whatever it is, I'm against it).

As Enzo Siciliano noted of *Salò, or The 120 Days of Sodom* and its portrayal of the victims:

> Their passivity as victims is petrifying – since, being victims, they cannot help weaving a poisonously consenting relationship with their executioners. What is frightening is their wavering between consent and refusal. The – highly regulated – anarchy of the situation ensures that in feeling themselves sometimes free, they delude themselves into thinking that they can offer their loving devotion to someone in full freedom. (ES, 388)

MORE PUNISHMENTS.

A change of pace and content follows the 'Circle of Shit' section: now *Salò, or The 120 Days of Sodom* invites us to contemplate a series of sex acts which, in contrast to everything else we've seen thus far, are apparently consensual and maybe even loving (eh? Love? In *Salò*?!). The Bishop is depicted being sodomized by one of the guards; two of the girls're glimpsed in a clinch in bed; and Ezio the Collaborator is shown fooling around with the black maid (a.k.a. the 'slave girl' – Ines Pellegrini).[19]

In the 'trilogy of life' movies, the omniscient narrator might've cut between each of the scenes of lovemaking without a commentary. In *Salò, or The 120 Days of Sodom*, however, the narration is dramatically denser: the Bishop is alerted to some victims breaking the rules (such as no liaisons without the permission of the libertines). Thus, each act leads from one to another, escalating from a photograph found under Graziella's pillow (of a beloved – Claudio Cicchetti), to a lesbian scene (Eva and Antiniska), and finally to an interracial sex scene, with Ezio and the maid. (In common with the 'trilogy of life' films, however, each of these vignettes is of a romantic/ erotic nature, the standard plots of farce).

In another truly preposterous moment in *Salò, or*

---

[19] Yes, we have several departures from white, heterosexual sex: homosexual sex, lesbian sex and interracial sex.

The 120 Days of Sodom (a movie which seems to have been designed to feature as many middle fingers raised to convention as possible), each of the libertines, armed with pistols, executes the naked Ezio (who defies them with the Communist salute, a classic Pasolinian touch, which takes them aback for a moment), and the maid. (Ezio is given a spectacular, multi-bullet demise – Pasolini does Peckinpah – turning Ezio into a modern St Sebastian, wounded with bullets instead of arrows. But the maid is seen off execution-style, mafia-style – with a single bullet to the head, as if she's not worth any more time, effort or ammo).

THE PORNOGRAPHY OF *SALO*.

Salò, or The 120 Days of Sodom's a film of Hell, the Inferno out of Dante Alighieri's *Divine Comedy* (the 1975 film's divided up, narratively, into Dantean 'circles' – (1) 'Anti-Inferno', (2) of manias, (3) of blood, and (4) of shit. Yes, this is a movie with pretentious title cards indicating just where we are among the Circles of Hell). It's a movie of death, sadism and torture taken to new, carnivalesque extremes. A film of the Marquis de Sade by way of Georges Bataille and Jean-Luc Godard. It's a film of distantiation, never getting close to the subject or the actors. Close-ups tend to be avoided, in favour of *tableau* staging, with the camera sometimes thirty or forty feet away from the action, shooting in wide shots (or from high angles). Filming from way back also of course hides the details of bodies which sidesteps film censorship.

There are also, significantly, no central, sympathetic characters to identify with (in fact, the cast aren't 'characters', but functions or tools of the movie). The viewpoint *Salò, or The 120 Days of Sodom* takes up is that of the perpetrators, which further problematizes the film (like other movies about fascism, such as *Schindler's List*, *The Damned*, *The Conformist* and *The Night Porter*). But it does also shift the viewpoint to the victims sometimes, as has been pointed out (which further complicates matters for the viewer. *Salò* doesn't 'take sides' in the usual clear-cut manner of most movies depicting military conflict). The ambiguous complicity of the captives adds more ideological and ethical problems (*Salò* isn't just four degenerate aristocrats and their wives perpetrating violent and degrading acts on totally unwilling victims; there is masochism here, too, as in other Pasolini films).

Salò, or The 120 Days of Sodom's a film of people obsessed with sex and death to the exclusion of everything else. They are endlessly fascinated with its rituals, its transgressions and subversions. Sex in all of its multiple possibilities. It's as if Pier Paolo Pasolini and the producers made a list of the acts and ideas that would appear shocking or intolerable to conventional bourgeois views (and what they could get away with showing in the new relaxation of film censorship in the 1970s), so there's lots of sadism (and, even more problematically, lots of masochism), sodomy, homosexuality, coprophilia and torture. Bourgeois rituals, such as marriage, are also mocked and transgressed. In the carnival of rituals in *Salò,* wedding ceremonies are satirically enacted (the bride and groom are made to kiss with shit-smeared mouths). The decadent aristos themselves dress up in women's clothing.

Salò, or The 120 Days of Sodom can be seen as about the pornography of death, rather than being 'pornographic' in itself. There's a lot of sex in the film, but it's not 'pornographic'. *Salò* isn't a 'sexy' film. At all. It's much more about death than sex. Or power. (Ultimately, it has nothing to do with sex whatsoever).

Most of the acts in *Salò, or The 120 Days of Sodom* occur with an audience – someone is looking at someone else for much of the time. And if there's no one around, a mirror will do. Certainly it enhances the suffering of the victims knowing that there are people, including their colleagues, watching all of this. (The libertines have created their own private club of sadomasochism, but the acts always have audiences, they're always partly public).

The 1975 film's also about power, as Pier Paolo

Pasolini maintained. Voyeurism is a recurring motif; in many (later) scenes, characters are watching other people have sex or get whipped or tortured. In the final torture scenes in *Salò*, the libertines sit on a throne-like chair (with a wooden eye on its back), looking out of a window with binoculars at the punishments enacted in the courtyard below (the perpetrators take in turns to sit on the perv's pew and observe their buddies in the courtyard hard at work. It's a condensed, film version of Michel Foucault's panopticon). There's a feeling that the movie itself is ambiguously enjoying these scenes, and not wholly condemning them. They're also problematic in implicating the viewer in the aristocrats' voyeurism, which you find in other movies which entangle the viewer in voyeurism – such as *Rear Window, Psycho* and *Peeping Tom*. (Meanwhile, the viewing room is another high culture environment, with art clustered around the walls like a museum, which exaggerates the contrast between culture and brutality, masters and slaves).

✻

The courtyard finale in *Salò, or The 120 Days of Sodom* is also preceded by another story. This one is about Tommy the Tortoise; he decides to have a surprise birthday party for his friends Billy the Badger and Rosie the Rabbit. On his happy, smiley way through the sunny, Summery fields to the baker's store, poor Tommy is kidnapped by German soldiers dressed as zombies, blindfolded and sodomized by 160 fairy tale characters. After 1,001 days of unspeakable degradation, Tommy emerges with a grin, shrugs off the experience, declares himself mysteriously purified, and toddles off home for a nice cup of tea.

IN THE COURTYARD.

The lengthy scenes of the tortures in the courtyard[20] (filmed on the backlot at Cinecittà) are among the most disturbing in *Salò, or The 120 Days of Sodom* – if we are

[20] Prior to the courtyard tortures, the victims, identified by a blue ribbon, have been stripped and told to sit in a bathtub filled with fæces and urine. This is the holding pen before they're taken outside.

still taking all of this straight (yet they also repeat scenes we've already seen, so they are redundant). Naked men hold naked victims face-down while the aristocrats take turns in torturing them: a girl has her head scalped; genitals and faces are burnt with a candle; tongues are cut off;[21] eyes are gouged out; some captives are naked, lying face-down and bound to stakes in the ground while someone sodomizes them; a woman is double-ended then hung from a rope. Some of the guards are the one-time victims, now complicit in the reign of terror.

These graphic scenes are shot with a long lens with a binocular mask attached to it through a window; there's no local sound (of screams or shouted instructions); some of the images are silent (which's creepiest of all); some have jazz music (Ennio Morricone was music adviser) or piano and other music over them; and some have the sound of distant war planes and bombing (this is an inventive (and cheap) way of reminding the audience[22] that this is taking place during WWII – it's 'apocalypse now' everywhere. At times, the sound of bombers is allowed to run underneath scenes for a long time, creating a bizarre, Gothic atmosphere).

Salò, or The 120 Days of Sodom cuts between long lens images through the window, C.U.s of the aristocrats holding the binoculars, and shots taken outside of the tortures.[23] The Duke smiles with devilish delight as the persecutions unfold (and he fondles the guard standing next to him). To heighten the layers of twisted scopophilia, the filmmakers have the Duke turn the binoculars around, so the view out of the window (of the men grappling the woman to the scaffold) is seen in wide angle.

The special make-up team (headed up by Sergio Chiusi, with Carboni-Roccohetti and Alfredo Tiberi), put over-size, plastic penises on the guys, as you do. (But, note, no over-large breast augmentations for the

---

21 This happens to poor Franco Merli, the star of *The Arabian Nights*.
22 The viewers that have stayed with the film to this point.
23 The finale of tortures, the culmination of the movie, is also covered in a matter-of-fact style: it's just another day at the office of totalitarianism and insitutionalized cruelty.

girls). Fake stomachs, fake scalps, fake tongues, fake necks, fake butts, fake nipples and the like were created for the trick shots of afflictions.

The music playing over the images offers the familiar extreme counterpoint to the horrors. Music is the best of humanity, the highest it can reach, I think, but the horrors enacted outside is humanity at its basest. From bliss to the abyss. During the shooting of the sequence (as the documentary footage reveals), Pasolini encouraged the actors to emote and suffer, only to erase all of those shrieks of agony not only in the dubbing, but out of the film entirely. (One of the perpetrators – the Bishop – shouts hysterically at the victims, and lashes out with a whip. His frenzy is all the more striking because we don't hear a word of it. It's apt that it's the Bishop, a Catholic authority figure, who loses it; the history of Christianity contains many incidents of over-the-top punishments).

The silent scream is one of cinema's most powerful dramatic devices (there are numerous examples). It's especially effective when the rest of the soundtrack dips out unexpectedly. It's an editor's trick – as is the replacement of the local sound with music (editors often cut films to temporary music – no doubt several records or tapes were pulled off the shelves and tried against the images in the cutting rooms in Roma. This part of filmmaking is a 'try it and see' process – you never quite know what's going to work until you actually see it and hear it. And it's striking that sometimes the music you planned to use (or that you thought would work), *doesn't* work; and also that suggestions of music that you reckon would be just silly, *do* work).

And when we cut back to the voyeurs' room in the villa, we see the radio, which reminds us that the music is playing in the room while each of the libertines observes the depredations outside (they remain in a cultured zone to the end – above, apart, aloof).

When one of the guards flips the rado dial to jazz music (provided by Ennio Morricone), it's a clear signal of a switch in generations, from classical music to modern jazz music, emphasizing the generational gap between the arisocrats and the guards (if the film had been set later – in, say, the 1960s – the jazz would be rock 'n' roll).

THE ENDING.

Salò, or The 120 Days of Sodom doesn't end: it stops. That is, it doesn't have an ending. Not a proper, satisfying ending which resolves or addresses (or does *something*) to or in or with the narrative, the plots, the characters, the goals, the motives, the whatevers. It just stops.

Because, after the graphic re-enactments of mediæval tortures,[24] the 1975 movie can't possibly go any further, doesn't want to go any further, and the audience has had enough already. Anyway, what're you going do if you kill all the victims? Go get another six million souls?

So *Salò, or The 120 Days of Sodom* doesn't have an ending, doesn't have any aftermath/ *dénouement* scenes, doesn't show the aristocrats patting themselves on the back for such a Grand 120 Days of Orgiastic Bliss *à la* de Sade (which they would surely do, before climbing into a limo, and driving away in style).

The libertines, bless 'em, get away with it all: there are no scenes of capture, of imprisonment, of punishment for these four freaks, their wives, their daughters, and their militia. No authorities from Italy, Germany, wherever, turn up and castigate the perpetrators. None of the family and friends of the victims gather into a mob and storm the villa. And no Allies enter the frame as 'deus ex machina' figures evoking the liberation of Europe at the end of the Second World War.

Instead, a number of endings to *Salò, or The 120 Days of Sodom* were considered. (1) Ethel Merman bursts into the Hall of Orgies dressed as the Pope and belts out, 'there's no business like show business!' (2) The cast and crew stake out director Pier Paolo Pasolini and producer Alberto Grimaldi in the courtyard and whip

---

24 As if, in the world of torture, you can't come up with anything new.

them repeatedly. (3) The camera spins round to show the remainder of the audience in the theatre, sprinting for the exits.

Several endings were tried out for *Salò, or The 120 Days of Sodom*, including the cast and the director dancing in the villa which had been hung with red flags (the idea of dancing ends the film, but in a more modest manner); a red flag with the words 'love you' was considered (but rejected for being too hippyish); in another ending, the libertines exit the mansion and considered the morality of their acts.

So *Salò, or The 120 Days of Sodom* closes, bizarrely, with a couple[25] of youths dancing in the voyeurs' viewing room to jazz music on the radio (when one of them switches the station, and the music changes to jazz).[26] Is it a smidgen of 'hope', a glimpse of the possibility that Life Will Continue, after the Apocalypse and Holocaust we've just witnessed? That these kids will leave the villa and go back to their girlfriends? No: because if the libertines have any sense, they will slaughter everyone involved, to make sure none of them squeal.

Is the ending of *Salò, or The 120 Days of Sodom* about 'normalizing' or transcending the degradations of the previous hour and forty-five minutes? So the film shows something modest, non-exploitative, non-violent, to offer a seemingly everyday scene. That kids will still want to dance and chat about their girlfriends (to them all of this has just been a job, some part-time work which they undertook for a short period,[27] then they'll go back to their lives). Or is it a suggestion not that 'ordinary life' will continue, but that *bourgeois life* will continue? That is, the middle classes will continue to perpetuate their preference for mundane, self-satisfied existence where they can't stop themselves dominating the classes underneath them?

---

[25] One of the boys is Claudio Tròccoli, a kid that Pasolini had met in the village of Chia (Pasolini had bought a tower in Chia where he retreated).
[26] To counter the notion that these boys are not homosexual, but are dancing for the fun of it, one of them asks the other about his girlfriend.
[27] It makes a change from a part-time Summer job waiting tables.

Yet it's also notable that the film ends with a depiction of the youths, not the libertines. That is, the younger generation, not the establishment. (Is the film guiltily handing over the final scene to the idea of youth, to these two youths (loads of people died, but these two survived), after staging numerous scenes where young people're tortured? We know that Pasolini hoped to address the youth of Italia).

THE CRITICAL RECEPTION OF *SALO*.

Salò, or The 120 Days of Sodom certainly does have a compelling power: *Salò* does compel the audience to witness it. Simply in terms of the sensational subject matter (and, of course, the sheer amount of nudity), it's going to guarantee a certain level of attention. In May 2006, *Time Out*'s Film Guide named it the Most Controversial Film of all time.

Salò, or The 120 Days of Sodom is one of those movies that presents a big challenge to a film critic. Because: (1) It can't be dismissed – this is an important work by a major talent. (2) It is a difficult film to describe in words, using the usual apparatus of film criticism. (3) It departs from many of the cinematic norms – in its form, its approach, and its relationship with the audience. (4) It's an art film, it has no stars, and it tackles very heavy material. (5) It instigates a problematic relation between the movie and the viewer. (6) It explores extremes of behaviour.

Inevitably, *Salò, or The 120 Days of Sodom* ran into numerous problems with film censors when it was released (it was withdrawn in Italia 3 weeks after its Dec 23, 1975 release). In some territories (such as Britain, Sri Lanka, Singapore, Vietnam, Malaysia, United Arab Emirates and Oz), it was banned outright (and the subsequent re-submission process of the movie for classification dragged on for decades – who was paying for that?). It wasn't released until 2000 in Albion. As with challenging movies of the era such as *The Devils, Straw Dogs* and *The Beast,* parts of *Salò* were cut out, and several versions have been released over the years.

(But that also occurs with 100s of movies, not only the 'controversial' ones, many of which are completely innocuous).

Even into the 2000s, for instance, *Salò, or The 120 Days of Sodom* was still problematic for the Australian film censors. It was banned in 1976, then passed in 1993, then banned again in 1998. *Salò* was submitted again in 2008, and rejected. It was passed 'R-18' in 2010. Several organizations protested about the film, including the Liberal Party, the Australian Christian Lobby and Family Voice.

In one extraordinary incident, the film canisters of *Salò, or The 120 Days of Sodom* were taken out into the streets of Roma and whipped by Catholic priests and religious zealots in white, pointy hats. No, not really.

Filmmakers such as Rainer Werner Fassbinder, Catherine Breillat and Michael Haneke have cited *Salò, or The 120 Days of Sodom* as one of their favourite films. For Raymond Murray, in *Images In the Dark: An Encyclopedia of Gay and Lesbian Film and Video*, *Salò* is

> an unbelievably bleak and depressing vision of the human condition which shocked audiences with its brutally graphic scenes of sexual degradation and oppressive violence. (108)

For Pasolini expert Sam Rohdie:

> It is Pasolini's most compelling film visually and his least watchable one: the shit his characters eat, the scalping, the tongue-cutting, the castrations, genitals burned, eyes gouged, masturbation, buggery, incest, killings, mouths blooded with razors. (48-49)

Many critics found it difficult to endure: for *TV Guide*, *Salò* was 'nearly unwatchable, extremely disturbing, and often literally nauseous'. Jonathan Rosenbaum called *Salò, or The 120 Days of Sodom* 'very hard to take, but in its own way an essential work'.

Geoff Andrew opined: 'it's very hard to sit through and offers no insights whatsoever into power, politics, history or sexuality'. 'The film is essential to have seen but impossible to watch', remarked Richard Brody. For Vincent Canby, *Salò* was theoretically interesting, 'but becomes so repugnant when visualized on the screen that it further dehumanizes the human spirit'. 'What *Salò* frequently looks like is self-revulsion pushed to an insane limit of absurdity, into an absurd kind of self-acceptance', as Gary Indiana put it (20). And Gideon Bachmann remarked, 'every scene attacks, every sensibility is ruthlessly crushed. Every form of sexual, sadistic, and psychopathic depravity is shown, but nothing separates these actions from the every day'.

In the 2013 book *Horror!*, John Coulthart remarked:

> Pasolini's minimal style offers no escape, with spartan sets, *vérité* camera work and an unrelenting march towards inevitable butchery. In the process it steers possibly closer than the director intended to a kind of vicarious pornography that at least ensures that viewers ask themselves why they're watching this parade of atrocities. (K. Newman, 188)

Bruce Kawin and Gerald Mast in *A Short History of the Movies* summarize *Salò, or The 120 Days of Sodom* thus:

> Pasolini fills the screen for two hours with orgies of sexual torture and oppression – buggery, voyeurism, casual murder, pornographic songs and stories (a vital part of the dirty old men's pleasure), mutilation, branding, scalping, the consumption of human feces. (338)

For some (such as David Thomson), *Salò, or The 120 Days of Sodom* is gratuitously violent and indulgent. Gratuitous – meaning, there's *too much*: *Salò* has made its key points by the 30-minute mark. After that, there is *more* – but it's simply *more of the same*.

Narrative progression is put aside in favour of variations on tortures, stories, images and music (like ladling more and more filth onto a plate. You get More – but it's More Of The Same Filth[28]). The patterns repeat, again and again, over the 120 days in Sodom and in Salò (it's a time loop of terror, a *Groundhog Day* of nausea). So, one of the libertines rushes into the next room to jerk off... so a girl is ordered to pee while a man watches... so a woman is fed bread (or cake) with nails in it and pierces her mouth...

Once the pattern is established, it revolves, repeatedly, or it looks at itself and repeats, like the big mirrors in the movie. Thus, the central section of *Salò, or The 120 Days of Sodom* could be re-arranged without altering much of anything. The only real narrative development occurs in the first and final acts.

Or does it? Not really: because, actually, the tortures simply carry on, tho', in the final act of *Salò, or The 120 Days of Sodom*, they move outside, and now the victims are being tortured simultaneously. The arrangement of the tortures alters, but not the narrative impact. And the 1975 movie comes to a stop: that is, the producers order the title card 'FINE' to be cut into the print after the scene of the two *ragazzi* dancing.

But the caption 'THE END' is a lie, because the movie *doesn't* end, because torture and coercion and power games *don't* end, because they never have ended, because there have always been bullies and victims, the haves and the have-nots.

Modern fascism, of the European (German and Italian) kind, might be a recent political phenomenon, but fascism is a very ancient political occurrence (and Italy is certainly one of the breeding grounds of the grandest fascisms – the Roman Empire, which was soon followed by the Catholic Church. Italy, you could say, does things Very Big. It makes the two contemporary superpowers, Russia and America, look like puppies).

---

[28] Just as consumerism and capitalism is more and more of the same junk.

SALO AND THE END OF EVERYTHING.

In this po-faced (poo-faced), Po Valley pantomime, everyone dies. Of course. The victims know that. The perpetrators know that. The accomplices know that. But this is not a prison camp movie, and there are no plans to break out, no concerted efforts to nobble the guards, no digging of tunnels, no attempts at making contact with the outside world, no calling down an air-strike. Sadly, there are no heroes who're going to Save The Day in this 1975 movie, and the entire narrative movement is downward...

...to *d-e-a-t-h*...

So the viewer is *not* rooting for the victims to survive, because, as in a Holocaust movie, the viewer knows all too well (and, bitterly, accepts) that:

1. There Is No Way Out.
2. That Will Be No Redemption.
3. That Nobody Will Be Saved.

Salò, or The 120 Days of Sodom is not a movie where the audience can *pretend* that the victims might be saved. They won't be. *Salò* is not a movie where the audience can look for glimmers of hope. There aren't any. *Salò* is not a movie where the possibility of escape for the victims (or come-uppance for the perpetrators) is entertained. There will be no escape and no come-uppance.

Everyone will die.

Oh sure, everyone will always die, everyone you've ever loved or ever known will die.

Every single one.

But in a movie, a slice of fiction, sometimes you hope that some kinda, sorta redemption or escape or transcendence is at least possible if not feasible.

But in *Salò*: *nothing*. Absolutely damn all.

This pompous, po-faced, poo-filled movie will beat you senseless.

✤

Salò, or The 120 Days of Sodom is a cold, calculating piece of work, self-consciously (even archly) *un*emotional, as if every camera angle and every image were chosen for its lack of emotive power – the opposite of mainstream cinema, of the traditional and modernist cinema of D.W. Griffith or Orson Welles, where everything works hard to enhance the dramatic impact. In the establishing scenes of *Salò*, shots are composed symmetrically, like the architectural, mathematical studies of Piero della Francesca in the Renaissance era (Italy does look lovely, though – the opening shot of *Salò, o Le 120 Giornate di Sodoma* of the lakes and the shore could be used in a tourist guide.[29] Mantua and Verona are famous for their beautiful lakeland scenery, and are well-known vacation spots).

Coldness, iciness, frigidity – these are clichés in art revaluating the fascist eras of the twentieth century.[30] The chilliness means blank expressions in the faces, unemotive acting styles, cool, medium shots and long shots, rectilinear, bland architecture (the courtyards and facades of the buildings which resemble the country estates of land-owners which've seen better days. Again in a Pier Paolo Pasolini movie, the choice of locations is superb, as is the adaptation and art direction of the spaces by production designer Dante Ferretti and company. They have captured a crumbling, decadent feeling of wealth in war-time: paintings line the floor, not the walls, as if just about to be carted away. It's a decaying realm of wealth, on the edge of falling apart, yet it's still able to run a tyrannical regime).

Yet *Salò, or The 120 Days of Sodom* is also too much like a lecture for me, too preachy, too obvious: it's Pier Paolo Pasolini admonishing the audience, beating it over the head with the holy spear yanked out of Christ's side. Let's face it, the target – of Western capitalism, of banal but all-pervasive consumerism, of

---

[29] There are overcast skies and a flat light, evoking North Italy, and not the familiar Italy of Rome and the South.

[30] In *Salò, or The 120 Days of Sodom*'s first act, the descent to the first circle of Hell, all is calm organization as the aristos and their fascist assistants prepare for their vacation orgy. The aristocrats are not sent up, there's a coolness, a politeness, and a feeling of just getting on with a job.

Part of *Salò, or The 120 Days of Sodom* is simply a film about how to organize and stage an orgy (something every 18th century libertine and 20th century *avant garde* intellectual needs to know).

the power relations between the aristocratic class and the peasant/ working class, of fascism in Italy in the 1930s and 1940s, of domination and submission, of power and coercion – it's all too easy or too obvious for a world-weary, veteran film director and poet like Pier Paolo Pasolini. Had *Salò* appeared <u>before</u> *Weekend* or *Persona* or *Battle of Algiers*, we might be celebrating it as a greater work (certainly its influence might've been stronger. Maybe it's a movie that Pasolini should've made five or more years earlier[31]).

And *Salò, or The 120 Days of Sodom* is simply too immature, too adolescent/ high school, too simplistically intellectual in its ideological analysis – it's like a diatribe from an out-of-work, Left Bank philosopher in Modern Marxism who's still seething because those ignorant dingbats at the Sorbonne cancelled his professorship.[32]

All of the political and ideological points in *Salò, or The 120 Days of Sodom* have been made better (and more economically) in other movies. It is a filmed lecture, a series of animated, photographic slides. You can practically hear Pier Paolo Pasolini's continuous voiceover commenting on the decline and fall of his beloved Italy: if Pasolini had recorded a narration to *Salò*, he wouldn't deliver a voiceover expounding on the action, he would produce one of his lengthy harangues[33] in which he rails against Italy's governments, its authorities (religious as well as secular), the decline of its working class culture, and his nostalgia for and mourning over the peasant way of life he idealized in his youth.

In this view, *Salò, or The 120 Days of Sodom* represents Pier Paolo Pasolini's denunciation of the people and powers he feels were responsible for ruining his beloved Italy and its working class and peasant class with ugly, superficial consumerism (yet, of course,

---

31 He was certainly getting there with *Theorem* and *Pigsty*, the two forerunners of *Salò*.
32 When he was caught in the restroom with a student.
33 Which you can hear in other Pasolini works, such as *Love Meetings* or *Appunti per un'Orestiade Africana*.

Pasolini can offer nothing in its place, cannot tell us how he would have changed things, and cannot define his utopia.[34] All intellectuals, Marxists, radicals, liberals, philosophers, poets and artists are like this: they can criticize society, deconstruct and lament society and its ills, but haven't got the faintest idea what to replace it with. Pasolini also can't explain away the fact that Italy's working class people *wanted* consumerist culture and Americana).

Pier Paolo Pasolini was the same: he spent an enormous amount of time and effort relating and analyzing the degeneration of modern Italy in fascism, decadence, mis-management, hypocrisy, greed, corruption, capitalist consumerism and all the rest, but could he suggest, in exact, concrete and practical terms, what he would do to fix it? No. Why didn't he spend some of that precious time constructing – in convincing and realistic and achievable terms – just what his utopian Italy would be?

That is, a *far* more compelling movie from Maestro Pasolini would've been a 120-minute statement of exactly what his utopia, his ideal world, would look like, how it would work, and what its societies and politics would be.

Because artists – and philosophers, intellectuals, radicals, rebels and politicians – *can't*.

SOME INTERTEXTS.

Blangis squats, shits, and forces Renata to eat his excrement, offering it to her on a spoon.[35] Renata has drawn attention to herself by weeping loudly over the death of her mother (during the round-up of the victims), in a scene where Blangis boasted of topping his mother. Pier Paolo Pasolini described the coprophagia scenes in *Salò or The 120 Days of Sodom* as a comment on the processed food industry. The scene

---

[34] Gary Indiana pointed out that Pasolini's polemics seem to have had more to do with 'proving the virtuousness of the attack', rather than actually trying to change things (18).

[35] 'This is the most notoriously unforgettable moment in *Salò*, a point of no return. After a quarter century it is still shocking and unassimilable in its raw cruelty', remarked Gary Indiana (73).

brings together matricide and sacrifice with faeces and cannibalism, ending with a scene of sadism as Blangis screams at Renata to 'eat!'

There are other movies which explore faeces and coprophilia. Like the over-eating Mr Creosote episode in *The Meaning of Life* (1983) from the Monty Python team; like *Blow-Out* (1973), directed by Marco Ferreri (he appeared in *Pigsty*); like Divine eating dog-doo in *Pink Flamingos* (1972); and like Marlon Brando ordering Maria Schneider to bugger him in *Last Tango In Paris* (1972), while wittering on about pigs and shit, etc. Italian trickster artist Piero Manzoni (1933-63) sold cans of his own turds as an artwork. Meanwhile, several rock acts in the early 1970s (such as Wayne County) simulated shit-eating on stage (using dog food). And it was part of *Pork*, the Andy Warhol play (using chocolate pudding).

We're Going To Eat You (a.k.a. *Hell HAs No Door, Hell Has No Gates, Kung Fu Cannibals* and *No Door To Hell*, 1980) is a wild and wonderful action comedy (directed by Tsui Hark and produced by Ng See Yuen and Kuen Cheung for Seasonal Film Corporation), which tackles the extreme theme of cannibalism with *very* black humour. *We're Going To Eat You*, one of Tsui Hark's incendiary early films, proves that you don't have to be po-faced, oh-so serious and arty in the Euro-intellectual manner to make all of the same points that every other movie about people eating people makes.

Another movie linked thematically to *Salò or The 120 Days of Sodom* is the *Erzsébet Báthory* episode in *Immoral Tales*, directed by Walerian Borowczyk in 1974. In *Immoral Tales*, Countess Báthory, the female Count Dracula, is a wealthy aristocrat who exploits the peasant class for her own selfish, narcissistic and superficial ends – capturing local peasant women, stripping and cleaning them, enjoying their caresses, then slaughtering them and bathing in their blood, to maintain her youthful appearance. (There are affinities in the stylistic approach, too: the large room the colour of dried blood in *Salò* is reminiscent of the bloody chamber in *Immoral Tales*.)

Mel Brooks, who kicked the Nazis savagely in many comical movies (from *The Producers*, a work of genius, onwards), made all of the points that Pier Paolo Pasolini and company want to make in *Salò, or The 120 Days of Sodom,* but achieves them in a much classier, cleverer and funnier manner.

SALO AND *1900.*

One of the filmic intertexts with *Salò or The 120 Days of Sodom* is *1900* (*Novecento,* 1976), a sprawling, flawed, awkward and similarly over-simplified exploration of Marxism, Communism and fascism in early-to-mid 20th century Italy. Alberto Grimaldi must've been *very* busy at this time, because he produced both *Salò or The 120 Days of Sodom* and *1900* – and he was producing *Casanova,* too (a Federico Fellini production which ran into financial and scheduling problems). Both *Salò* and *1900* were filmed around the same time (Spring, 1975), and they also shared similar locations (in the Po Valley),[36] like the huge country estates with their wide courtyards and long, low buildings, and the flat, green plains of Northern Italy (around the River Po; much of *Salò or The 120 Days of Sodom* was filmed in or near Mantua).[37]

Like Pier Paolo Pasolini, Bernardo Bertolucci, who directed *Novecento,* can't quite achieve a satisfying balance between poetry and politics, melodrama and Marxism. Are Bertolucci and co-writers Franco Arcalli and Giuseppe Bertolucci celebrating, denouncing, analyzing, re-coding, poeticizing, or spiritualizing? All at once, of course (film directors always like to have things all ways – like any artist).

Like *Salò o Le 120 Giornate di Sodoma, 1900* contained plenty of potentially controversial scenes. Among the silliest was Robert de Niro masturbating

---

[36] And personnel, such as Nico Naldini. Meanwhile, Pasolini regular Laura Betti was in *1900.*

[37] At the time, Pasolini and Bertolucci had fallen apart somewhat; during a soccer game between the two film productions, they were reconciled. (Pasolini's team lost).

Laura Betti with a gun! Closely followed by an ageing Burt Lancaster being fondled by a teenage girl. (1975 was still an era when Euro-art directors were keen on pushing the boundaries of cinema in terms of explicit material, just as Pasolini tried to do with *Salò*).

THEORETICAL APPROACHES TO *SALO*.

Salò or The 120 Days of Sodom is a movie that's tailor-made for critical assessments by high school students, literature and film students, PhD students, and film critics with a penchant for employing philosophical theory (tho' some colleges and universities would likely prefer that *Salò or The 120 Days of Sodom wasn't* chosen for study. After all, there are movies which make all of the same points but don't include scenes of shit-eating, rape and murder). *Salò* is one of those movies that contains its own deconstructions within it, which're easy to see and decode. The cinema of Jean-Luc Godard, and movies like *Persona, Blow Up, Performance, Blade Runner* and *Alien*, also have this cultural analysis built-in (hell, *Salò* even provides the eager viewer with an 'Essential Bibliography'!).

Here are some theoretical approaches to *Salò or The 120 Days of Sodom* which are delightfully obvious (there are many, many others):

1. Sigmund Freud and Freudian psychoanalysis (œdipal complexes, oral and anal drives, and – hey! – sex!).

2. Marxism and materialism (power, exploitation, capital (gold), excrement, etc).

3. Communism and Marxism: the death of the left.

4. Postmodernism (surface not depth, meaning's emptied out, nothing has any effect/ affect, etc, *à la* Jean Baudrillard).

5. Semiotics (a plethora of signs *à la* Roland Barthes[38]).

6. Repression, the 'return of the repressed' of Slavoj Zizek.

7. Kristevan abjection (the abjected matter in

---
[38] One of the authors cited in the 'Essential Bibliography'.

Julia's Kristeva's theory of abjection).

8. The politics of power and ideology (sin, guilt, punishment, etc, *à la* Michel Foucault[39]).

SALO AND KRISTEVAN ABJECTION.

I'll take the brilliant theory of abjection developed by French-Romanian philosopher Julia Kristeva (b. 1941) as one example of approaching *Salò or The 120 Days of Sodom* theoretically. For Kristeva, abjection is a useful theory which throws light on issues such as Freudian œdipalism (which's absolutely foundational to Pier Paolo Pasolini's art); the psychosexual development of the child; to creativity and art; and to the history of religion. Kristeva's concept of abjection is a more sophisticated approach to issues such as religion, art and early psychosexual growth, I would argue, than Freudian psychoanalysis, or Barthesian semiotics, or Baudrillardian postmodernism, or Lacanian psychology. Kristeva takes up Freud and Lacan, but goes beyond them; in doing so, she also provides a more convincing (and, incidentally, a less sexist and sex-obsessed) philosophy.

For Julia Kristeva, the artist activates the tensions between the realms of the symbolic and the semiotic, between expression and repression, between the maternal and the individual (we are here talking about the young artist (or individual): that is, about those primal and primary zones of the womb, fluids, the maternal, the first few months of existence outside of the mother.)

In the first stages of differentiation, identity is still shaky, and the individual confuses her/ himself with the maternal image. The way out of this confusion, in the classic scenario, is via the age-old œdipal triangle (which you can see played out in all of Pier Paolo Pasolini's movies: vivid and consciously autobiographical examples occur in the present day scenes in *Oedipus Rex*). The (male) child must split up his mother in order to take up his masculine gender: she is split

---
[39] Why are so many of the eggheads cited French? Discuss.

into the abject and the sublime, Julia Kristeva says in her book *Powers of Horror* (157). Abjecting the mother enables the child to separate itself from the mother. To counter the mother becoming a phobic object, if she is only abjected, the phobic substitutes a sign for the absent object (ib., 45). Abjection thus operates in an in-between zone, as Kristeva calls it in *Powers of Horror*, 'of phobia, obsessions, and perversion' (ibid.). Her definition of abjection is striking: 'the abject is the violence of mourning for an "object" that has always already been lost'. If you think about that, it's very revealing![40] (It certainly echoes throughout the cinema of Pasolini).

The flipside of the empowering notion of the *chora* (Julia Kristeva's term for the pre-œdipal, semiotc realm) in the role of the artist is abjection: Kristeva sees the artist's project as the purifying of abjection (this can be applied directly to *Salò, or The 120 Days of Sodom*). Abjection lies behind the history of religions: the abject is simultaneously the 'land of oblivion' (the phrase might describe the world of *Salò*), and that 'veiled infinity', the moment 'when revelation bursts forth', Kristeva remarked in *Powers of Horror* (9).

For Julia Kristeva, sociality and subjectivity are founded on abjection, on the expulsion of the unclean and the disorderly (we see this actively at work in *Salò, or The 120 Days of Sodom*). But the abject can never be totally eliminated, and accompanies, in sublimated form, society. The abject is the borderland of ambiguity, a total subjectivity (the links between abjection and fascism and exploitation are strikingly portrayed in *Salò*). Ironically, it is *jouissance* that

> alone causes the abject to exist as such. One does not know it, one does not desire it, one joys in it. Violently and painfully. A passion. (9)

The abject is a 'space of simultaneous pleasure and danger', commented Elizabeth Grosz in her essay "The

---

[40] Julia Kristeva's abject thus has a Lacanian subtext: it relates to Jacques Lacan's lack and *objet a*.

Body of Signification" (1990, 94).

Food, urine, vomit, tears and saliva are the things that create abjection – associated with the orifices and body surfaces which later become the erotic zones. Abjection is linked to the body's waste fluids, to those materials which produce disgust (spit, fæces, urine, mucus, blood: *Salò, or The 120 Days of Sodom* happily foregrounds all of those fluids). The fluids of abjection remind society of the body's limitations, its boundaries, its cycles and fatality. These excremental products signify 'the danger to identity that comes from without', Julia Kristeva remarked in *Powers of Horror* (71).

The subject, in abjection, is never distinct from the objects of abjection. The abject is neither inside nor outside (like the skin on milk), neither dead nor alive (like the corpse). The abject relates to the insecurity of the body image noted Elizabeth Grosz (1992, 198). Menstrual blood, however, indicates a different kind of fear, to do with fecundity and the subject's refusal to recognize the 'corporeal link to the mother'.[41]

In her pre-œdipal, semiotic incarnation, the mother is the phallic mother; as the post-œdipal or symbolic mother, she is castrated; the woman who is not or doesn't want to be a mother is seen as suffering from a masculinity complex (ib., 94). The abject, though, is not an object, not something that can be named, not something assimilable, not something definable. The abject is not the Other, nor is it otherness; it is not, either, the subject's correlative. The only quality that the abject has is that it is opposed to the 'I', the subject. The abject worries, nags, seduces desire; yet it cannot be assimilated, so desire rejects it. Even so, there is an impetus or spasm, a leap that is made 'towards an elsewhere as tempting as it is condemned', as Kristeva put it in *Powers of Horror* (1).

As Elizabeth Grosz points out in "The Body of Signification", the abject aspects of society don't go away: rather,

---
41 E. Grosz, 1990, 92.

> it is impossible to exclude the threatening or anti-social elements with any finality. They recur and threaten the subject not only in those events Freud described as the 'return of the repressed' – that is, in psychical symptoms – they are also a necessary accompaniment of sublimated and socially validated activities, such as the production of art, literature, and knowledges, as well as socially unacceptable forms of sexual drives. (1990, 87)

For Elizabeth Grosz (in "The Body of Signification"), naming the abject 'established a distance or space which may keep its dangers at bay. To speak of the object is to protect oneself against it while at the same time relying on its energetic resources' (ib., 93).

The different means of purifying the abject becomes the history of religions in Julia Kristeva's view in *Powers of Horror* (17). For the monotheic religions, abjection persists as taboo or exclusion, associated with defilement and pollution. When the abject encounters Christianity it becomes 'a threatening otherness – but always nameable, always totalizeable' (ib., 17). Out of the encounter with the sacred, the abject is written by the artist (you can see how this applies directly to Pier Paolo Pasolini's entire artistic output): art continues the work that religion does, and art will continue, when religion finally dies, to perform this catharsis. Kristeva wrote in *The Power of Horror*:

> In a world in which the Other has collapsed, the æsthetic task – a descent into the foundations of the symbolic construct – amounts to retracting the fragile limits of the speaking being, closest to its dawn, to the bottomless "primacy" constituted by primal repression. Through that experience, which is nevertheless managed by the Other, "subject" and "object" push each other away, confront each other, collapse, and start again – inseparable, contaminated, condemned, at the boundary of what is assimilable, thinkable. Great modern literature unfolds over that terrain: Dostoyevsky, Lautréamont, Proust, Artaud, Kafka, Céline. (ib., 18)

MORE ON INTERPRETING *SALO*.

What is *Salò, or The 120 Days of Sodom* about? *Salò* can be unpicked in numerous ways, starting with the simplest: the hunter and the hunted, the exploiters and the exploited, the oppressors and the oppressed, the killers and the killed, the eaters and the eaten. It's about bosses and workers (on multiple levels, including Communist politics), where the bosses are also prostitutes. It's about capitalism as prostitution (a common view in 1960s and 1970s political cinema – Jean-Luc Godard is one of the chief exponents), where we are all slaves, where we all exist in states of coercion, where social hierarchies're strictly enforced, where there's always someone above you (and always someone below you), where you are exploiting someone else – and somebody is exploiting you.

Salò, or The 120 Days of Sodom is a critique of political systems, in particular of Communism, and of the relation of Italian Communism to Italy's political life, and of the relation between Communism and fascism (at both local levels and ideological levels).

All of these ways of looking at *Salò, or The 120 Days of Sodom*, from the political and the social to the philosophical and religious, are built in to the piece, and rendered obvious to all. The best essay you could write on *Salò, or The 120 Days of Sodom* would be to show the movie again. For your M.A. thesis at Princeton University, you simply include a copy of the film (don't forget the legal notice about permissions and copyright, or you might be dragged outside and burnt with candles!).

Yes, *Salò, or The 120 Days of Sodom* is an essay masquerading as a movie, or a movie based on a film script based on a lecture based on an essay based on a series of ideas. A movie of ideas – *Salò, or The 120 Days of Sodom* is so powerful partly because the conception is so strong (in contrast to most movies, and certainly most Hollywood movies of recent times, where a flamboyant, noisy and fussy delivery masks emptiness).

And this is partly why all of the analyses of *Salò*,

or The 120 Days of Sodom you've ever read seem completely redundant. Sure, it's interesting (but only mildly) to see what So-and-So thought of *Salò, or The 120 Days of Sodom*, but *Salò* is a movie which contains its own analysis – and *multiple* analyses. So writing 3,000 words, 5,000 words or 10,000 words, whatever, about *Salò* is sort of useless. None of the critical deconstructions of *Salò* you've read tell you anything that can't already be found in the movie itself.

Thus, as with many of the movies directed by Jean-Luc Godard, the best thing is simply to watch the film again.

Critical reviews of *Salò, or The 120 Days of Sodom* tend to say similar things: it's scary, it's confrontational, it's controversial, it's tough to watch, it challenges the film-viewer relationship, it's about power, about fascism, about Communism, about capitalism, about consumerism, about exploitation, blah blah blah.

Every essay or piece on *Salò, or The 120 Days of Sodom* also notes: (1) the death of Pier Paolo Pasolini so close to the film's release in November, 1975; (2) the mystery of the murder, the theft of the film cans, etc; (3) and of course Pasolini's politics, Marxism and homosexuality.

Salò, o Le 120 Giornate di Sodoma is a perfect movie for studying in schools and colleges – because it's one of those films that deconstructs itself, that offers a commentary on itself throughout, and that even includes a reading list in the credits! However, with its outrageous material and controversial status, it likely wouldn't be selected for the classroom! (You can imagine what would happen when little, rosy-cheeked Sally skips home with a *tra-la-la* through the sunny forest carrying the DVD of *Salò* to show her folks what they're studying in school!).

Pier Paolo Pasolini in Rome, 1967 (by Franco Vitale).

APPENDICES

QUOTES BY
PIER PAOLO PASOLINI

I love life fiercely, desperately. And I believe that this fierceness, this desperation will carry me to the end... Love of life for me has become a more tenacious vice than cocaine. I devour my existence with an insatiable appetite. (1970)

-

...cinema is already a dream

-

...to make films is to be a poet

-

One can cheat in everything except style.

-

Even a sound image, say thunder booming in a clouded sky, is somehow infinitely more mysterious than even the most poetic description a writer could give of it. A writer has to find oniricity through a highly refined linguistic operation, while the cinema is much nearer to sounds physically, it doesn't need any elaboration. All it needs is to produce a clouded sky with thunder and straight away you are close to the mystery and ambiguity of reality.

-

...a tree photographed is poetic, a human face photographed is poetic because physicity is poetic in itself, because it is an apparition, because it is full of mystery, because it is full of ambiguity, because it is full of polyvalent meaning, because even a tree is a sign of a linguistic system. But who talks through a tree? God, or reality itself. Therefore the tree as a sign puts us in communication with a mysterious speaker.

•

When I make a film I'm always in reality, among the trees and among the people; there's no symbolic or conventional filter between me and reality as there's in literature. The cinema is an explosion of my love for reality. I have never conceived of making a film that would be a work of a group, I've always thought of a film as a work of an author, not only the script and the direction but the choices of sets and locations, the characters, even the clothes. I choose everything, not to mention the music. (1971)

•

The cinema is a language which expresses reality with reality. So the question is: what is the difference between the cinema and reality? Practically none.

•

Reality is divine. That is why my films are never naturalistic. The motivation that unites all of my films is to give back to reality its original sacred significance. (1968)

•

I avoid fiction in my films. I do nothing to console, nothing to embellish reality, nothing to sell the goods. (1973)

•

I've never wanted to make a conclusive statement. I've always posed various problems and left them open to consideration. (1971)

NOTES ON RENAISSANCE ARTISTS

MASACCIO.

Pier Paolo Pasolini responded to the flattened perspectives of Early Renaissance art, to the *tableau* approach to grouping figures, and to the separation of foreground and background. Pasolini didn't need to 'quote' particular painters of the Renaissance, or individual paintings, because his visual approach in cinema is already informed by a frontal perspective, which arranges the action (the figures) at right angles to the camera lens.

Each painter in the Renaissance re-shaped space to his/ her own liking. Art historians dutifully record the development of illusionistic space in a progression of artists – from Cimabue and Giotto di Bondone to Masaccio, Domenico Veneziano and Masolino da Panicale, from Fra Filippo Lippi and Fra Angelico through Sandro Botticelli and Filippino Lippi, Giovanni Bellini and Raphael de Sanzio, finding an apotheosis of depth and *sfumato* in Leonardo da Vinci, but deepening in darkness still further with Michelangelo di Caravaggio, and, later, Rembrandt van Rijn.

In the art of Masaccio (1401-28), space begins to open up from the spaceless, golden backgrounds of Byzantine art. The *Crucifixion* from Masaccio's *Pisa Altarpiece* (in Naples) depicts four figures (Jesus and the 'three Marys') against a gold background which suggests, as gold always does in Renaissance painting, power and divinity. With the *Trinity* (in Santa Maria Novella, Florence), Masaccio's space deepens. The evocation of the architecture in Masaccio's *Trinity* is very powerful. He creates a barrel vault between two pilasters, seen from a low viewpoint. The architectonics of the *Trinity* are showy, theatrical, like a stage set. Masaccio monumentalizes his subjects, making God the apex of that strongest of all geometric shapes, the triangle or pyramid.

GIOTTO.

Giotto di Bondone (*c.* 1267-1337) was one of the premier artists in Italy of the 14th century, celebrated by Dante Alighieri, and seen today as one of the key architects of the focus in Early Renaissance art on the human figure. Giotto created works in Naples, Assisi, Padua, Florence and Rome; however, only the famous fresco cycle in Padua (in the Arena Chapel) is recognized as definitely authored by Giotto.

In the art of Giotto, the landscape is still very much a *background*, flattened spatially, so the action in the foreground is not connected with it. Early Renaissance landscape is full of marvellous passages of detail and light, but it is flat and relatively undynamic. In the background of Giotto's *Lamentation*, one of the chief works by Giotto, where the weeping angels swarm like crazed birds in the sky, the landscape is hardly painted in: the suggestions of rocks, a tree, and not much more.

In *The Decameron*, Pasolini cast himself as Giotto (as the artist appeared in the fiction of Giovanni Boccaccio). The Giottoan set-piece in *The Decameron* was a quasi-historical representation of the artist painting a fresco commission in a church (alluding to the Paduan fresco cycle).

PIERO DELLA FRANCESCA.

Piero della Francesca (*c.* 1410/ 20-92) has one of the most special and distinctive forms of space in painting. Piero's sense of space stands out from other painters, as with Paul Cézanne, Rembrandt van Rijn and Mark Rothko. The bright, timeless spaces of Piero are instantly recognizable, and critics sometimes evoke Greek sculpture in connection with Piero's paintings.[1] One might also see in Piero's hermetic, ritualized, timeless paintings the art of Chinese landscape painting, with its evocations of emptiness, which hints at the radical void of Eastern mysticism (in Zen Buddhism and Taoism). Piero's hypnotic art coolly melds science with art, space with spirit, the personal with the cosmic, and history, myth and religion with time.

For Piero della Francesca, geometry, proportion, perspective and mathematics had a magical quality. His art exalts, on one level, a *jouissance* of mathematics and measurement, in which the 'science' of Renaissance perspective is joyously explored. Piero seemed to lean towards the cool, impersonal, impassive scientific inquiry of Aristotlean philosophy, rather than the more sensuous, more obviously mystical aspects of Platonic philosophy: he is regarded by Bernhard Berenson as 'impersonal' (1960, 136). Not a few critics have noted the cool, detached, 'impersonal' approach of Piero's art. R. Vischer calls Piero a 'realist': 'above all he wishes to be a realist, to draw in a realist manner'.[2] A. Stokes regards Piero as the first Cubist, a common view of Piero;[3] while for Kenneth Clark, Piero was a fully 'classic artist'.[4] In his *Tratto della Nabilta della Pittura*, Alberti called Piero 'the greatest geometrician of his age.'[5] F.M. Godfrey was equally breathless, claiming that '[n]ever before has art blended so nobly

---

[1] Like the art of Ancient Greece, Piero della Francesca's paintings rejoice in eternal brilliance, an architectonic precision, and a 'Classical' sense of proportion and harmony. In Piero's epoch, perspective, proportion and geometry attained a fetishistic quality.
[2] R. Vischer: *Luca Signorelli and the Italian Renaissance*, 1879.
[3] A. Stokes: *The Stones of Rimini*, 1929.
[4] Kenneth Clark: *Piero della Francesca*, Phaidon, 1969.
[5] Alberti: *Tratto della Nabilta della Pittura*, 1585.

with a mathematical purity of space-construction'.[6] Other art critics, though, have not been so convinced of Piero's talents. Lawrence Wright pointed out that 'his geometry is by our standards involved and laborious.[7]

MICHELANGELO MERISI DA CARAVAGGIO.

Of the many Renaissance and post-Renaissance painters, including those of the Baroque and Mannerist eras, the art of Michelangelo Merisi da Caravaggio (1573-1610) stands out as having marked affinities with the æsthetics of Pier Paolo Pasolini. Not, in contrast to the Early Renaissance artists, in the sense of space and visuals, but in subject matter, and in a tragic view of life. And Carvaggio's own life: he was a homosexual with a penchant for the rough trade of the streets (which he famously painted); his career was filled with controversy (and occasional violence); he had a troubled relationship with the authorities; he lived much of the time, like Pasolini, in Roma; and he died, like Pasolini, in mysterious circumstances, way before his time. Caravaggio is a Pasolinian personality, ideal for the subject of a biopic (altho' Pasolini much preferred the Early Italian Renaissance artists, like Masaccio and Giotto, to the Mannerists and Baroque artists).[8]

---

[6] F.M. Godfrey: *A Student's Guide to Italian Paintings 1250-1800*, Alec Tiranti 1965, 88.
[7] Lawrence Wright: *Perspective in Perspective*, Routledge 1983, 75.
[8] The Pasolinian devotee, Derek Jarman, produced a very disappointing biographical movie about Caravaggio in the 1980s.

Piero, Madonna del Parto

Giotto, The Dream of St Gregory, The Legend of St Francis

Michelangelo da Caravaggio, The Lute Player, Hermitage Museum

FILMOGRAPHY

SALO, OR THE 120 DAYS OF SODOM

Dec 23, 1975 (Italy). 118 mins.

CAST

Paolo Bonacelli – the Duke
Giorgio Cataldi – the Judge
Uberto Paolo Quintavalle – the Bishop
Aldo Valletti – the President
Caterina Boratto – Signora Castelli
Elsa De Giorgi – Signora Maggi
Hélène Surgère – Signora Vaccari
Sonia Saviange – the piano player
Sergio Fascetti – Victim (Maschio)
Bruno Musso – Carlo Porro – Victim (Maschio)
Antonio Orlando – Tonino – Victim (Maschio)
Claudio Cicchetti – Victim (Maschio)
Franco Merli – Victim (Maschio)
Umberto Chessari – Victim (Maschio)
Lamberto Book –(Gobbi) – Victim (Maschio)
Gaspare Di Jenno – Rino – Victim (Maschio)
Giuliana Melis – Victim (Femmina)
Faridah Malik – Fatimah – Victim (Femmina)
Graziella Aniceto – Victim (Femmina)

Renata Moar – Victim (Femmina)
Dorit Henke – Doris – Victim (Femmina)
Antiniska Nemour – Victim (Femmina)
Benedetta Gaetani – Victim (Femmina)
Olga Andreis – Eva – Victim (Femmina)
Tatiana Mogilansky – Figlia
Susanna Radaelli – Figlia
Giuliana Orlandi – Figlia
Liana Acquaviva – Figlia
Rinaldo Missaglia – Militare
Giuseppe Patruno – Militare
Guido Galletti – Militare
Efisio Etzi – Militare
Claudio Troccoli – Collaborator
Fabrizio Menichini – Collaborator
Maurizio Valaguzza – Collaborator
Ezio Manni – Collaborator
Paola Pieracci – Ruffian
Carla Terlizzi – Ruffian
Anna Maria Dossena – Ruffian
Anna Recchimuzzi – Ruffian
Ines Pellegrini – Serva
Alessandro Gennari – Ufficiale della O.V.R.A.
Marco Lucantoni – Prima Victim Maschio
Dante Trazzi – Reclutatore Ragazzi
Anna Troccoli – First Victim Femmina

CREW

Produced – Alberto Grimaldi, Alberto De Stefanis and Antonio Girasante
Directed – Pier Paolo Pasolini
Script – Pier Paolo Pasolini, Sergio Citti and Pupi Avati
Cinematography – Tonino Delli Colli
Film Editing – Nino Baragli
Production Design – Dante Ferretti
Set Decoration and make-up – Osvaldo Desideri

Costume Design – Danilo Donati
Giusy Bovino – hair stylist
Alfredo Tiberi – makeup artist
Renzo David – production supervisor
Alberto De Stefanis – unit manager
Antonio Girasante – production manager
Alessandro Mattei – production supervisor
Angelo Zemella – production supervisor
Umberto Angelucci – first assistant director
Fiorella Infascelli – second assistant director
Maria-Teresa Barbasso – draughtswoman
Italo Tomassi – painter
Fausto Ancillai – sound mixer
Massimo Anzellotti – sound effects editor
Gilles Barberis – audio restorer
Alessandro Biancani – audio restorer
Giorgio Loviscek – sound
Domenico Pasquadibisceglie – sound
Giuseppina Sagliano – boom operator
Alfredo Tiberi – special effects
Deborah Imogen Beer – still photographer
Emilio Bestetti – camera operator
Carlo Tafani – camera operator
Sandro Battaglia – first assistant camera
Giancarlo Granatelli – second assistant camera
Vanni Castellani – costume assistant
Ugo De Rossi – assistant editor
Alfredo Menchini – assistant editor
Enzo Ocone – post-production coordinator
Arnaldo Graziosi – musician: piano
Ennio Morricone – music consultant
Beatrice Banfi – script supervisor
Vittorio Cudia – assistant secretary
Maurizio Forti – administrator
Alberto Grimaldi – presenter
Pietro Innocenti – administrator
Nico Naldini – publicist
Marco Bellocchio – voice dubbing: Aldo Valletti
Laura Betti – voice dubbing: Hélène Surgère
Giorgio Caproni – voice dubbing: Giorgio Cataldi

Aurelio Roncaglia – voice dubbing: Umberto Paolo Quintavalle

Giancarlo Vigorelli – voice dubbing: Paolo Bonacelli

Thanks:

Roland Barthes – bibliography: Sade, Fourier, Loyola

Maurice Blanchot – bibliography: Lautréamont et Sade

Simone de Beauvoir – bibliography: Faut-il brûler Sade?

Pierre Klossowski – bibliography: Sade mon prochain – Le Philosophe scélérat

Philippe Sollers – bibliography: L'écriture et l'expérience des limites

PIER PAOLO PASOLINI

FILMOGRAPHY AND BIBLIOGRAPHY

FEATURE FILMS

Beggar (*Accattone,* 1961)
Mother Rome (*Mamma Roma,* 1962)
Love Meetings (a.k.a. *Lessons In Love*, *Comizi d'Amore*, 1964)
The Gospel According To Matthew (*Il Vangelo Secondo Matteo*,1964)
The Hawks and the Sparrows (*Uccellacci e Uccellini,* 1966)
Oedipus Rex (*Edipo Re*, 1967)
Theorem (*Teorma,* 1968)
Pigsty (*Porcile*, 1969)
Medea (*Medea,* 1969)
The Decameron (*Il Decamerone,* 1971)
The Canterbury Tales (*I Racconti di Canterbury*, 1972)
The Arabian Nights (*Il Fiore Delle Mille e Una Notte,* 1974)
Salò, or The 120 Days of Sodom (*Salò, o le Centoventi Giornate di Sodoma,* 1975)

SHORT FILMS

The Anger (*La Rabbia,* 1963)
Curd Cheese (*La Ricotta,* episode in *RoGoPaG*, 1963)
The Earth Seen From the Moon (*La Terra Vista Dalla Luna,* episode in *The Witches = Le Streghe*, 1967)
What Are the Clouds? (*Che Cosa Sono le Nuvole?,* episode in *Caprice Italian Style = Capriccio all'Italiana,* 1968)
The Sequence of the Flower Field (*La Sequenza del Fiore di Carta,* episode in *Love and Anger = Vangelo '70/ Amore e Rabbia,* 1969)

DOCUMENTARIES

Location Hunting In Palestine (*Sopralluoghi in Palestina Per Il Vangelo secondo Matteo*, 1965)
Notes For a Film In India (*Appunti Per un Film Sull'India*, 1969)
Notes For a Garbage Novel (*Appunti Per un romanzo dell'immondizia*, 1970)
Notes Towards an African Oresteia (*Appunti Per un'Orestiade Africana*, 1970)
The Walls of Sana'a (*Le Mura di Sana'a*, 1971)
12 December 1972 (*12 Dicembre 1972*, 1972)
Pasolini and the Shape of the City (*Pasolini e la forma della città*, 1975)

SCRIPTS

The River Girl (1954)
Il Prigioniero della montagna (1955)
Manon: Finestra 2 (1956)
Nights of Cabiria (1956)
A Farewell To Arms (1957)
Marisa la Civetta (1957)
Giovani Mariti (1958)
Grigio (1958)
La Notte Brava (1959)
Marte di un Amico (1960)
From a Roman Balcony (1960)
Il Carro armato dell'8 settembre (1960)
I Bell'Antonio (1960)
La Lunga Notte del '43 (1960)
Accattone, F.M., Rome, 1960
La Ragazza In Vetrina (1961)
La Commare Secca (1962)
Mamma Roma, Rizzoli, Milan, 1962
Il Vangelo secondo Matteo, Garzanti, Milan, 1964
Uccellacci e uccellini, Garzanti, Milan, 1966
Oedipus Rex, Garzanti, Milan, 1967/ Lorrimer Publishing, 1984
Requiescant (1967, uncredited)
Il Ragazzo-motore (1967)
Theorem, Garzanti, Milan, 1968
Medea, Garzanti, Milan, 1970
Ostia, Garzanti, Milan, 1970
Storie Scellerate (1973)
Trilogia della vita, Cappelli, Bologna, 1975
San Paolo, Einaudi, Turin, 1977

WORKS AFTER PASOLINI'S DEATH

Laboratorio teatrale di Luca Ronconi (1977)
Mulheres... Mulheres (1981)
Calderon (1981)
Die Leiche murde nie gefunden (1985)

L'Altro enigma (1988)
Who Killed Pasolini? (1995)
Complicity (1995)
Il Pratone del casilino (1996)
Le Bassin de J.W. (1997)
Una Disperata vitalità (1999)
Orgia (2002)
Salò: Yesterday and Today (2002)
Pasolini prossimo nostro (2006)
'Na specie de cadavere lunghissimo (2006)
La Rabbia di Pasolini (2008)
Pilades (2016)

POETRY

Poesie e Casarsa, Libreroa Antiqua Mario Landi, Bologna, 1942
Poesie, Stamperia Primon, 1945
Diarii, 1945
I Pianti, Publicazioni dell-Academiuta, Casarsa, 1946
Dove la mia patria, Publicazioni dell-Academiuta, Casarsa, 1949
Poesia dialettale del Novecento, Guanda, Parma, 1952
Tal cour di un frut, Edizioni Friuli, Tricesimo, 1953/ 1974
Dal Diario, Salvatore Sciascia, Caltanisetta, 1954
Il Canto popolare, La Meridiana, Milan, 1954
La Meglio gioventu, Sansoni, Florence, 1954
Le Ceneri di Gramsci, Garzanti, Milan, 1957
L'Usignolo della Chiesa Cattolica, Loganesi, Milan, 1958/ Turin, 1976
Roma 1950, Milan, 1960
Sonetto primaverile, Milan, 1960
La Religione del mio tempo, Garzanti, Milan, 1961
Poesia in forma di rosa, Garzanti, Milan, 1964
Poesie dimenticate, Società Filologica Friulana, Udine, 1965
Potentissima Signora, Longanesi, Milan, 1965
Poesie, Garzanti, Milan, 1970/ 1999
Transumanar e organizzar, Garzanti, Milan, 1971
Le Poesie, Garzanti, Milan, 1975
La Nuova gioventu, Einaudi, Turin, 1975
Poesie e pagine ritrovate, 1980
Poems, New York, 1982
Sette Poesie e due lettere, 1984
Roman Poems, City Lights, 1986
Poems, 1996
Poems Scelte, 1997
Poesie rifiutate, 2000
La Nuova gioventu, 2002
Tutte le poesie, 2003
Meditazione orale, 2005
Poeta delle ceneri, 2010

FICTION

Ragazzi di Vita, Garzanti, Milan, 1955/ London, 1989
Una Vita Violenta, Garzanti, Milan, 1959
Donne di Roma, Il Saggiatore, Milan, 1960
A Dream of Something, 1962
Roman Nights and Other Stories, 1965
La Divina Mimesis, 1975
Amado mio, Aitti impuri, 1982
Petrolio, 1992/ 2005
Stories From the City of God, 1995
Romanzi e racconti, 1998
Il re dei giapponesi, 2003

BIBLIOGRAPHY

PIER PAOLO PASOLINI

Pasolini On Pasolini, ed. Oswald Stack, Thames & Hudson, London, 1969
Entretiens avec Pier Paolo Pasolini, Belfond, Paris, 1970
Interview, *Lui*, no. 1, June, 1970
Empirismo eretico, Garzanti, Milan, 1972
Interview, *The Guardian*, Aug 13, 1973
Con Pier Paolo Pasolini, ed. E. Magrelli, Bulzoni, Rome, 1977
Il dialogo, il potere, la morte: la critica e Pasolini, ed. L. Martellini, Cappelli, Bologna, 1979
"Sopralluoghi o la ricerca dei luoghi perduti" (1973), in M. Mancini & G. Perella, 1982
Lutheran Letters, tr. S. Hood, Carcanet Press, 1987
A Future Life, Rome, 1989
"The Lost Pasolini Interview", *Celluloid Liberation Front*, 2012

OTHERS

- G. Aichele. "Translation as De-canonization: Matthew's *Gospel According to Pasolini*", *Cross Currents*, 2002
- T. Aitken. "The Greatest Story – Never Told", *The Tablet*, Dec 23, 1995
- H. Alpert. *Fellini: A Life*, Paragon House, New York, N.Y., 1988
- R. Altman, ed. *Sound Theory, Sound Practice*, Routledge, London, 1992
- —. *Film/Genre*, British Film Institute, London, 1999
- D. Andrew. *The Major Film Theories*, Oxford University Press, Oxford, 1976
- —. *Concepts In Film Theory*, Oxford University Press, Oxford, 1984
- —. ed. *Breathless*, Rutgers University Press, New Brunswick, N.J., 1987
- G. Andrew. *The Film Handbook*, Longman, London, 1989
- G. Annovi. *Pier Paolo Pasolini*, Columbia University Press, 2017
- S. Arecco. *Pier Paolo Pasolini*, Partisan, Rome, 1972
- G. Austin. *Contemporary French Cinema*, Manchester University Press, Manchester, 1996

B. Babington. *Biblical Epic and Sacred Narrative In the Hollywood,* Manchester University Press, Manchester, 1993

G. Bachmann. "Pasolini on de Sade", *Film Quarterly,* vol. 29, no. 2, 1975-76

—. "The 220 Days of Sodom", *Film Comment,* vol. 12, no. 2, Mch-Apl, 1976 (and in *Scraps From the Loft,* June 7, 2018)

M. Barker, ed. *The Video Nasties: Freedom and Censorship In the Media,* Pluto Press, London, 1984

—. & J. Petley, eds. *Ill Effects: The Media/ Violence Debate,* Routledge, London, 1997

R. Barthes. *S/Z,* Hill and Wang, New York, N.Y., 1974

—. *The Pleasure of the Text,* Hill and Wang, New York, N.Y., 1975

—. *Image, Music, Text,* tr. S. Heath, Fontana, London, 1984

G. Bataille. *Literature and Evil,* Calder & Boyars, London, 1973

—. *The Story of the Eye,* Penguin, London, 1982

L. Bawden, ed. *The Oxford Companion To Film,* Oxford University Press, Oxford, 1976

J. Baxter. *An Appalling Talent: Ken Russell,* M. Joseph, London, 1973

—. *Fellini,* St Martin's Press, New York, 1993

A. Bazin. *What Is Cinema?,* University of California Press, Berkeley, C.A., 1960, 2 vols

—. "Cinema and Theology", *South Atlantic Quarterly,* 91, 2, 1992

M. Beja. *Film and Literature: An Introduction,* Longman, London, 1979

—. ed. *Perspectives On Orson Welles,* G.K. Hall, Boston, M.A., 1995

D. Bellezza. *Morte di Pasolini,* Milan, 1981

R. Bellour & M. Bandy, eds. *Jean-Luc Godard,* Museum of Modern Art, N.Y., 1992

Maurizio De Benedictis. *Sergio Citti. Lo "straniero" del cinema italiano,* Lithos, 2008

Bernard Berenson: *The Italian Painters of the Renaissance,* Phaidon 1952/ Fontana 1960

A. Bergala & J. Narboni, eds. *Pasolini Cinéaste,* Paris, 1981

R. Bergan & R. Karney. *Bloomsbury Foreign Film Guide,* Bloomsbury, London, 1988

D. Bergman. *Gaiety Transfigured,* Madison, 1991

I. Bergman. *Bergman On Bergman, Interviews with Ingmar Bergman,* eds. S. Björkman *et al,* tr. P. B. Austin, Touchstone, New York, N.Y., 1986

—. *The Magic Lantern: An Autobiography*, London, 1988

—. *Images: My Life In Film,* Faber, London, 1994

A. Bertini. *Teoria e tecnica del film in Pasolini,* Rome, 1979

B. Bertolucci. *Bertolucci By Bertolucci,* with E. Ungari and D. Ranvard, Plexus, London, 1987

P. Biskind. *Easy Riders, Raging Bulls: How the Sex 'n' Drugs 'n' Rock 'n' Roll Generation Saved Hollywood,* Bloomsbury, London, 1998

V. Boarini. *Da Accattone a Salo,* Bologna, 1982

P. Bogdanovitch. *This Is Orson Welles,* Da Capo, New York, 1998

L. Bolton & C.S. Manson, eds. *Italy On Screen: National Identity*

and Italian Imaginary, New Studies in European Cinema Series, Peter Lang, 2010
J. Boorman, ed. *Projections 4*, Faber, London, 1995
—. *Projections 4 1/2*, Positif Editions/ Faber, London, 1995
D. Bordwell & K. Thompson. *Film Art: An Introduction*, McGraw-Hill Publishing Company, New York, N.Y., 1979
—. *The Films of Carl-Theodor Dreyer*, University of California, Berkeley, 1981
—. et al. *The Classical Hollywood Cinema: Film Style and Mode of Production To 1960*, Routledge, London, 1985
—. *Narration In the Fiction Film*, Routledge, London, 1988
—. *Ozu and the Poetics of Cinema*, British Film Institute, London, 1988
—. *Making Meaning*, Harvard University Press, Cambridge, M.A., 1989
—. & N. Caroll, eds. *Post-Theory: Reconstructing Film Studies*, University of Wisconsin Press, Madison, W.I., 1996
—. *The Way Hollywood Tells It*, University of California Press, Berkeley, C.A., 2006
—. & K. Thompson. *Film History*, McGraw-Hill, 2010
F. Brady. *Citizen Welles*, Scribner's, New York, 1989
P. Braunberger. *Pierre Braunberger*, Centre National de la Cinématographie, Paris, 1987
D. Breskin. *Inner Voices: Filmmakers In Conversation*, Da Capo, New York, 1997
R. Bresson, *Notes On the Cinematographer*, Quartet, London, 1986
F. Brevini, ed. *Pasolini*, Mondadori, Milan, 1981
R. Brody. *Everything Is Cinema: The Working Life of Jean-Luc Godard*, Faber, London, 2008
R. Brown, ed. *Focus On Godard*, Prentice-Hall, N.J., 1972
Gian Piero Brunetta. *The History of Italian Cinema*, Princeton University Press, 2009
S. Bukatman. *Terminal Identity: The Virtual Subject In Postmodern Science Fiction*, Duke University Press, Durham, N.C., 1993
P.J. Burgard, ed. *Nietzsche and the Feminine*, University Press of Virginia, Charlottesville, 1994
R. Burgoyne. *Bertolucci's 1900*, Wayne State University Press, Detroit, M.I., 1991
F. Burke and M. Waller, eds. *Federico Fellini: Contemporary Perspectives*, University of Toronto Press, 2002
I. Butler. *Religion In the Cinema*, A.S. Barnes, New York, N.Y., 1969
J. Butler. *Gender Trouble: Feminism and the Subversion of Identity*, Routledge, London, 1990
R. Butter *et al*, eds. *Displacing Homophobia: Gay Male Perspectives In Literature and Culture*, London, 1989
I. Cameron, ed. *The Films of Jean-Luc Godard*, Praeger, N.Y., 1969
A. Carotenuto. *L'Autunno della Conscienza*, Turin, 1985
N. Carroll. *Mystifying Movies: Fads and Fallacies of Contemporary Film Theory*, Columbia University Press, New

York, N.Y., 1988
S. Casi. *Desiderio di Pasolini*, La Sonda, Turin, 1990
J. Caughie, ed. *Theories of Authorship: A Reader*, Routledge, London, 1988
—. & A. Kuhn, eds. *The Sexual Subject: A* Screen *Reader In Sexuality*, Routledge, London, 1992
Centro Studi sul Cinema e sulle Communicazioni di Massa. *La Giovani generazioni e il cinema di Pier Paolo Pasolini, La Scene e lo schermo*, Dec, 1989
G. Chester & J. Dickey, eds. *Feminism and Censorship: The Current Debate*, Prism Press, Bridport, Dorset, 1988
M. Ciment. *Projections 9: French Filmmakers On Filmmaking*, Faber, London, 1999
H. Cixous. *The Newly Born Woman*, tr. B. Wing, Minnesota University Press, Minneapolis, 1986
—. *The Hélène Cixous Reader*, ed. Susan Sellers, Blackwell, Oxford, 1994
D.A. Cook. *A History of Narrative Film*, W.W. Norton, New York, N.Y., 1981, 1990, 1996
P. Cook & M. Bernink, eds. *The Cinema Book*, 2nd ed., British Film Institute, London, 1999
T. Corrigan. *A Cinema Without Walls: Movies and Culture After Vietnam*, Rutgers University Press, N.J., 1991
P. Cowie. *The Cinema of Orson Welles*, Da Capo, New York, N.Y., 1973
—. *Ingmar Bergman*, Secker & Warburg, London, 1982
R. Crittenden, ed. *Fine Cuts: The Art of European Film Editing*, C.R.C. Press, 2012
M. Crosland, ed. *The Marquis de Sade Reader*, Peter Owen, 2000
J. Davidson. *The Greeks and Greek Love*, Weidenfeld & Nicholson, London, 2007
G. Day & C. Bloch, eds. *Perspectives On Pornography: Sexuality In Film and Literature*, Macmillan, London, 1988
L. De Giusti, *I Film di Pier Paolo Pasolini*, Gremese, Rome, 1990
T. de Lauretis & S. Heath, eds. *The Cinematic Apparatus*, St Martin's Press, New York, N.Y., 1980
—. *Alice Doesn't: Feminism, Semiotics, Cinema*, Indiana University Press, Bloomington, I.N., 1984
—. *Technologies of Gender*, Macmillan, London, 1987
G. Deleuze & F. Guattari. *Cinema 1: The Movement Image*, Athlone Press, London, 1989
—. *Cinema 2: The Time Image*, Athlone Press, London, 1989
—. *What Is Philosophy?*, Verso, London, 1994
J. Derrida: *Of Grammatology*, Johns Hopkins University Press, Baltimore, M.D., 1976
—. *Spurs: Nietzsche's Styles*, University of Chicago Press, Chicago, I.L., 1979
—. *Writing and Difference*, University of Chicago Press, Chicago, I.L., 1987
—. *Archive Fever*, University of Chicago Press, Chicago, I.L., 1999
G. DeSanti *et al. Perchè Pasolini*, Guaraldi, Florence, 1978
J. Distefano. "Picturing Pasolini", *Art Journal*, 1997

W.W. Dixon. *The Films of Jean-Luc Godard*, State University of New York Press, Albany, N.Y., 1997

J. Dollimore. *Sexual Dissidence*, Oxford, 1991

J. Duflot. *Entretiens avec Pier Paolo Pasolini*, Pierre Belfond, Paris, 1970

R. Durgnat. *Films and Feelings*, Faber, London, 1967

A. Dworkin. *Pornography: Men Possessing Women*, Women's Press, London, 1984

—. *Intercourse*, Arrow, London, 1988

—. *Letters From a War Zone: Writings, 1976-1987*, Secker & Warburg, London, 1988

A. Easthope, ed. *Contemporary Film Theory*, Longman, London, 1993

M. Eliade. *Ordeal by Labyrinth*, University of Chicago Press, Chicago, I.L., 1984

—. *Symbolism, the Sacred and the Arts*, Crossroad, New York, N.Y., 1985

A. Eliot. "*Oedipus Rex* by Pier Paolo Pasolini", *Literature Film Quarterly*, 2004

T. Elsaesser. *European Cinema*, Amsterdam University Press, Amsterdam, 2005

P. Ettedgui. *Production Design & Art Direction*, RotoVision, 1999

Etudes cinématographiques, special Pasolini number, 109-111, 1976

D. Fairservice. *Film Editing*, Manchester University Press, Manchester, 2001

M. Farber. *Negative Space*, Studio Vista, London, 1971

C. Fava & Aldo Vigano. *The Films of Federico Fellini*, Citadel, New York, N.Y., 1990

F. Fellini. *Fellini On Fellini*, Delacorte, New York, N.Y., 1976

—. *Fellini On Fellini*, ed. C. Constantin, Faber, 1995

—. *I'm a Born Liar: A Fellini Lexicon*, ed. D. Pettigrew, Abrams, New York, 2003

A. Ferrero. *Il Cinema di Pier Paolo Pasolini*, Marsilio, Venice, 1977

J. Finler. *The Movie Directors Story*, Octopus Books, London, 1985

—. *The Hollywood Story*, Wallflower Press, London, 2003

John Fletcher & Andrew Benjamin, ed. *Abjection, Melancholia and Love: The Work of Julia Kristeva*, Routledge, London, 1990

K. Forni. "A "cinema of poetry": What Pasolini Did To Chaucer's *Canterbury Tales*", *Literature Film Quarterly*, 2002

G.E. Forshey. *American Religious and Biblical Spectaculars*, Praeger, Westport, CT, 1992

M. Foucault. *The History of Sexuality*, Penguin, London, 1981

—. *The Use of Pleasure: The History of Sexuality*, vol. 2, Penguin, London, 1987

—. *Politics, Philosophy, Culture: Interviews and Other Writings, 1977-1984*, ed. L.D. Kritzmon, Routledge, New York, N.Y., 1990

J. Franklin. *New German Cinema*, Columbus Books, 1986

K. French, ed. *Screen Violence*, Bloomsbury, London, 1996

P. French *et al. The Films of Jean-Luc Godard*, Blue Star House, 1967

A. Frisch. "Francesco Vezzolini: Pasolini Reloaded", interview, Rutgers University Alexander Library, New Brunswick, N.J.

Diana Fuss. *Essentially Speaking*, Routledge, New York, 1989

—. ed. *Inside/ Out: Lesbian Theories, Gay Theories*, Routledge, London, 1991

F. Gado. *The Passion of Ingmar Bergman*, Durham, N.C., 1986

J. Gallagher. *Film Directors On Directing*, Praeger, New York, N.Y., 1989

H. Geduld, ed. *Filmmakers On Filmmaking*, Indiana University Press, Bloomington, I.N., 1967

J. Geiger & R. Rutsky, eds. *Film Analysis*, Norton & Company, New York, N.Y., 2005

J. Gelmis. *The Film Director As Superstar*, Penguin, London, 1974

D. Georgakas & L. Rubenstein, eds. *Art Politics Cinema: The Cineaste Interviews*, Pluto Press, London, 1985

F. Gérard. *Pier Paolo Pasolini*, Seghers, Paris, 1973

—. *Pasolini ou le mythe de la barbarie*, Université de Bruxelles, 1981

J. Gerber. *Anatole Dauman: Pictures of a Producer*, British Film Institute, London, 1992

M. Gervais. *Pier Paolo Pasolini*, Paris, 1973

L. Gianetti: *Godard and Others*, Tantivy, 1975

—. *Understanding Movies*, Prentice-Hall, N.J., 1982

P.C. Gibson & R. Gibson, eds. *Dirty Looks: Women, Pornography, Power*, British Film Institute, London, 1993

Jean-Luc Godard. *Godard On Godard*, ed. A. Bergala, Cahiers du Cinéma, Paris, 1985

—. *Godard On Godard*, eds. J. Narobi & T. Milne, Da Capo, New York, N.Y., 1986

—. *Interviews*, ed. D. Sterritt, University of Mississippi Press, Jackson, 1998

—. *Godard On Godard 2*, ed. A. Bergala, Cahiers du Cinéma, Paris, 1998

—. *Histoire(s) du cinéma*, Galimard-Gaumont, Paris, 1998

—. "An Audience With Uncle Jean-Luc", *The Guardian*, Feb 11, 2000

J. Gomez. *Ken Russell*, Muller, 1976

R. Gottesman, ed. *Focus On Orson Welles*, Prentice-Hall, Englewood Cliffs, N.J., 1976

P. Grace. *The Religious Film: Christianity and the Hagiopic*, Wiley-Blackwell, Sussex, 2009

D. Graham, ed. *Film and Religion*, St Mungo Press, 1997

B.K. Grant, ed. *Film Genre*, Scarecrow Press, Metuchen, N.J., 1977

—. ed. *Crisis Cinema: The Apocalyptic Idea In Postmodern Narrative Film*, Maisonneuve Press, 1993

—. *Film Genre Reader II*, University of Texas Press, Austin, T.X., 1995

J. Green. *The Encyclopedia of Censorship*, Facts on File, New York, N.Y., 1990

N. Greene. *Pier Paolo Pasolini: Cinema As Heresy*, Princeton

University Press, N.J., 1990

Elizabeth Grosz. "Philosophy, Subjectivity and the Body", in C. Pateman, 1986

—. "Desire, the body and recent French feminism", *Intervention*, 21-2, 1988

—. *Sexual Subversions*, Allen & Unwin, London, 1989

—. "The Body of Signification", in J. Fletcher, 1990

—. "Fetishization", in E. Wright, 1992

—. *Volatile Bodies,* Indiana University Press, Bloomington, I.N., 1994

—. *Space, Time and Perversion*, Routledge, London, 1995

B. Groult: "Les portiers de nuit", in *Ainsi soit-elle*, Grasset, Paris, 1975, and in E. Marks, 1981

L. Hanlon. *Fragments: Bresson's Film Style*, Farleigh Dickinson University Press, Rutherford, 1986

S. Harwood. *French National Cinema,* Routledge, London, 1993

P. Hartnoll, ed. *The Oxford Companion To the Theatre,* Oxford University Press, Oxford, 1985

S. Hayward & G. Vincendeau, eds. *French Film*, Routledge, London, 1990

S. Heath. *Questions of Cinema*, Macmillan, London, 1981

—. *Cinema and Language*, University Presses of America, 1983

W. Herzog. *Herzog On Herzog*, ed. P. Cronin, Faber & Faber, London, 2002

G. Hickenlooper. *Reel Conversations: Candid Interviews With Film's Foremost Directors and Critics*, Citadel, New York, N.Y., 1991

C. Higham. *Orson Welles,* St Martin's Press, New York, N.Y., 1985

J. Hill & P.C. Gibson, eds. *The Oxford Guide To Film Studies*, Oxford University Press, Oxford, 1998

J. Hillier, ed. *Cahiers du Cinéma: The 1950s, New-Realism, Hollywood, New Wave*, Harvard University Press, Cambridge, M.A., 1985

—. *The New Hollywood*, Studio Vista, London, 1992

L.C. Hillstrom, ed. *International Dictionary of Films and Filmmakers: Directors*, St James Press, London, 1997

D. Holmes & A. Smith, eds. *100 Years of European Cinema*, Manchester University Press, Manchester, 2000

H. Hughes. *Cinema Italiano*, I.B. Tauris, London, 2011

G. Indiana. *Salò*, British Film Institute, London, 2000

—. "Pasolini, *Mamma Roma,* and *La Ricotta"*, Criterion, 2004

A. Insdorf. *Indelible Shadows: Film and the Holocaust*, Cambridge University Press, Cambridge, 1989

L. Irigaray. *The Irigaray Reader,* ed. M. Whitford, Blackwell, Oxford, 1991

F. Jameson. *Signatures of the Visible*, Routledge, New York, N.Y., 1990

—. *Postmodernism, or the Cultural Logic of Late Capitalism*, Verso, London, 1991

D. Jarman. *Modern Nature*, Century, London, 1991

P. Kael. *Kiss Kiss Bang Bang*, Bantam, New York, N.Y., 1969

—. *Going Steady*, Bantam, New York, 1971

—. *Taking It All In*, Marion Boyars, 1986
—. *State of the Art*, Marion Boyars, London, 1987
—. *Movie Love*, Marion Boyars, London, 1992
A. Kaes. *From Hitler To Heimat: The Return of History As Film*, Harvard University Press, Cambridge, M.A., 1989
E. Ann Kaplan, ed. *Psychoanalysis and Cinema*, Routledge, London, 1990
B.F. Kawin. *Mindscreen: Bergman, Godard and First-Person Film*, Princeton University Press, Princeton, N.J., 1978
—. *How Movies Work*, Macmillan, New York, N.Y., 1987
P. Keough, ed. *Flesh and Blood: The National Society of Film Critics On Sex, Violence, and Censorship*, Mercury House, San Francisco, C.A., 1995
T. Kezich. *Fellini: His Life and Work*, Faber and Faber, New York, N.Y., 2006
G. Kindem. *The International Movie Industry*, Southern Illinois University Press, Carbondale, I.L., 2000
R. Kinnard & T. Davis. *Divine Images: A History of Jesus On the Screen,* Citadel Press, New York, N.Y., 1992
C. Klimke. *Kraft der Vergangenheit: Zu Motiven der Filme von Pier Paolo Pasolini,* Frankfurt, 1988
T. Jefferson Kline. *Bertolucci's Dream Loom: A Psychoanalytic Study of Cinema*, University of Massachusetts Press, Amherst, 1987
P. Kolker. *The Altering Eye: Contemporary International Cinema*, Oxford University Press, New York, N.Y., 1983
—. *Bernardo Bertolucci*, British Film Institute, London, 1985
—. *A Cinema of Loneliness: Penn, Stone, Kubrick, Scorsese, Spielberg, Altman*, Oxford University Press, New York, N.Y., 1988/ 2000
S. Kracauer. *Theory of Film*, Princeton University Press, Princeton, N.J., 1997
L. Kreitzer. *The New Testament In Fiction and Film*, J.S.O.T., 1993
—. *The Old Testament In Fiction and Film*, Sheffield Academic Press, Sheffield, 1994
J. Kristeva. *Powers of Horror: An Essay On Abjection*, tr. L.S. Roudiez, Columbia University Press, New York, 1982
—. *Desire In Language: A Semiotic Approach To Literature and Art*, ed. L.S. Roudiez, tr. Thomas Gora, Alice Jardine & L.S. Roudiez, Blackwell, Oxford, 1982
—. *Revolution In Poetic Language*, tr. Margaret Walker, Columbia University Press, New York, 1984
—. Article in *Art Press*, 4, 1984-85
—. *The Kristeva Reader*, ed. T. Moi, Blackwell, Oxford, 1986
—. *Tales of Love*, tr. L.S. Roudiez, Columbia University Press, New York, N.Y., 1987
—. *Black Sun: Depression and Melancholy,* tr. L.S. Roudiez, Columbia University Press, New York, N.Y., 1989
—. *Strangers To Ourselves*, tr. L.S. Roudiez, Harvester Wheatsheaf, Hemel Hempstead, 1991
A. Kuhn. *Women's Pictures: Feminism and the Cinema*, Routledge & Kegan Paul, London, 1982

A. Kurosawa. *Something Like an Autobiography*, Vintage, New York, N.Y., 1983

J. Lacan. *Écrits: A Selection*, tr. Alan Sheridan, Tavistock, 1977

—. and the École Freudienne. *Feminine Sexuality*, eds. J. Mitchell and J. Rose, Macmillan, London, 1988

R. Lapsley & M. Westlake, eds. *Film Theory: An Introduction*, Manchester University Press, Manchester, 1988

A. Lawton. *The Red Screen: Politics, Society, Art In Soviet Cinema*, Routledge, London, 1992

B. Leaming. *Orson Welles*, Viking, New York, 1985

V. Lebeau. *Psychoanalysis and Cinema*, Wallflower, London, 2001

P. Leprohan. *The Italian Cinema*, tr. R. Greaves & O. Stallybrass, Secker & Warburg, London, 1972

E. Levy. *Cinema of Outsiders: The Rise of American Independent Film*, New York University Press, New York, N.Y., 1999

J. Lewis. *Whom God Wishes To Destroy: Francis Coppola and the New Hollywood*, Duke University Press, Durham, N.C., 1995

—. ed. *New American Cinema*, Duke University Press, Durham, N.C., 1998

—. *Hollywood v. Hard Core: How the Struggle Over Censorship Created the Modern Film Industry*, New York University Press, New York, N.Y., 2000

—. ed. *The End of Cinema As We Know It: American Film In the Nineties*, New York University Press, New York, N.Y., 2002

J. Leyda, ed. *Filmmakers Speak*, Da Capo, New York, 1977/ 84

—. *Kino: A History of the Russian and Soviet Cinema*, 3rd edition, Allen & Unwin, London, 1983

M. Litch. *Philosophy Through Film*, Routledge, London, 2002

P. Livington. *Ingmar Bergman and the Rituals of Art*, Cornell University Press, Ithaca, N.Y., 1982

V. LoBrutto. *Sound-On-Film*, Praeger, New York, N.Y., 1994

—. *Stanley Kubrick*, Faber, London, 1997

Y. Loshitzky. *The Radical Faces of Godard and Bertolucci*, Wayne State University Press, Detroit, M.I., 1995

L. Lourdeaux. *Italian and Irish Filmmakers In America: Ford, Capra, Coppola and Scorsese*, Temple University Press, Philadelphia, P.A., 1990

L. Lucignani & C. Molfese, eds. *Per Conoscere Pasolini*, Bulzoni, Rome, 1978

C. MacCabe. *Godard, Images, Sound, Politics*, Macmillan/ British Film Institute, London, 1980

—. *Godard: A Portrait of the Artist At 70*, Faber, London, 2003

—. *"The Decameron"*, Criterion, 2012

M. Macciocchi, ed. *Pasolini*, Grasset, Paris, 1980

A. Maggi. *The Resurrection of the Body: Pier Paolo Pasolini From St Paul To Sade*, University of Chicago Press, 2009

P. Malone. *Movie Christs and Antichrists*, Crossroad, 1990

R. Maltby. *Harmless Entertainment: Hollywood and the Ideology of Consensus*, Scarecrow Press, Metuchen, N.J., 1983

—. *Hollywood Cinema*, 2nd ed., Blackwell, Oxford, 2003

M. Mancini & G. Perella. *Pier Paolo Pasolini: corpi e luoghi*, Theorema, Bologna, 1982

Mao Tse-tung. *The Little Red Book (Quotations From Chairman Mao Tse-tung)*, Foreign Language Press, Peking, 1967

E. Marks & I. de Courtivron, eds. *New French Feminisms: an anthology*, Harvester Wheatsheaf, Hemel Hempstead, 1981

T. Martin. *Images and the Imageless: A Study In Religious Consciousness and Film,* Bucknell University Press, 1981

G. Mast *et al,* eds. *Film Theory and Criticism: Introductory Readings*, Oxford University Press, New York, N.Y., 1992a

—. & B Kawin, *A Short History of the Movies*, Macmillan, New York, N.Y., 1992b

T.D. Matthews. *Censored*, Chatto & Windus, London, 1994

J.R. May & M. Bird, eds. *Religion In Film*, University of Tennessee Press, Knoxville, 1982

—. *Image and Likeness: Religious Vision In American Film Classics,* Paulist, 1992

—. *New Image of Religious Film*, Sheed & Ward, London, 1996

J. Mayne. *The Woman At the Keyhole: Feminism and Women's Cinema*, Indiana University Press, Bloomington, I.N., 1990

M. Medved. *Hollywood vs. America*, HarperCollins, London, 1992

P. Mellencamp & P. Rosen, eds. *Cinema Histories, Cinema Practices*, University Publications of America, Frederick, M.D., 1984

—. *A Fine Romance: Five Ages of Film Feminism*, Temple University Press, Philadelphia, P.A., 1995

M. Miles. *Seeing and Believing: Religion and Values In the Movies*, Beacon, Boston, M.A., 1996

M.C. Miller. ed. *Seeing Through Movies*, Pantheon, New York, N.Y., 1990

Wu Ming. "The Police vs. Pasolini, Pasolini vs the Police", Verso Books, 2016

T. Modleski, ed. *Studies In Entertainment*, Indiana University Press, Bloomington, I.N., 1987

—. *The Women Who Knew Too Much: Hitchcock and Feminist Theory*, Methuen, London, 1988

—. *Feminism Without Women: Culture and Criticism In a 'Postfeminist' Age*, Routledge, London, 1991

T. Moi. *Sexual/ Textual Politics: Feminist Literary Theory*, Methuen, London, 1983

J. Monaco. *The New Wave: Truffaut, Godard, Chabrol, Rohmer, Rivette*, Oxford University Press, New York, N.Y., 1977

I. Moscati. *Pasolini e il teorema del sesso*, Milan, 1995

P. Mosley. *Ingmar Bergman*, Marion Boyars, London, 1981

R. Murphy, ed. *The British Cinema Book*, Palgrave/ Macmillan, London, 2nd edition, 2009

R. Murray. *Images In the Dark: An Encyclopedia of Gay and Lesbian Film and Video*, Titan Books, London, 1998

S. Murri. *Pier Paolo Pasolini*, Rome, 1984

N. Naldini. *Nei camp dei Friuli: La giovanezza di Pasolini,* Pesce d'Oro, Milan, 1984

—. *Pasolini, una vita,* Einaudi, Turin, 1989

J. Naremore. *The Magic World of Orson Welles,* Southern Methodist University Press, Dallas, T.X., 1989

- J. Natoli. *Hauntings: Popular Film and American Culture 1990-92*, State University of New York Press, Albany, N.Y., 1994
- —. *Speeding To the Millennium: Film and Culture 1993-1995*, State University of New York Press, Albany, N.Y., 1998
- —. *Postmodern Journeys: Film and Culture, 1996-1998*, State University of New York Press, Albany, N.Y., 2001
- S. Neale. *Cinema and Technology*, Macmillan, London, 1985
- —. & B. Neve. *Film and Politics In America*, Routledge, London, 1992
- J. Nelmes, ed. *An Introduction To Film Studies*, Routledge, London, 1996
- R. Neupert. *The End: Narration and Closure In the Cinema*, Wayne State University Press, Detroit, M.I., 1995
- K. Newman & J. Marriott. *Horror! The Definitive Companion To the Most Terrifying Movies Ever Made*, Carlton Books, London, 2013
- G. Nowell-Smith. *Visconti*, British Film Institute, London, 1973
- —. ed. *The Oxford History of World Cinema*, Oxford University Press, Oxford, 1996
- —. & S. Ricci, eds. *Hollywood and Europe*, British Film Institute, London, 1998
- —. *Making Waves: New Cinemas of the 1960s*, Bloomsbury, 2013
- J. Orr & C. Nicholson, eds. *Cinema and Fiction*, Edinburgh University Press, Edinburgh, 1992
- —. *Cinema and Modernity*, Polity Press, Cambridge, 1993
- —. *Contemporary Cinema*, Edinburgh University Press, Edinburgh, 1998
- C. Ostwalt. "Religion & Popular Movies", *Journal of Religion and Film*, 2, 3, 1998
- R. Palmer, ed. *The Cinematic Text*, A.M.S., New York, N.Y., 1989
- A. Panicali & S. Sestini, eds. *Pier Paolo Pasolini*, Nuovo Salani, Florence, 1982
- E. Passannanti. *Il Corpo & Il Potere*, Joker, 2004
- —. *La Ricotta*, Mask Press, 2007
- —. *Il Cristo dell'Eresia*, Joker, 2009
- —. *La Nudita del Sacro nei Film di Pier Paolo Pasolini*, Brindin Press, 2019
- Carole Pateman & Elizabeth Grosz, eds. *Feminist Challenges*, Allen & Unwin, Sydney, 1986
- A. Pavelin. *Fifty Religious Films,* A.P. Pavelin, Chiselhurst, Kent, 1990
- C. Penley, ed. *Feminism and Film Theory*, Routledge, London, 1988
- —. et al, eds. *Close Encounters: Film, Feminism and Science Fiction*, University of Minnesota Press, Minneapolis, 1991
- V.F. Perkins. *Film As Film: Understanding and Judging Movies*, Penguin, London, 1972
- T. Peterson. *The Paraphrase of an Imaginary Dialogue: The Poetics and Poetry of Pier Paolo Pasolini*, New York, 1994
- S. Petraglia. *Pier Paolo Pasolini*, Nuova Italia, Florence, 1974
- D. Petrie. *Screening Europe: Image and Identity In Contemporary European Cinema*, British Film Institute, London, 1992

G. Phelps. *Film Censorship*, Gollancz, London, 1975

K. Phillips. *New German Filmmakers*, Ungar, New York, N.Y., 1984

L. Polezzi & C. Ross, eds. *In Corpore: Bodies In Post-Unification Italy*, Fairleigh Dickinson University Press, 2007

C. Potter. *Image, Sound and Story: The Art of Telling In Film*, Secker & Warburg, London, 1990

N. Power & G. Nowell-Smith. "Subversive Pasolini", 2012-13, ninapower.net, 2017

P. Powrie, ed. *French Cinema In the 1990s*, Oxford University Press, Oxford, 1999

R. Prendergast. *Film Music*, W.W. Norton, New York, N.Y., 1992

S. Prince. *Savage Cinema: Sam Peckinpah and the Rise of Ultra-violent Movies*, University of Texas Press, Austin, T.X., 1998

—. ed. *Screening Violence*, Athlone Press, London, 2000

—. *A New Pot of Gold: Hollywood Under the Electronic Rainbow*, Scribners, New York, N.Y., 2000

S. Projansky. *Watching Rape: Film and Television In Post-feminism Culture*, New York University Press, New York, N.Y., 2001

T. Pugh. "Chaucerian Fabliaux, Cinematic Fabliau: Pier Paolo Pasolini's *I racconti di Canterbury*", *Literature Film Quarterly*, 2004

M. Pye & Lynda Myles. *The Movie Brats: How the Film Generation Took Over Hollywood*, Faber, London, 1979

T. Rayns, ed. *Fassbinder*, British Film Institute, London, 1979

K. Reader. *Robert Bresson*, Manchester University Press, Manchester, 2000

A. Reinhartz. "Jesus in Film: Hollywood Perspectives on the Jewishness of Jesus", *Journal of Religion and Film*, 2, 2, 1998

A. Restivo. *The Cinema of Economic Miracles: Visuality and Modernization In the Italian Art Film*, Duke University Press, 2002

La Revue d'estgétique, special Pasolini number, 3, 1982

J. Rhodes. *Stupendous, Miserable City: Pasolini's Rome*, University of Minnesota Press, 2007

P. Rice & P. Waugh, eds. *Modern Literary Theory: A Reader*, Arnold, London, 1992

J. Richards, ed. *Films and British National Identity*, Manchester University Press, Manchester, 1997

M. Richardson. *Surrealism and Cinema*, Berg, New York, N.Y., 2006

D. Richie. *The Films of Akira Kurosawa*, University of California Press, Berkeley, C.A., 1965

R. Rinaldi. *Pier Paolo Pasolini*, Mursia, Milan, 1982

D. Robinson. *World Cinema*, Methuen, London, 1981

G. Rodgerson & E. Wilson, eds. *Pornography and Censorship*, Lawrence & Wishart, London, 1991

S. Rohdie. *Antonioni*, British Film Institute, London, 1990

—. *The Passion of Pier Paolo Pasolini*, British Film Institute, London, 1995

J. Romney & A. Wootton, eds. *Celluloid Jukebox: Popular Music*

and the Movies Since the 50s, British Film Institute, London, 1995
- P. Rosen, ed. *Narrative, Apparatus, Ideology: A Film Theory Reader*, Columbia University Press, New York, N.Y., 1986
- A. Rosenstone, ed. *Revisioning History: Film and the Construction of a New Past*, Princeton University Press, Princeton, N.J., 1995
- R. Roud. *Jean-Luc Godard*, Thames & Hudson, London, 1970
- R. Ruiz. *The Poetics of Cinema*, Dis Voir, Paris, 1995
- P. Rumble & B. Testa, eds. *Pier Paolo Pasolini*, University of Toronto Press, Toronto, 1994
- —. *Allegories of Contamination: Pier Paolo Pasolini's Trilogy of Life*, University of Toronto Press, Toronto, 1996
- K. Russell. *A British Picture: An Autobiography*, Heinemann, London, 1989
- M. Russell & J. Young. *Film Music,* RotoVision, 2000
- V. Russo. *The Celluloid Closet: Homosexuality In the Movies*, Harper & Row, New York, N.Y., 1981
- M. de Sade. *The 120 Days of Sodom*, tr. A. Wainhouse & R. Seaver, Arrow, London, 1996
- J. Sanford. *The New German Cinema*, Da Capo Press, New York, N.Y., 1982
- A. Sarris, ed., *Interviews With Film Directors*, Avon, New York, N.Y., 1969
- T. Schatz. *Hollywood Genres,* Random House, New York, N.Y., 1981
- —. *Old Hollywood/ New Hollywood*, U.M.I. Research Press, Ann Arbor, M.I., 1983
- —. *The Genius of the System: Hollywood Filmmaking In the Studio Era*, Pantheon, New York, N.Y. 1988
- Naomi Schor. *Breaking the Chain: Women, Theory and French Realist Fiction*, New York, 1985
- —. & Elizabeth Weed, eds. *Differences: More Gender Trouble: Feminism Meets Queer Theory*, 6, 2-3, Indiana University Press, Summer, 1994
- P. Schrader. *Transcendental Style In Film: Ozu, Bresson, Dreyer*, Da Capo Press, 1972
- M. Schumacher. *Francis Ford Coppola*, Bloomsbury, London, 2000
- B. Schwartz. *Pasolini Requiem*, Vintage Books, New York, 1995
- P. Schwenger. *Phallic Critiques: Masculinity and 20th Century Literature,* London, 1984
- O. Schweitzer. *Pier Paolo Pasolini*, Hamburg, 1986
- Bernhart Schwenk & Michael Semff, eds. *Pier Paolo Pasolini and Death,* Ostfildern 2005
- M. Scorsese. *Scorsese On Scorsese*, ed. D. Thompson & I. Christie, Faber, London, 1989, 1995
- *Screen Reader I: Cinema/ Ideology/ Politics*, Society for Education in Film & TV, 1977
- *Screen Reader II: Cinema and Semiotics*, British Film Institute, London, 1982
- C. Sharrett, ed. *Crisis Cinema*, Maisonneuve Press, Washington, D.C., 1993

D. Shipman. *The Story of Cinema*, Hodder & Stoughton, London, 1984

—. *Caught In the Act: Sex and Eroticism In the Movies*, Hamish Hamilton, London, 1986

T. Shone. *Blockbuster: How the Jaws and Jedi Generation Turned Hollywood Into a Boom-Town*, Scribner, London, 2005

E. Showalter, ed. *The New Feminist Criticism,* Virago, London, 1986

Enzo Siciliano. *Pasolini: A Biography*, tr. John Shepley, Random House, New York, 1982

L. Sider *et al*, eds. *Soundscapes: The School of Sound Lectures 1998-2001*, Wallflower Press, London, 2003

M. Silberman. *German Cinema,* Wayne State University Press, Detroit, M.I., 1995

K. Silverman. *The Subject of Semiotics*, Oxford University Press, New York, N.Y., 1983

—. *The Acoustic Mirror: The Female Voice In Psychoanalysis and Cinema*, Indiana University Press, Bloomington, I.N., 1988

—. *Male Subjectivity At the Margins*, Routledge, London, 1992

—. & H. Farocki. *Speaking About Godard,* New York University Press, New York, N.Y., 1998

P. Adams Sitney, ed. *The Film Culture Reader*, Praeger, New York, N.Y., 1970

—. *Vital Crises In Italian Cinema*, University of Texas Press, Austin, T.X., 1995

S. Snyder. *Pier Paolo Pasolini*, Twayne, 1980

V. Sobchack, ed. *The Persistence of History: Cinema, Television, and the Modern Event*, Routledge, London, 1995

A. Solomon. *20th Century-Fox: A Corporate and Financial History*, Scarecrow Press, Metuchen, N.J., 1988

J. Solomon. *The Ancient World In the Cinema*, London, 1978

—. *The Ancient World In the Cinema*, Yale University Press, New Haven, CT, 2001

P. Sorlin. *The Film In History: Restaging the Past*, Blackwell, Oxford, 1980

S. Spignesi. *The Woody Allen Companion*, Plexus, London, 1994

George Stambolian & Elaine Marks, eds. *Homosexuality and French Literature: Cultural Contexts/ Critical Texts,* Cornell University Press, Ithaca, 1979

B. Steene. *Ingmar Bergman*, Twayne, Boston, M.A., 1968

—. *Ingmar Bergman: A Guide To References and Resources*, Boston, M.A., 1987

N. Steimatsky. "Pasolini on Terra Sancta: Towards a Theology of Film", *Yale Journal of Criticism*, 11, 1, 1998

L. Stern. *The Scorsese Connection*, British Film Institute, London, 1995

D. Sterritt. *The Films of Jean-Luc Godard*, Cambridge University Press, Cambridge, 1999

P. Steven, ed. *Jump Cut: Hollywood, Politics and Counter Cinema*, Between the Lines, Toronto, 1985

G. Stewart. *Between Film and Screen: Modernism's Photo Synthesis*, University of Chicago Press, Chicago, I.L., 1999

C. Sylvester, ed. *The Penguin Book of Hollywood*, Penguin, London, 1999

Y. Tasker. *Spectacular Bodies: Gender, Genre and the Action Cinema*, Routledge, London, 1993

M. Temple & J. Williams, eds. *The Cinema Alone: Essays On the Work of Jean-Luc Godard, 1985-2000*, Amsterdam University Press, Amsterdam, 2000

—. *et al*, eds. *Godard For Ever*, Black Dog Publishing, London, 2004

S. Teo. *Hong Kong Cinema*, British Film Institute, London, 1997

N. Thomas, ed. *International Dictionary of Films and Filmmakers: Films*, St James Press, London, 1990

K. Thompson. *Breaking the Glass Armor: Neoformalist Film Analysis*, Princeton University Press, Princeton, N.J., 1988

—. & D. Bordwell. *Film History: An Introduction*, McGraw-Hill, New York, N.Y., 1994

—. *Storytelling In the New Hollywood*, Harvard University Press, Cambridge, M.A., 1999

D. Thomson. *A Biographical Dictionary of Film*, Deutsch, London, 1995

C. Tohill & P. Tombs. *Immoral Tales: Sex and Horror Cinema In Europe 1956-1984*, Titan Books, London, 1995

Sergio Toffetti. *La Terra vista dalla luna: il cinema di Sergio Citti*, Lindau, 1993

C. Tonetti. *Luchino Visconti*, Columbus Books, 1985

—. *Bernardo Bertolucci*, Twayne, Boston, M.A., 1994

E. Törnqvist. *Between Stage and Screen: Ingmar Bergman Directs*, Amsterdam University Press, Amsterdam, 1995

J. Trevelyan. *What the Censor Saw*, Michael Joseph, London, 1973

H. Trosman. *Contemporary Psychoanalysis and Masterworks of Art and Film*, New York University Press, New York, N.Y., 2000

F. Truffaut. *The Films In My Life*, tr. L. Mayhew, Penguin, London, 1982

P. Tyler. *Sex Psyche Etcetera In the Film*, Horizon, New York, N.Y., 1969

—. *Screening the Sexes: Homosexuality In the Movies*, Doubleday, New York, N.Y., 1973

M. Valck & M. Hagener, eds. *Cinephilia: Movies, Love and Memory*, Amsterdam University Press, Amsterdam, 2005

K. Van Gunden. *Fantasy Films*, McFarland, Jefferson, NC 1989

M. Viano. *A Certain Realism: Making Use of Pasolini's Film Theory and Practice*, University of California Press, Berkeley, 1993.

G. Vincendeau, ed. *Encyclopedia of European Cinema*, British Film Institute, London, 1995

—. ed. *Film/ Literature/ Heritage: A Sight & Sound Reader*, British Film Institute, London, 2001

P. Virilio & S. Lotringer. *The Aesthetics of Disappearance*, tr. P. Beitchman, Semiotext(e), New York, N.Y., 1991

—. *The Vision Machine*, tr. J. Rose, Indiana University Press, Bloomington, I.N., 1994

J. Vizzard. *See No Evil: Life Inside a Hollywood Censor*, Simon & Schuster, New York, N.Y., 1970

A. Vogel. *Film As a Subversive Art*, Weidenfeld & Nicolson, London, 1974

A. Walker. *Sex In the Movies*, Penguin, London, 1968

—. *Hollywood, England: The British Film Industry In the Sixties*, Harrap, London, 1986

J. Wasko. *Movies and Money*, Ablex, N.J., 1982

—. *Hollywood In the Information Age*, Polity Press, Cambridge, 1994

P. Webb. *The Erotic Arts*, Secker & Warburg, London, 1975

E. Weiss. & J. Belton, eds. *Film Sound: Theory and Practice*, Columbia University Press, New York, N.Y., 1989

O. Welles. *This Is Orson Welles*, HarperCollins, London, 1992

—. *Orson Welles: Interviews*, ed. M. Estrin, University of Mississippi Press, Jackson, 2002

Helen Wilcox *et al*, eds. *The Body and the Text: Hélène Cixous, Reading and Teaching*, Harvester Wheatsheaf, Hemel Hempstead, Herts., 1990

P. Willemen, ed. *Pier Paolo Pasolini*, British Film Institute, London, 1977

L. Williams, ed. *Viewing Positions: Ways of Seeing Film*, Rutgers University Press, New Brunswick, N.J., 1995

L.R. Williams. *Critical Desire: Psychoanalysis and the Literary Subject*, Arnold, London, 1995

—. *Sex In the Head*, Harvester Wheatsheaf, Hemel Hempstead, 1995

W. Willimon. "Faithful to the Script", *Christian Century*, 2004

S. Willis. *High Contrast: Race and Gender In Contemporary Hollywood Film*, Duke University Press, Durham, N.C., 1997

R. Wilson & W. Dissanayake, eds. *Global/ Local: Cultural Production and the Transnational Imaginary*, Duke University Press, Durham, N.C., 1996

E. Wistrich. *'I Don't Mind the Sex It's the Violence': Film Censorship Explored*, Marion Boyars, London, 1978

M. Wolf. *The Entertainment Economy*, Penguin, London, 1999

P. Wollen: *Signs and Meaning In the Cinema*, Secker & Warburg, London, 1972

B. Wood. *Orson Welles*, Greenwood Press, Westport, CT, 1990

P. Wood, ed. *Scorsese: A Journey Through the American Psyche*, Plexus, London, 2005

R. Wood. *Ingmar Bergman*, Praeger, New York, N.Y., 1969

—. *Hollywood From Vietnam To Reagan... and Beyond*, Columbia University Press, New York, N.Y., 2003

T. Woods. *Beginning Postmodernism*, Manchester University Press, Manchester, 1999

Elizabeth Wright, ed. *Feminism and Psychoanalysis: A Critical Dictionary*, Blackwell, Oxford, 1992

J. Wyatt. *High Concept: Movies and Marketing In Hollywood*, University of Texas Press, Austin, T.X., 1994

E.C.M. Yau, ed. *At Full Speed: Hong Kong Cinema In a Borderless World*, University of Minnesota Press, Minneapolis, MN, 1998

- J. Young, ed. *The Art of Memory: Holocaust Memorials In History*, Prestel, New York, N.Y., 1994
- G. Zigaini. *Pasolini e la morte*, Marsilio, Venice, 1987
- J. Zipes, ed. *The Oxford Companion To Fairy Tales*, Oxford University Press, 2000
- —. *Sticks and Stones: The Troublesome Success of Children's Literature From Slovenly Peter To Harry Potter*, Routledge, London, 2002
- —. *The Enchanted Screen: The Unknown History of Fairy-tale Films*, Routledge, New York, N.Y., 2011
- —. *The Irresistible Fairy Tale*, Prince University Press, Princeton, N.J., 2012
- S. Zizek. *Looking Awry*, Verso, London, 1991
- —. *Enjoy Your Symptom: Jacques Lacan In Hollywood and Out*, Routledge, New York, N.Y., 1992
- —. ed. *Everything You Always Wanted To Know About Lacan (But Were Too Afraid To Ask Hitchcock)*, Verso, London, 1992
- —. *The Metastases of Enjoyment*, Verso, London, 1994
- —. *The Indivisible Remainder*, Verso, London, 1996
- —. *The Fright of Real Tears: The Uses and Misuses of Lacan In Film Theory*, British Film Institute, London, 1999

Websites for Pasolini-related material include:

pierpaolopasolini.com
pasoliniroma.com
jclarkmedia.com
bernardobertolucci.org

JEREMY ROBINSON has published poetry, fiction, and studies of J.R.R. Tolkien, Samuel Beckett, Thomas Hardy, André Gide and D.H. Lawrence. Robinson has edited poetry books by Novalis, Ursula Le Guin, Friedrich Hölderlin, Francesco Petrarch, Dante Alighieri, Arseny Tarkovsky, and Rainer Maria Rilke.

Books on film and animation include: *The Akira Book* • *The Art of Katsuhiro Otomo* • *The Art of Masamune Shirow* • *The Ghost In the Shell Book* • *Fullmetal Alchemist* • *Cowboy Bebop: The Anime and Movie* • *The Cinema of Hayao Miyazaki* • *Hayao Miyazaki: Pocket Guide* • *Princess Mononoke: Pocket Movie Guide* • *Spirited Away: Pocket Movie Guide* • *Blade Runner and the Cinema of Philip K. Dick* • *Blade Runner: Pocket Movie Guide* • *The Cinema of Donald Cammell* • *Performance: Donald Cammell: Nic Roeg: Pocket Movie Guide* • *Pasolini: Il Cinema di Poesia/ The Cinema of Poetry* • *Salo: Pocket Movie Guide* • *The Trilogy of Life Movies: Pocket Movie Guide* • *The Gospel According To Matthew: Pocket Movie Guide* • *The Ecstatic Cinema of Tony Ching Siu-tung* • *Tsui Hark: The Dragon Master of Chinese Cinema* • *The Swordsman: Pocket Movie Guide* • *A Chinese Ghost Story: Pocket Movie Guide* • *Ken Russell: England's Great Visionary Film Director and Music Lover* • *Tommy: Ken Russell: The Who: Pocket Movie Guide* • *Women In Love: Ken Russell: D.H. Lawrence: Pocket Movie Guide* • *The Devils: Ken Russell: Pocket Movie Guide* • *Walerian Borowczyk: Cinema of Erotic Dreams* • *The Beast: Pocket Movie Guide* • *The Lord of the Rings Movies* • *The Fellowship of the Ring: Pocket Movie Guide* • *The Two Towers: Pocket Movie Guide* • *The Return of the King: Pocket Movie Guide* • *Jean-Luc Godard: The Passion of Cinema* • *The Sacred Cinema of Andrei Tarkovsky* • *Andrei Tarkovsky: Pocket Guide*.

'It's amazing for me to see my work treated with such passion and respect. There is nothing resembling it in the U.S. in relation to my work.'
(Andrea Dworkin)

'This model monograph – it is an exemplary job, and I'm very proud that he has accorded me a couple of mentions… The subject matter of his book is beautifully organised and dead on beam.'
(Lawrence Durrell, on *The Light Eternal: A Study of J.M.W. Turner*)

'Jeremy Robinson's poetry is certainly jammed with ideas, and I find it very interesting for that reason. It's certainly a strong imprint of his personality.'
(Colin Wilson)

'*Sex-Magic-Poetry-Cornwall* is a very rich essay… It is a very good piece… vastly stimulating and insightful.'
(Peter Redgrove)

ARTS, PAINTING, SCULPTURE

web: www.crmoon.com • e-mail: cresmopub@yahoo.co.uk

The Art of Andy Goldsworthy
Andy Goldsworthy: Touching Nature
Andy Goldsworthy in Close-Up
Andy Goldsworthy: Pocket Guide
Andy Goldsworthy In America
Land Art: A Complete Guide
The Art of Richard Long
Richard Long: Pocket Guide
Land Art In Great Britain
Land Art in Close-Up
Land Art In the U.S.A.
Land Art: Pocket Guide
Installation Art in Close-Up
Minimal Art and Artists In the 1960s and After
Colourfield Painting
Land Art DVD, TV documentary
Andy Goldsworthy DVD, TV documentary
The Erotic Object: Sexuality in Sculpture From Prehistory to the Present Day
Sex in Art: Pornography and Pleasure in Painting and Sculpture
Postwar Art
Sacred Gardens: The Garden in Myth, Religion and Art
Glorification: Religious Abstraction in Renaissance and 20th Century Art
Early Netherlandish Painting
Jasper Johns
Brice MardenLeonardo da Vinci
Piero della Francesca
Giovanni Bellini
Fra Angelico: Art and Religion in the Renaissance
Mark Rothko: The Art of Transcendence
Frank Stella: American Abstract Artist
Alison Wilding: The Embrace of Sculpture
Vincent van Gogh: Visionary Landscapes
Eric Gill: Nuptials of God
Constantin Brancusi: Sculpting the Essence of Things
Max Beckmann
Gustave Moreau
Caravaggio
Egon Schiele: Sex and Death In Purple Stockings
Delizioso Fotografico Fervore: Works In Process 1
Sacro Cuore: Works In Process 2
The Light Eternal: J.M.W. Turner
The Madonna Glorified: Karen Arthurs

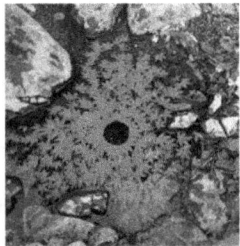

POETRY

Ursula Le Guin: *Walking In Cornwall*
Peter Redgrove: Here Comes The Flood
Peter Redgrove: Sex-Magic-Poetry-Cornwall
Dante: Selections From the *Vita Nuova*
Petrarch, Dante and the Troubadours
William Shakespeare: *The Sonnets*
William Shakespeare: Complete Poems
Blinded By Her Light: The Love-Poetry of Robert Graves
Emily Dickinson: Selected Poems
Emily Brontë: Poems
Thomas Hardy: Selected Poems
Percy Bysshe Shelley: Poems
John Keats: Selected Poems
John Keats: Poems of 1820
D.H. Lawrence: Selected Poems
Edmund Spenser: Poems
Edmund Spenser: *Amoretti*
John Donne: Poems
Henry Vaughan: Poems
Sir Thomas Wyatt: Poems
Robert Herrick: Selected Poems
Rilke: Space, Essence and Angels in the Poetry of Rainer Maria Rilke
Rainer Maria Rilke: Selected Poems
Friedrich Hölderlin: Selected Poems
Arseny Tarkovsky: Selected Poems
Paul Verlaine: Selected Poems
Novalis: *Hymns To the Night*
Arthur Rimbaud: Selected Poems
Arthur Rimbaud: *A Season in Hell*
Arthur Rimbaud and the Magic of Poetry
D.J. Enright: By-Blows
Jeremy Reed: *Brigitte's Blue Heart*
Jeremy Reed: *Claudia Schiffer's Red Shoes*
Gorgeous Little Orpheus
Radiance: New Poems
Crescent Moon Book of Nature Poetry
Crescent Moon Book of Love Poetry
Crescent Moon Book of Mystical Poetry
Crescent Moon Book of Elizabethan Love Poetry
Crescent Moon Book of Metaphysical Poetry
Crescent Moon Book of Romantic Poetry
Pagan America: New American Poetry

MEDIA, CINEMA, FEMINISM and CULTURAL STUDIES

J.R.R. Tolkien: The Books, The Films, The Whole Cultural Phenomenon
J.R.R. Tolkien: Pocket Guide
The *Lord of the Rings* Movies: Pocket Guide
The Ghost Dance: The Origins of Religion
The Cinema of Hayao Miyazaki
Hayao Miyazaki: *Princess Mononoke*: Pocket Movie Guide
Hayao Miyazaki: *Spirited Away*: Pocket Movie Guide
The Peyote Cult
HomeGround: The Kate Bush Anthology
Tim Burton : Hallowe'en For Hollywood
Ken Russell
Cixous, Irigaray, Kristeva: The *Jouissance* of French Feminism
Julia Kristeva: Art, Love, Melancholy, Philosophy, Semiotics and Psychoanalysis
Luce Irigaray: Lips, Kissing, and the Politics of Sexual Difference
Hélène Cixous I Love You: The *Jouissance* of Writing
Andrea Dworkin
'Cosmo Woman': The World of Women's Magazines
Women in Pop Music
Discovering the Goddess (Geoffrey Ashe)
The Poetry of Cinema
The Sacred Cinema of Andrei Tarkovsky
Andrei Tarkovsky: Pocket Guide
Andrei Tarkovsky: *Mirror*: Pocket Movie Guide
Walerian Borowczyk: Cinema of Erotic Dreams
Jean-Luc Godard: The Passion of Cinema
Jean-Luc Godard: Pocket Guide
John Hughes and Eighties Cinema
Ferris Buller's Day Off: Pocket Movie Guide
The Cinema of Richard Linklater
Liv Tyler: Star In Ascendance
Blade Runner and the Films of Philip K. Dick
Paul Bowles and Bernardo Bertolucci
Media Hell: Radio, TV and the Press
Detonation Britain: Nuclear War in the UK
Feminism and Shakespeare
Wild Zones: Pornography, Art and Feminism
Sex in Art: Pornography and Pleasure in Painting and Sculpture
Sexing Hardy: Thomas Hardy and Feminism

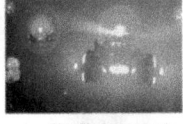

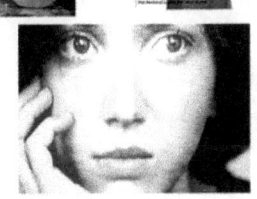

The Light Eternal *is a model monograph, an exemplary job. The subject matter of the book is beautifully organised and dead on beam.* (Lawrence Durrell)
It is amazing for me to see my work treated with such passion and respect. (Andrea Dworkin)
Sex-Magic-Poetry-Cornwall *is a very rich essay... It is like a brightly-lighted box.* (Peter Redgrove)

CRESCENT MOON PUBLISHING   P.O. Box 1312, Maidstone, Kent, ME14 5XU, Great Britain
0044-1622-729593   cresmopub@yahoo.co.uk   www.crmoon.com